THE

PHENOMENA OF SPIRITUALISM.

THE

PHENOMENA OF SPIRITUALISM

Scientifically Explained and Exposed.

BY THE

REV. ASA MAHAN, D.D.,

FIRST PRESIDENT OF OBERLIN COLLEGE, OHIO,

Author of "Science of Intellectual Philosophy," "Science of Logic," "Doctrine of the Will," "Science of Moral Philosophy," etc.

"There are more things in heaven and earth, Horatio,
Than are dreamt of in your philosophy."

A. S. BARNES AND CO.,

NEW YORK, CHIGAGO, AND NEW ORLEANS.

MDCCCLXXVI.

PREFACE.

PERHAPS we cannot better introduce the reader to the treatise before him, than by giving a short statement of the circumstances which led us to adopt the views therein developed in regard to Spiritualism. Since the year 1850, our residence has been in several of the grand centres of this movement, and where, consequently, the mysterious phenomena were continuously forced upon our attention. One of the circumstances which first impressed our mind as we reflected upon what was passing before us, was the utter incompatibility of the fundamental characteristics of these facts, as reported even by spiritualists themselves, with the supposition that they are the *intended* results of intelligent minds who are communicating with us from the heavenly or infernal world. By no laws of mind known to us could we account for the facts by a reference to such an origin. When they were referred to good spirits, our reply was: good spirits cannot falsify as these do; for these falsify when spirits, if present, cannot but know the truth; profess knowledge when they must know themselves ignorant, and make positive affirmations when they must know that they are only guessing. Good spirits cannot thus act. When they were referred to bad spirits, our reply was: these spirits do not lie like men in the flesh, nor as any spirits would do whose conduct is governed by any laws known to us. There is a certain "*method*" even in lying, wherever it appears, and here is lying which has no such method, or any method at all which can properly be ascribed to spirits aiming at some intelligent end, good or bad. When individuals told us that they had had communications with their spirit friends, our reply was: the spirit here speaking says some things that that of your mother, if present, might and no doubt would say. Your mother, however, when alive and with you, never falsified as this spirit does, and would not thus falsify, if now present. We therefore rejected the *ab extra* spirit hypothesis, as wholly incompatible with the facts.

We were first led to refer the facts to tricks of the mediums. Soon, however, we were confronted with phenomena wholly incompatible with such a supposition. We met, for example, with evidences, which we could not resist and maintain our integrity, of the reality of physical manifestations of a very startling and impressive character. We ourselves personally witnessed such facts as we could account for by no reference to conscious or unconscious muscular action. We also met with individuals of the first intelligence and integrity, and who utterly repudiate the spirit theory, who had themselves witnessed such phenomena. In the Congregational Society's Rooms in Boston, for example, an orthodox Congregational clergyman, of unquestionable intelligence and integrity, affirmed to us, in the presence of several other clergymen, that on one occasion he saw a medium place her hands gently upon a marble-topped table, no other person being near; that after holding them there awhile, the object began to move after her around the room, that he himself got under the table, and taking hold of its legs, attempted to hold it still, and that he was, with the table, drawn quite a distance over the floor, all his efforts to the contrary notwithstanding. From many others we received precisely similar and equally credible statements. We found, then, that we had to admit the facts, or take the ground that no strange events can be established by testimony. How, then, could we ask the world to believe in Christian miracles? We found equally valid evidence for the reality of the facts of Spiritualism, as far as the *intelligent communications* are concerned. We found ourselves necessitated, therefore, in moral honesty, to admit the facts, and then to seek an explanation of them on some mundane hypothesis, as their character precluded any other supposition than their exclusively mundane origin.

As we reflected upon the facts under consideration, we were forcibly struck with this suggestion, that they seemed evidently to imply the existence in nature of a *polar force* not yet distinctly recognised in philosophy, a force having, when developed, very strong attractive and repulsive power; a force, the direction of whose action, when certain conditions are fulfilled, accords with mental states, and is determined by the same; a force, finally, through which the mental states of one mind may be reproduced in others, and thus embodied, as in these communications. The existence of precisely such a force seemed demanded by the facts, whether we supposed it governed, in the production of these manifestations, by spirits in the body or out of the body. We were also deeply impressed with the obvious correspondence of these manifestations, physical and mental, with the phenomena of mesmerism and clairvoyance, on the one hand, and those of another class which from time to time have, in all ages, startled and troubled mankind, and which philosophers now refer to a power in nature denominated the Odylic Force, on the other. This led to a careful examination and classification of each of these classes of phenomena, and to an equally careful comparison of the results thus obtained with the spirit-phenomena, physical and intellectual.

The following are some of the conclusions to which we were thus conducted: 1. There is in nature a force having the identical properties above specified, and which we denominate the Odylic Force. 2. This force is identical with the cause of all the mesmeric and clairvoyant phenomena, on the one hand, and with the immediate cause of these manifestations, on the other. 3. By a reference to the properties and laws of this force as developed in the spirit-circles, and to its relations to the minds constituting the same, we can account most fully for all the spirit-phenomena, of every kind, without the supposition of the presence or agency of disembodied spirits. Consequently, the hypothesis of Spiritualism is wholly unsustained by any valid evidence whatever. 4. The entire real facts of Spiritualism demand the supposition that this force in the production of these communications is controlled exclusively, for the most part unconsciously, by the minds in the circles, and not by disembodied spirits out of the same. 5. We finally found, what we did not at first expect, that we had developed facts and principles which gave an equally ready and satisfactory explanation of the phenomena of witchcraft, necromancy, fortune-telling, etc., etc., phenomena which from time to time have been the wonder and terror of mankind in all ages. 6. Other consequences of equal and far greater importance seemed undeniably to follow from our facts and deductions. The results of our investigations the reader will find embodied in the following treatise.

Facts of recent occurrence have fully prepared the public mind, as we judge, to receive a scientific explanation of the real phenomena of Spiritualism, the *impositions* of the system having been so fully exposed. Since the following treatise was put into the printer's hands, in every remaining place not therein referred to, where ghosts have been professedly exhibited—in the United States, for example—the impositions have been fully exposed, "the spirits" having been caught, and demonstrated to be men or women in the flesh. With these suggestions the work before us is commended to the careful and candid examination of the reader.

THE AUTHOR.

LONDON, *April 27th*, 1875.

CONTENTS.

INTRODUCTION.

CHAPTER I.

ELECTRICITY, MAGNETISM, AND ANIMAL MAGNETISM DISTINGUISHED.

CHAPTER II.

THE ODYLIC, ODIC, OR PSYCHIC FORCE.

CHAPTER III.

PHYSICAL AND INTELLECTUAL MANIFESTATIONS ELUCIDATED.

CHAPTER IV.

POSITIVE AND CONCLUSIVE PROOF THAT ALL THESE COMMUNICATIONS AND MANIFESTATIONS ARE THE EXCLUSIVE RESULT OF MUNDANE CAUSES, AND NOT OF THE AGENCY OF DISEMBODIED SPIRITS.

CHAPTER V.

TENDENCY OF SPIRITUALISM.

CHAPTER VI.

MISCELLANEOUS TOPICS.

PHENOMENA OF SPIRITUALISM

SCIENTIFICALLY EXPLAINED AND EXPOSED.

INTRODUCTION.

A GENTLEMAN, while in Egypt, asked an intelligent citizen of that country what he really thought of their most celebrated necromancer. The reply received was this: "I regard him as pretty much of a humbug. Yet, I think that there is *something* real in the art which he practises." If we will carefully scrutinize the public sentiment of Europe and America, we shall find, we judge, that the above answer most correctly expresses the popular conviction in respect to modern Spiritualism. That the great mass of phenomena presented under that name is gross humbuggery and imposition, no well-informed individual, who would maintain his self-respect, will question. That, at the basis of these phenomena, there are important facts requiring a scientific explanation, the most intelligent men, who have made the nearest approach to these facts, do not entertain any doubt. The celebrated juggler, Signor Blitz, for example, after the most careful scrutiny of these phenomena, affirmed, that there were facts there which the art he practised could never explain. Such has been the result of our researches after a correct knowledge of the real character and cause of these phenomena. As a teacher of youth, and president of important colleges, we ever regarded it as an important duty to be well informed on our part in respect to all subjects of public interest, that we might be qualified so to instruct our pupils that they should be able to distinguish between truth and error. Discerning, as we early did, the fact, that the so-called spirit-phenomena would become objects of even world-wide interest, we at once commenced a careful inquiry into their real character and causes. We commenced our investigations with the distinct and avowed impression, that *all* these phenomena were the exclusive result of trickery and imposture. We had not proceeded far in our investigations, however, before we found ourselves confronted with palpable facts which admitted of no such explanation. We found, for example, that individuals could go into these spirit-circles, and there obtain specific answers to any number of purely *mental* questions, and that, too, when the questions pertained to facts so remote and foreign to all minds but their own in the circles, as to preclude the possibility of trickery or deception. We will, for example, go into any circle in any part of England, a circle which can, by no possibility, know anything whatever of us or of our place of residence. When the proper conditions have been fulfilled, we will ask the question: Is the spirit we are now thinking of present? the spirit being that of our mother. On receiving an affirmative answer, we will request the spirit to answer the question which we now mentally put, the question being: Will you designate the names of your children, and that in the order of their birth? These specific names, in the order mentally designated, will be given. Facts of a precisely similar character, as will be rendered demonstrably evident in the progress of this treatise, are being repeated in thousands of circles, the world over. In regard to the so-called physical phenomena, "deeds of darkness" excepted, we found that we could produce them ourselves, and that upon objects of our own selection, and when alone in our own room; and we obtained undeniable evidence of the existence of precisely similar facts wherever proper experiments were tried. From such undeniable facts, the existence of which will be hereafter abundantly verified, we deduced two inferences:

that there is a power, or force, in nature—a force not yet generally recognised by scientists—a force which, when developed from any cause, occasions these wonders; and that, in the spirit-circles, this force is so controlled, and that by *some* intelligent cause, as to secure specific responses to our most secret thoughts.

From these facts spiritualists infer that it is spirits outside of this mundane sphere that control this force in the production of these phenomena. With this exposition in mind, we return to the case of our mother. In answer to a purely mental question, the real names of all her children have been given, and that in the specific order above designated. For the purpose of self-satisfaction in regard to the question whether it is, in fact, the spirit of our mother, or any extra-mundane spirit, that is communicating with us, we, mentally as before, request a second answer to the question previously put, mentally suggesting, at the same time, that great care shall be used to give the right answer, as important deductions may be based upon the answer received. The answer received in the first case, the correct one too, was, Asa, Polly, Betsey. The response, in this second case, is, Shadrach, Meshach, and Abednego. We here state cases which, as we shall show hereafter, are perfectly parallel to facts everywhere occurring in these circles, whenever and wherever thinkers visit them, and put questions there with wise discretion and full self-possession. In reflecting upon these cases we call to mind the conscious fact, that at the time when each name was designated, our thought was directed to that specific name, and so directed in the first three cases without reflecting upon any inferences to be deduced from the answers received, and in the last three for the specific purpose of obtaining facts for the solution of an important problem in science. The facts strictly common to these two cases are these: that, in each case alike, there was a definite response to a purely mental question, of the character of which none but we could be conscious; and that the *name* given, in every instance, accorded with the identical one upon which our thought was, at the moment, definitely fixed. Hence the question arises, to wit: Did *our* mental states determine the action of the force through which these responses were obtained, or was the determining cause the mental states of a spirit from another sphere? Here, on the hypothesis that such facts do exist, we have the question imposed upon science to settle. All must agree, as we have said, that the action of this force in the production of these phenomena, supposing them to be real, is determined by the mental states of minds within these circles, or by those of spirits from another sphere. The question for science is: Which of these hypotheses is the true one?

It may be a matter of interest and profit to the reader, perhaps, should we here indicate the *method* of inquiry in conformity to which we have endeavoured to obtain a scientific answer to this question. Several years ago, an instrument, or machine, called Planchette, was very extensively sold and used throughout the United States. The instrument consisted of a thin piece of board fixed upon a frame that moved upon wheels or rollers, so arranged that the instrument could be readily moved in any direction. When a pencil was so fixed to the end of the instrument, that the point of the pencil would touch a sheet of paper upon the table, all was in readiness for the desired experiments. When individuals place their hands upon the top of the instrument and hold them there for a time, it begins to move, and letters, sentences, and answers to questions mental and verbal, are written out upon that sheet of paper. What is very peculiar about the Planchette is, that by no acts of will can it, by any possibility, be made to move the pencil so as to write a single letter, word, or sentence. It is only as the ends of the fingers touch the surface of the board referred to, and all volitions are suspended, that any letters, words, or sentences will be written out. Here, spiritualists exclaim, is palpable evidence of the agency of spirits in moving the instrument so as to produce these results. A company of educated minds formed themselves into a circle for the purpose of discovering the specific cause of these phenomena. After the most careful and extended investigation, they found that the most fixed relation existed between every one of these phenomena and a specific, and corresponding, mental state pre-existing in some mind, or minds, within the circle. So it was found everywhere, when corresponding inquiries were made, and Planchette took its place among the abortions of the past.

About this time, another instrument was invented, and called Planchette Out-done. On a thin board circles were drawn, circles within one another, and circles from the centre of which lines were drawn to such words as Yes and No, to the days of the week, and to numerals from one to one hundred, etc. Taking between the fingers the end of a silk thread, to the other end of which a small metallic ball was affixed, and holding the ball over the centre of these circles, we might put any questions we pleased, and the motion of the ball would be in the directions which would indicate specific answers to said questions. Here, as before, spiritualists affirmed the demonstrated presence of spirit-agency. Wishing to determine the real character and cause of these facts, we approached the instrument in this manner: withholding vision totally from the location of any words and figures upon the circles, we held the ball as required, and asked the question: Am I about to take a journey? it being my purpose to do so. Under these circumstances, the ball absolutely refused to move in any direction. We willed it to move, and entreated the spirits, if any were present who had the power to do so, to move that ball in some direction. There it remained, however, utterly motionless. At length, we looked out the locality of the term Yes, and then repeated the question: Am I about to take a journey? Instantly the ball moved in the direction which indicated the right answer. In utter ignorance of the locality of the name of any day of the week, I then put the question: On what day of the week shall I start on this journey? In this state of things, no action of my will, nor any "spirit from the vasty deep," would move that ball. When the inquiry was repeated, after the location of the right day was known, the right answer was obtained. The same identical facts attended the inquiries: How long shall I be absent from home? What is my age? and many others. We from hence drew the following deductions: that there may be in nature a force whose activity is determined by mental states—a force not yet, as before stated, generally recognised by scientific men; that in the cases under consideration, the mental states determining the action of this force were undeniably mundane, and not extra-mundane; and that we may have here a key which will unlock all the mysteries of Spiritualism, a principle which will enable us to explain all these so-called spirit-phenomena. With this specific inquiry distinctly in mind, namely, Is the cause of these phenomena mundane or extra-mundane? we have investigated these phenomena. These investigations we have pursued after having clearly determined what the essential characteristics of these facts must be—if their cause is mundane, on the one hand, or supra-mundane, on the other. Of this fact we are absolutely assured, that when these phenomena shall be investigated in accordance with a strictly scientific method, all mystery about them will disappear, and they will be found to be as readily reducible to fixed laws of nature, and as explicable by said laws, as are any other classes of known facts; and that, admitting all spirit-facts that can, with any show of reason, be affirmed to be real, we have no more occasion to call in the agency of extra-mundane spirits to explain these facts, than we have to do the same thing to explain the facts pertaining to the transit of Venus.

THE DIVERSE THEORIES PERTAINING TO THESE PHENOMENA, AND THE METHODS OF INQUIRY, AND LAWS OF EVIDENCE BY WHICH ANY ONE OF THEM CAN BE VERIFIED.

Before we can proceed intelligently in the investigation of any class or classes of facts, we must, first of all, settle definitely the proper *method of inquiry* to be observed, and the specific *laws of evidence* applicable in such cases. We propose now to do this relatively to the phenomena under consideration. All the theories which have been put forward for the explanation of these facts may be classed under the following denominations, namely, the Humbug Theory, that which refers all these phenomena to trickery and imposition; the Satanic Agency Theory, that which admits the facts to be real, and their determining cause supra-mundane, but affirms that cause to be the Father of Lies; the Spirit Theory, that which, not only admits and affirms the facts to be real, but refers, for their causes and explanation, to the agency of disembodied spirits who have left this world; and the Mundane Theory, that which also admits the facts, and refers, for their explanation, to mundane causes exclusively. We propose to consider each of these theories in the order stated; our present object being, not to prove or disprove any one of them, but to fix and determine the proper *method* of inquiry in each case, and the immutable *conditions* on which each can be scientifically verified, provided such verification is possible. We begin with

The Humbug Theory.

All the other theories, it will be borne in mind, admit, that among the so-called spirit-phenomena there are real and important facts—facts which have no connexion with trickery and imposture, facts which require a scientific scrutiny and explanation. On what conditions can this Humbug Theory be verified? It is no verification of this theory, we reply, to prove that very many and very important classes of these so-called spirit-phenomena are deliberate impositions, or even that all of these "dark room showings" are of this character. If we grant all this, as we readily do, a large residuum of essential facts will be left—facts against which no such charge has ever yet been sustained. What gave Spiritualism its chief influence in America was the fact, that, for a long time, its claims were opposed on the hypothesis that it was either true, or was, in all its facts, a gross and intentional imposition upon the public; the mediums being everywhere able to convince all who entered their circles that their leading facts were no impositions. The first medium we ever personally knew was one of our own pupils, who utterly repudiated Spiritualism in all its claims. In circles in which he was the medium, all the phenomena which appeared in any of the spirit-circles were developed, and that when all present with him utterly repudiated the system under consideration. One of the best table-movers I ever saw was an aged and venerable member of my own church. At any of our houses, or in any circle, he would take a stand or table, and after laying his hands or fingers gently upon its surface for a little time, the object would begin to move, and perform antics which no one could induce by any manipulations controlled by the will. I can affirm, without fear of contradiction, that no well-informed American will deny, that in our country all the essential physical and intellectual phenomena of Spiritualism have been, not only witnessed, but produced, in many circles in which no single spiritualist was present, and where the exclusive object was to determine by experiment what phenomena can be developed by the means employed in the spirit-circles. Individuals, under such circumstances, have no motives for imposing upon themselves or others. It is a well-known fact, that in America, in England, and on the Continent—in France especially—all the essential physical and intellectual spirit-phenomena have been produced in circles formed for no other purpose than determining by experiment what is and is not true in respect to these phenomena. To charge such persons with the intention to practise deception upon the public, is but to evince that we ourselves are too much the creatures of prejudice to discern facts as they are in the world around us. Those who would verify this Humbug Theory, must not adduce mere admitted deceptions, but take into account the facts affirmed by spiritualists in common with intelligent non-believers in this system—individuals whose judgments are based upon independent experiments of the most reliable character, and whose veracity is unimpeachable.

The Satanic Agency Theory.

This theory admits and affirms the phenomena of Spiritualism, the phenomena generally claimed to be real, and refers them to satanic agency as their determining cause. On what conditions can this theory be verified? On three conditions, we answer, exclusively: proof that the cause of these facts must be extra-mundane, in the first instance; in the next, that this cause cannot be spirits from this world, but must be of an exclusively satanic character; and, finally, that these phenomena are controlled in accordance with the *revealed* character of the devil as the arch-deceiver of the race. Will any thinker attempt to verify all the above propositions? each of which must be proven, or this theory must be abandoned. That Satan desires that Spiritualism should become the accepted faith of the race, we have no doubt. To prove that even the mass of these accepted facts are the exclusive results of his direct and immediate agency, is quite another matter. If it shall be shown, as we believe it will be, that the cause of these phenomena is exclusively mundane, then this santanic hypothesis becomes a demonstrated error. If, granting the supra-mundane cause of these facts, it should appear that we have as good evidence of their being produced by departed spirits, as we have of their satanic origin, then the theory under consideration cannot be verified. Finally, if it should appear that the revelations of Spiritualism are uniformly of an order so low, inane, and so palpably self-contradictory, as to preclude the idea of their origin with such an intelligence as Satan undeniably is, the dogma that he is the immediate and exclusive author of these revelations becomes absurd. Satan may "transform himself into an angel of light." He is not, however, a fool. A system of error originated by him for the people of this century, it is quite safe to say, would bear a character for *greatness* in some respects corresponding to the intelligence of this century. Satan must be aware of facts in the universe in advance of scientific discovery, and events in the world around us in advance of our present knowledge. How easy it would be for him, in his sovereign control over these communications, to render his circles *reliable* sources of information on all such subjects, and thus impart to Spiritualism itself a most plausible verification. Are there circles of this character? The advocates of this Satanic Agency Theory must show that such are the real facts of the case, or, to be self-consistent, they must abandon their theory. If it should be found that these circles are, on no subjects not known to us, *reliable* sources of information; that in respect to facts of which we are not informed all these communications are void of higher credibility than mere imagining, or "prudent guessing," no prudent thinker will regard them as controlled by a being of such vast powers of knowledge and sources of information as Satan undeniably possesses. Satan does not *care* to lie when a lie will not answer his end. To suppose that he will lie when a lie will defeat, and giving right information will accomplish, his ends, is to impute to him greater folly than revelation or common sense will allow.

The Spiritualistic Theory.

The common doctrine of all who admit the leading facts of Spiritualism is, that these phenomena are the *direct* and *immediate* result of the action of *some* force in nature, by whatever name that force is designated; and that these phenomena are *effects* of the action of the said force as controlled by spirits in the circles or from some extra-mundane sphere. This common doctrine implies the existence in nature of a force the action of which, when the proper conditions are fulfilled, accords with, and is controlled by, *mental states.* The question for science, in this case, is whether these mental states pertain to spirits in, or out of, these circles—spirits dwelling in bodies in this mundane sphere, or coming into these circles from some other spheres. The doctrine of Spiritualism is, that the phenomena under consideration are produced through the action of this force as directed and controlled by the mental states of spirits who were once in the flesh as members of our race, but are now inhabitants of the spirit-realm. Through this force, mankind are now in communication with the disembodied realm of spiritual existences; just as in the matter of intellectual intercourse the people of England are, by means of telegraphic and other sources of intercourse, in communication with the peoples on the other side of the Atlantic. If this is really and truly the case, then the two kinds of intercommunication will, and must, have the same essential characteristics. In the same essential particulars in which one is a *reliable*, or *unreliable*, source of information, the other will be. We do not send messages across the ocean to obtain answers in respect to questions about which we are as perfectly informed as they are, but to obtain *information* in respect to subjects about which *they* may be informed and *we* are ignorant. The information thus obtained, also, is found to be so reliable that the most important business transactions are prudently regulated by it. If we are through these spirit-mediums, also, in real communication with the realm of minds, not living in the flesh on the other side of the Atlantic, but dwelling in the undiscovered country, we shall find that intercommunication in this latter case has, in all essential particulars, the same characteristics of reliability and unreliability as in the former. We have, for example, a mother in the spirit-land. While she lived these were the fixed characteristics of her communications to us. In all particulars in which we were both alike well-informed, we, of course, ever found her perfectly truthful. Equally trustworthy did we invariably and especially find her in respect to facts known to her, but about which we were ignorant or misinformed. In these relations, with perfect reliability, she would with special care enlighten our ignorance, or correct our errors, as the case might be. We enter a spirit-circle, and are there professedly put into communication with the same mind that, while in the body, we called our mother. As the immutable condition of identification, we are bound to require that her present communications shall have, in all essential respects, the same characteristics of reliability as her earthly ones had. There are many facts of which we are both fully and equally informed. There are many others about which she has a perfect knowledge, and we are wholly ignorant, or misinformed, and have the means of ascertaining the truth as it is. Suppose, now, that we should find that all her communications have, in all respects, the same identical characteristics of reliability that her living ones had. We should, in such case, be bound, as we judge, to admit that we are in actual communication with the spirit of that mother. Suppose, on the other hand, that on all subjects in respect to which we and she must be equally informed, we find all answers to be true; and that on all subjects about which we are ignorant or misinformed, and she perfectly informed, all communications and responses have the immutable characteristics of utter unreliability, making no nearer approach to the truth than common imaginings and guessings do. In such case we should dementate ourselves and gracelessly slander our mother, if we should admit that it is her spirit which is communicating with us. Answers to questions about which she and we are equally informed have no bearing whatever upon the question of her presence or absence, it being as probable, to say the least, that *our* thoughts determined these answers, as that *hers* did. In respect to the unreliable communications, we cannot admit that they came from her without affirming that, since her residence among the spirits, she has become a lawless liar, and we are perpetrating an act of self-dementation in so doing. As these responses have no other characteristics than vain imaginings or imprudent guessings, we are bound by all the principles of logical integrity to conclude that these lying imaginings and guessings are unconsciously our own, and not consciously hers, as they must be conscious lies, if they proceed from her at all.

No candid thinker will question the validity of the test of identification now under consideration, and the necessity, if we would not be most senselessly deceived in a matter of grave importance, of subjecting the claims of Spiritualism to the most rigid application of this test. In illustration of the manner in which this criterion has been applied in numberless instances in the United States, we will here allude to a fact stated in full in the body of this treatise. A gentleman, while sitting in a circle in the city of Boston, became impressed with the conscious fact, that the answers and communications obtained invariably accorded with specific thoughts previously, and at the time, present in his own mind. Hence, the question arose, whether his own thoughts, and not those of spirits supposed to be present, had determined these responses and communications. To satisfy his own mind on a question of such fundamental importance, he entered upon a series of experiments, so conducted as not at all to disturb the harmony of the circle, or awaken a suspicion in any mind of his intent. After extensive trials, he found, that by a conscious and secret regulation of his own thoughts, he could wholly suspend these phenomena, or give any direction to these communications he pleased. He would put a question, for example, and then fix his thoughts upon a specific answer which he knew to be false, and about which, as he was equally aware, the spirit assumed as present was well-informed; and that specific error would invariably be affirmed as true. The same fixed correspondence between the communications received and his own voluntarily-determined secret thoughts, obtained in all other instances. The conclusion which the inquirer deduced from such facts need not be specified. This individual understood at once the reason why, in all cases in which the inquirer and the spirit supposed to be present were both well-informed of the facts inquired about, the answers received were correct; that in cases where the inquirer was in error and the spirit well-informed, the error of the inquirer, and not the truth as it must have been known to the spirit, if present, was reported; and, finally, why, in all cases where the inquirer was wholly ignorant, and the spirit, if present, must have been well-informed, the answers had the fixed characteristics of unreliability which peculiarize mere guessing. Suppose, now, that, in the progress of this treatise, it shall be rendered fully and undeniably evident, that the above are the fixed characteristics of the intellectual communications obtained in all the circles throughout the wide domain of Spiritualism, then, in the judgment of all minds not desirous of being deceived, the high claims of the system "vanish into nought." If, on the other hand, the advocates of the system can show that these communications have, as far as we can test them, the known characteristics of reliability which peculiarize communications between individuals in this world, then the claims of the system must be admitted.

It will also be claimed by spiritualists, and that with truth, that in these circles, entirely *new* information is sometimes obtained—information in respect to subjects about which the inquirers, and all persons present, are totally uninformed. What test, to determine the fact of spirit-presence or absence, shall be applied in such cases? The answer is obvious To prove that such information has come from "the spirits" it must be rendered undeniably evident, that this same *kind* of information is never derived from the action of exclusively mundane causes. If, on comparing the facts presented, we find them to be identical, in all essential characteristics, with other facts originated in circumstances where the presence and action of "the spirits" are not at all to be presumed, then all evidence in favour of the claims of Spiritualism—evidence based upon such facts—totally disappears. No test is more evidential and important than this; and to its application the system will be held to the strictest account, provided our object is truth. We should dementate ourselves, if we should admit, as proof of spirit-presence and agency, facts of the same character as are known to result from exclusively mundane causes.

We here notice the capital error on which the claims of Spiritualism have thus far, dark-room *séances* aside, been, for the most part, based. An individual enters a circle, and puts a question to a spirit assumed to be present—a question pertaining to a subject about which, as he well knows, all in the circle, himself excepted, must be absolutely ignorant; a subject about which, as he is equally aware, himself and the spirit supposed to be present are perfectly informed. It is assumed here, that if the right answer is now given, the action of the force through which the answer is obtained *must* have been directed by the mental states of the spirit referred to. Here is a fundamental error. How do we know but that the action of this force may have been determined by the mental states of the inquirer, and not by those of any disembodied spirit at all? This is the very question to be determined by a careful investigation of the facts before us. Take away, as we must do, or violate all the laws of scientific deduction, the evidence derived from this one source, and all the most essential evidences of Spiritualism disappear at once.

Again: amid the multitudinous false communications which are continuously obtained in the spirit-circles, once in a while some statement is made relatively to some fact about which all present are profoundly ignorant—a statement which turns out to be true. This fact is at once heralded abroad as proof absolute of the claims of Spiritualism, and this without any inquiry whether precisely similar information is not often obtained through exclusively mundane causes. What an infinite and presumptuous leap in logic we have here! Before any valid inference whatever can be based upon such facts, it must be rendered undeniably evident that no such facts are ever originated through causes acting in the world around us.

A company of individuals seat themselves around a table, and place their hands upon its surface. Soon the object begins to move and to perpetrate wonderful antics; singular effects are also produced upon the bodies of individuals in the circles; or, from unknown causes, articles in a room or house begin to be strangely and spontaneously moved towards and from one another. We are compelled to admit that the era of old superstition has come again, when people infer merely from such facts, that "the spirits" are acting in our midst. Yet it is upon such unindicative facts as these, that the claims of Spiritualism are almost exclusively based. Leave such facts out of the account, as they undeniably should be, and the claims of the system vanish into nought.

The Mundane Theory.

We have already indicated much which pertains to the proper presentation of the character of this hypothesis. The advocates of this hypothesis admit the leading facts claimed by spiritualists as real, the reality of the force through which these phenomena are produced, and the agency of *mind* in the control of this force, as far as intellectual communications are concerned. What it claims is that the mental states by which this force is controlled in the production of such phenomena belong to minds in these circles, and not to spirits from any higher or lower sphere. We must bear in mind here, that the force by which these phenomena are produced, is developed by the circles in which these communications are obtained, and that that force is here developed by exclusively mundane causes. Without absolute proof to the contrary, we should conclude, that the causes which developed this force within these circles, control it while acting there. The burden of proof undeniably lies with the spiritualist, and not with the advocate of this mundane theory. All that is requisite to annihilate utterly the claims of Spiritualism, and to vindicate for that under consideration perfect claims to our regard as the true hypothesis, is to show conclusively that all these phenomena may be the exclusive result of mundane causes. If we should be able to go further than this, and to show, undeniably, that a large portion of these phenomena, and these among the most essential, *must* be regarded as being the result of exclusively mundane causes, and that the entire residuum of spirit-facts can be readily accounted for by reference to such causes, then, as all will admit, this mundane hypothesis will have received a strictly scientific verification. This is what we propose to accomplish in our future presentations.

In regard to our leading facts, we would say, that, in a work previously published, the mass of these facts have been before the American public for more than fifteen years, and the reality, and correctness of the statement, of not one of them has been questioned even by spiritualists themselves. Since his views were first made public, the author has been watching the progress of facts bearing upon the subject, and setting them in order for the establishment of the truth. All the facts which have come to his notice tend but in one direction—the confirmation of the mundane hypothesis as he has developed it. Through letters and verbal communications from leading minds in many parts of the United States, we have been advised and urged to give to the public, in a newly-arranged form, what we have formerly published, and have since gathered, upon a subject which may be truly said to be attracting the attention of Christendom. It is in accordance with such advice, and our own convictions of what the public interests demand, that the present work has been prepared, and is now commended to the careful and candid examination of the friends of truth. The principles laid down in this introduction will, as we judge, fully prepare the reader to appreciate the bearing of the facts and arguments which may be presented.

THE AFFIRMED VISIBLE, TANGIBLE, AND AUDIBLE MANIFESTATIONS OF SPIRITUALISM.

Before proceeding to a direct consideration of the facts before us, it may be deemed important that we say a few words upon the affirmed visible, tangible, and audible manifestations of the spirits—manifestations which have attracted so much attention during the few years past. In America, permit us to say, all these manifestations, the latest-invented ones not excepted, are "known and read of all men" as *detected* and *exposed* impositions. These wonders had their origin in an obscure town in Southern Ohio, and individuals travelled hundreds of miles, and paid very heavy admission fees, to enjoy the exalted privilege, as was afterwards demonstrated, of being miserably humbugged. When the imposition was exposed in that locality, similar and still greater wonders attracted public attention in others. Among the most celebrated of these impostors were the Davenport family, their performances being simply more inexplicable than those which had been exhibited elsewhere. In many of the places in which they appeared, however, they were detected in their impositions in the very act. For what they did in the city of Adrian, or are believed to have done, nobody supposes that any but the vilest spirits from the lower regions would keep them company. In the city of New York, they were proclaimed in all the papers as having been openly detected while in the act of perpetrating their detestable impositions. At this time, we read in a number of the

Banner of Light, the central organ of Spiritualism in the United States, a full account of these disclosures. In this article these Davenports were affirmed to be a family of vile and detected impostors, and the public were warned against them as such, and were protested to against holding Spiritualism as in any way responsible for the doings of these individuals. The manner in which the impositions of such individuals were exposed, was various. Sometimes, for example, the orifices of the trumpets, which the spirits were affirmed to blow in the darkness, were secretly covered with paint, which was found to cover the lips of the villains when the light was restored. At one time, when there was a show of spirit-hands, at the opening in the front of the dark closet, individuals were permitted to touch those hands. One strong man suddenly grasped one of those hands, and held it fast. The spirit struggled desperately to get free. The hand was held, however, until the fact was rendered demonstrably evident to the audience, that that hand belonged to a lying spirit in a human body skulked away in that dark closet. Here the most mysterious of their feats were copied. An individual well known in the city where we reside when at home, said to some friends of ours, from whom we received the account, "Go and get a rope; and having tied me just as you did them, leave me alone, as you left them, and see what the result will be." This was done. After the man was left alone a little time, the door—the only one by which the room could be entered—was opened, and there sat the man with the rope in his hand. This man affirmed that no spirit but his own had anything to do in "loosing his hands," and laughed, as well he might, at the spectators for supposing that none but spirits could untie ropes under such circumstances. The manner in which the Davenports were exposed in the city of New York was on this wise. The individual who was to extinguish the lights, left one of the burners lighted so slightly that the fact was not perceived. When the performance in the deep darkness was at its height, the noise of trumpets, stringed instruments, etc., being at the loudest, and individuals were being touched by spirit-hands, the light was suddenly let on; and there stood the whole Davenport family engaged in their fiendish impositions. By similar means were they, time and again, detected and exposed; yet, they would go into communities where they had not been before, and by their satanic impositions persuade multitudes of people that these elsewhere detected and exposed impostors were attended with audible, visible, and tangible manifestations of the presence of disembodied spirits. After deceiving many in America, they passed over to England, and palmed off upon untold multitudes here their impositions, which had become stale and intolerably offensive on the other side of the Atlantic. Yet we may safely challenge spiritualists to produce, through any of their *séances*, higher evidence of spirit-presence than has been furnished by these detected and exposed Davenports. All the showings of all the other mediums are of the same identical character, and are no more inexplicable than are the doings of these men.

One of the most popular means of convincing the people of the presence of spirits, was experiments of this kind. The medium would request individuals to write out sentences on pieces of paper, and then lay them, the blank surface upwards, upon the table. The spirits were then requested to read the writings on the slips, and afterwards guide the hand of the medium to write out what was contained on each slip. To convince the audience that all was done with perfect integrity, one man was appointed to sit at the table and watch the medium, and another to take up the papers in succession, and then, after the medium had read what the spirits had guided his or her hand to write, to read what was upon the paper in his hands. While such *séances* were being held in the city of Kalamazoo, in the state of Michigan, the late Squire Haskal, editor of one of the daily papers in the city, noticed that before the spirit-writing occurred, something was said, or done, evidently with design, to draw away the eyes and attention of people from the table and fix them upon some object in a distant part of the room, giving the medium time to lift the slips and read what was on them. He accordingly suggested to some friends, that at the next *séance* he should be appointed to sit at the table and watch the medium. This was agreed upon. As preparatory for what was to follow, Squire Haskal prepared two papers exactly like one another, and wrote upon each a sentence unlike what was written upon the other. When seated at the table, he laid one of these papers before the medium, and requested the spirits to reveal what was written thereon. After the usual act of diverting attention on her part, he took occasion to make some remarks, in the progress of which he, for a moment, diverted the attention of the medium and all others, as she had before done. During this moment, the papers were exchanged. When attention was restored to the business in hand, Squire Haskal requested that the present should be considered by the spirits, the medium, and the audience, as a *test* experiment, and hence, he would earnestly request the spirits to read with the greatest care that paper again. All this was agreed to by the audience, the medium, and, as affirmed through her, by the spirits. The medium, as moved by the spirits, wrote out what they had read upon

Squire Haskal's paper, and she, with great assurance, read what they had guided her to write. The man appointed to do so then took up the paper, and read that. To the amazement of the medium, and the surprise of the audience, the two were found not to agree at all. Squire Haskal then requested the man to read the other paper, and this was found to have been exactly copied by "the spirits." The medium was terribly enraged, and demanded that Squire Haskal should leave the platform at once. This he avowed himself well pleased to do, as he had exposed to the audience the cheat which was being played upon them. We state the facts as related to us by Mr. Haskal himself. It was by such disclosures as these that these *séance* wonders, the occasional newly-invented ones excepted, lost their interest and influence in America. We would here remark also, that the art of thus reading communications, and that without the aid of spirits, has now been carried much further than was ever done by spiritualists.

Another important fact demands special attention here. Not only have these wonder-workers been exposed as deliberate impostors, but their impositions, in all essential particulars, have been copied. Everything which they can do by the affirmed aid of spirits, has been, and is being, performed, not only in America, but in London and Paris; and far more mysterious things than these so-affirmed spirit-mediums can do is being done also. We have referred to the manner in which these wonders have been copied in America. Let any individual visit the nightly exhibitions of Maskelyne and Cook at the Egyptian Hall, London, and he will witness the performance, and that avowedly without the aid of spirits, of all that is claimed to have been done by their aid in the spirit-*séances.* We will refer to a few facts which we and other friends witnessed there. On a carpeted platform, everywhere in full view of the audience, stands a cabinet eight or ten feet high. This box stands upon rollers, and is freely moved in all directions. In front is a door with double openings, and at the right side, a little higher than the doors, is an opening into the cabinet—an opening in the form of a diamond. When the door or doors are opened, the audience have a full view of the entire inside of the box. A committee from the audience carefully examine this box within and without, rolling it in all directions to find whether it has any secret exterior connexions. Having fully satisfied themselves, they report that the cabinet is a strictly honest affair. In other parts of the room, and wholly disconnected with this box, are a table, chairs, etc.

The main exercises of the evening commenced with a striking exhibition of table-moving. A gentleman and lady seated themselves at the ends of a table, and placed their fingers upon the top of the same. The object immediately becomes violently agitated, moving in various directions, and finally turning bottom-side upwards, at quite a distance from the floor. This feat over, the lady leaves the table, and advances near the centre of the platform, where no visible object touches her but the carpet on which she stands. While standing there, she begins to ascend, as if borne upward by invisible powers. When she has reached a height of from two to four feet from the floor, and while she is standing thus "in mid air," an individual strikes with a cane under her feet, to prove that she is sustained there by nothing between her and the floor. After remaining in this position for some time, she is quietly let down to the floor, and takes her leave of the audience.

The time has now come for the cabinet exhibitions. Two men enter the box, and seat themselves opposite each other. The committee now enter, and with cords fasten the hands and feet of the men to bolts, which have been previously examined with all care. Everything is made as fast and secure as the committee know how to do it. When the committee leave the cabinet, the men become visible to the audience, and all see them fastened with cords as securely as human ingenuity knows how to do it, seals being placed upon the knots of the cords. Musical and other instruments are laid in the centre of the box, and placed out of contact with the men. The doors are now closed upon these men, and they are "left alone in their glory." Hardly have the doors been closed, however, when "spirit-hands" appear at the opening referred to, and an arm is put out quite to the elbow. Then the instruments are played upon and sounded, and a great "spirit-racket" is made inside that box. "After the uproar has ceased," the doors are opened, and the men appear, as securely fastened as before. The committee go in and find that not a bolt or cord has been apparently moved. A metallic ring, large enough to be passed over the hand on to the arm, is presented to the committee. The object, after being examined and found to be solid throughout, and marked so that it may be known when seen a second time, is placed in the box, with the request that one of the men would place it upon his left arm. After the usual time the doors were opened, and the ring was found upon the right arm of one of the men. He was reminded of his mistake, and was requested to change the ring from the right to the left arm. This was accordingly done. Then, the doors being closed again, the ring was immediately thrown out upon the platform. The doors being opened, and all found secure as before, one of the men was requested, as the next performance, to take off his coat. The doors being closed and then opened as before, the man's coat was found upon the bottom of the box, and he in his shirt-sleeves. A request was then made that someone in the audience would lend his coat, that "the medium" might put it on. This request was complied with, and after a little time the garment was found upon the back of the man in the box. The entire room was then darkened for a few moments, and when the light was thrown on again, the coat was found to have been taken from the back of the "medium," and laid in its owner's lap. The door of the box was then closed, with the request that the men inside should release themselves from their bonds. In about one minute the doors were opened and the men were seen standing there, with the cords lying at their feet. Between each experiment the men in the box were not only exposed to the full view of the audience, but the committee made a careful examination of the bolts, cords, knots, and seals, to see that all were in the same state as at the first.

After a little period, all the lights were extinguished, and we found ourselves in "the palpable obscure." Soon, objects, made partly visible by phosphorescent light attached to them, passed all about over our heads; a hand and arm appeared holding a tambourine; and notes of wind and stringed instruments were heard in the atmosphere of the room all above us. When the din ceased, and the lights were restored, nothing was visible to account for the phenomena which we had witnessed.

"The *séance*" closed with what seemed more mysterious than anything we had witnessed before. A trunk was placed upon the platform, and when opened a man came forward and laid himself down in the trunk. We all saw him lying there. A bit of a straw was given him, to be put out through a hole after the trunk should be closed. The lid was then put down and locked, and the trunk was bound with cords as securely as could be desired, and upon the knots of the cords seals were placed. When all was done, the bit of straw was put out of the hole designated, to render it demonstrably evident that the man was in the trunk. The trunk was then put into the box; and after it had remained closed less than two minutes, the doors were opened, and there stood the man, while nothing about the trunk was, to all appearance, changed at all. All the above, which are exact copies of the highest wonders of Spiritualism, were affirmed before the audience to have been performed by legerdemain, and without any help whatever from "the spirits."

Still more seemingly inexplicable, and explanatory of "the spirit-wonders," are the feats of legerdemain as nightly performed in the Hondin Theatre in Paris.

The French Government, finding that its authority over the people of Algiers was endangered by the Mahometan priests, and that the power of the latter over the former was sustained mainly by affirmed spirit-manifestations of the identical character which are occurring among spiritualists in Europe and America, sent over to Algiers a Mr. Robert Hondin, one of the most distinguished legerdemain wonder-workers in France. The mission of Mr. Hondin was to repeat before the people all the affirmed spirit-miracles of the priests, to add to these many others which they could not copy, and then reveal openly the manner in which all such deceptions were perpetrated. This was done, and the power of the priests over the people was broken. The wonders which Mr. Hondin performed in Algiers are now being repeated in the Hondin Theatre in Paris, and there modern spirit-wonders are not only being re-enacted, but far out-done. We will present two of these performances, as related to us from original observation by Professor Gregory, President of the Illinois Industrial University, in the United States, and Dr. Shurfey, formerly a surgeon in the United States army. The first performance to which we refer was on this wise. A young lad came out before the audience, and while standing in open view, and in the clearest light in their immediate presence, an individual approached and placed over the lad an object in the shape of a barrel. The man stepped back, and drawing a pistol from his pocket, fired it at the object before him. No sooner had the report of the pistol died away, than the voice of the lad was heard from the gallery announcing himself unhurt. The barrel was then taken up and found to be empty.

A large trunk was then brought upon the stage, shown to the audience to be empty, affirmed by the committee selected by the audience to be in that state, was locked, and the key retained by them. The trunk was then most thoroughly bound round in every direction by cords, which were firmly tied together and seals placed upon the knots. After this, a thick canvas covering was placed over and buckled firmly around the trunk. The whole was then bound round with cords fastened together, and sealed as in the first case. On being called, an individual looking like a Moor comes forward, with something like a bag upon his arm, and is asked if he can put himself into that bag, tie it over his head, as a bag of meal is tied up, and then put himself into that trunk without disturbing any of its fastenings. On his expressing his belief that he can perform the feat, circular curtains are let down around the trunk. When all has been fully examined by the committee and pronounced in due order, the stranger passes in where the trunk is, the committee standing all around to guard against deception. After standing there for a while, the curtains are raised, and nothing appears but the trunk, with no appearance whatever of having been disturbed. The committee now uncover, and open the trunk, and find lying in it something looking like a bag of meal tied up firmly at the top. The object, in full view of the audience, is taken out, placed on end, and untied at the top. The covering drops down, and there stands the Moor, as he passed into that curtained environment. While all the wonder-doings of the spiritualists are fully copied, such additional wonders are performed without the aid of "the spirits," and to expose the impositions of Mahometan priests, and spirit-mediums in Christendom.

The people of England may be interested to learn somewhat of the doings in America of Katie King, who occupied for some time the thoughts of the citizens of London. According to reports in the papers here, the portion of her hair which she allowed to be clipped, appears as veritable human hair, and her garments, the portion which she also allowed to be cut off, to be of English manufactory. In the reports we have read of her manifestations, it would seem very difficult, if not impossible, to account for her appearances and disappearances, or for her entrances and departures from the house where she appears, on the supposition that she is a spirit in a veritable human body. Hence the inference that she must be a visitant from the spirit-spheres. The idea that she is such a spirit might account, perhaps, for her *bodily* appearances and disappearances, entrances and exits, but not at all for similar facts relatively to her English manufactured clothing. If this home-made outer garment could be made to enter and pass out of that house, and to appear and disappear in it, the same, as it would appear to a philosopher, might be true of a human body inside of that garment. We leave these suggestions to the reflections of the reader.

According to American accounts, the cloth cut from Katie's garments is unlike any produced in any manufactory known to the people of London. Granting this, the case is not altered at all. The cloth is of a kind which can be cut and sewed like any other, and has the same characteristics of solidity, durability, and earthliness as any other cloth. Now, put a human body into garments made of such cloth, and it is, undeniably, no more difficult to account for the entrance into and exit from, or for the appearance and disappearance in, any room, of that body, than it is to account for similar facts relatively to the garments which that body wears. If we should judge otherwise, we should be compelled to admit that our logic and common sense both were in an abnormal state. Katie, then, as far as the facts under consideration are concerned, is no validly-evinced spirit-presence from any higher sphere than this.

Katie, however, after entertaining the people of London for a time, informed them that, having been called to a higher sphere, she must leave them for ever, or, at least, for the present. In regard to her new and more exalted sphere, we are now able to report its location. She left the small village of London and was transferred to the second story of a brick house in Ninth Street, in the great city of Philadelphia, in the United States of America; the first floor being occupied as a music store. Here she appears in the service of two mediums, Mr. and Mrs. Holmes, formerly well know in London. Her manifestations in this city, as reported in the American papers (our statements being taken from *Leslie's Illustrated Weekly*, as given from original observations)—her manifestations here, we say, are mainly a repetition of those in London, with this difference, that she here allowed herself to be sketched at full length. We would say, that if hers is a fair example of countenances among the celestials, we have but poor hopes of physical improvement there; and from Katie's verbal communications we are compelled to infer that she has been but a dull scholar during two centuries of schooling in the upper spheres. Katie did not make a long stay among the people of Philadelphia; being ambitious, no doubt, of occupying a still higher sphere, and she makes her next appearance, under the guardianship of Mr. and Mrs. Holmes, in the great city of Blissfield—a city located ten miles east of our residence when at home—a city of somewhat less than two thousand inhabitants, and located in the state of Michigan. Here, on the first floor of a common frame house, the people from all parts around were, when our last daily papers of the *Adrian Times* arrived, being entertained with the same spirit-manifestations with which Katie had previously "astonished the natives" of Philadelphia and London. Our *Times*' reporter gives a very clear account of the mysterious facts which he witnessed in one of these *séances*. The facts detailed are identical with the mysteries witnessed in Philadelphia and London. The reporter, however, found the people of Blissfield, from certain facts which they had noticed, almost, or quite, unanimous in the belief that the whole affair is deceptive, and the *séance* reported was suddenly brought to a close by some noises heard outside the house. The people, as the reporter affirms, manifest no disposition whatever for acts of disorder or violence. Their avowed plan is this—to watch the house on all sides and know whether any clandestine entrances occur; and if Katie shall appear in the *séance* room, to have several persons there who shall seize her, and hold her fast until she shall vanish from sight and touch, or be compelled to reveal herself as a human being. Had the London examiners manifested similar wisdom, Katie would now be "known and read of all men" as a veritable "spirit-presence" on the earth, or as "a deceiving spirit" in a human body. While watching the house outside, an individual in man's clothes was dimly seen slyly approaching the back part of the house, in the vicinity of a bedroom contiguous to that in which the *séances* are held. This individual was caught, and, after breaking a gutta percha cane into three parts about the head and shoulders of the man by whom he was caught and held, confessed himself a woman. After being refused the most earnest request to be permitted to approach and rap three times on the outside of the house where the *séance* was to be held, the man-woman was, at her piteous entreaties not to be compelled to be seen by the multitude, told to "go and sin no more." While a Katie was thus caught outside the house, no Katie King appeared in the *séance* room that evening, and Mr. Holmes the next day sent a man to Adrian to purchase a cane like that which had been broken. The people of Blissfield will have it that the real Katie King has been caught and verified as a woman in man's clothes in their midst. What is singular about the matter is, that, on an attempt to hold another *séance*, the people being on the alert, Mrs. Holmes, after the visitors had paid their money and were seated in readiness for the "spirit-manifestations," had a fit, from which she could not be recovered, and the audience left with less money and, perhaps, with more wisdom than they had before they were treated to "just nothing at all." The reason assigned by Mr. and Mrs. Holmes for these failures, as reported from them in the *Adrian Times*, is the following :—

"They gave the *séance* in good faith, and the fact that they had no manifestations from materialized spirits was on account of the plan laid by the parties in attendance, that, should Katie appear, they would seize her. This would cause the spirit, as well as the mediums, much pain. The spirits were, of course, aware of this, and refused to appear. Further than this they had no explanations to make."

To us, it appears that the public will not accept these as sufficient reasons for such non-appearance. Had Katie been caught, or suffered herself to be caught, and then vanished, as she might have done, had she been the spirit she pretended to be, the fact of such disappearance would have convinced the world of her real spirit-character. Her refusal to meet such a test lost her a golden opportunity to verify her pretensions, and throws more than suspicion over them all.

The messenger of the *Times* now went down to Blissfield, and agreed with Mr. and Mrs. Holmes for a *test séance*, the individuals to be selected by the messenger, and to be constituted equally of believers and unbelievers in Spiritualism. When the conditions were submitted to Katie, this answer, as reported by the mediums, was received from her. We give her response with facts and remarks as stated in the *Times*:—

" She will not consent to appear while the bed-room in the rear of the cabinet is occupied. Parties will, doubtless, put their own construction on this change of programme. To many it will be evidence of the truth of the Blissfield theory, that with the bed-room occupied and the doors leading to the main room guarded, 'Katie' is unable to appear. It is certain that when, on the occasion of a recent *séance*, Mr. Blaisdell, of Blissfield, occupied the bed-room, 'Katie' stated that she 'gained strength' from him. But then her appearance was preceded by a dark *séance*, and the doors leading to the main room were not carefully guarded."

Lest anyone should affirm, that we have in America a *pseudo*-Katie, we will give the account of her manifestations as given in Frank Leslie's *Illustrated Newspaper*, and the *Adrian Times*. After describing the preliminaries, Mr. Leslie's account thus proceeds:—

"The light being now lowered a little, but not so as to render surrounding objects invisible in any degree, we were one and all requested to join in singing, for the purpose, it was said, of "harmonizing the influences." Preferring to keep our eye upon the small openings, and the cabinet door, that, after our inspection, had been closed and latched, we declined to give any specimen of our vocal powers, although those about us began to sing, and most tunefully, some melody that was unknown to us. In the course of a few moments, we thought that we perceived the curtain that hung before the lower pentagonal aperture move; and scarcely had the idea taken possession of us when the white and shapely arm of a woman was thrust through the opening, and the latch that fastened the door lifted, by apparently soft, taper fingers, out of the staple. The arm was now withdrawn, and almost instantly afterwards a sweet, young face appeared at the same aperture, with a soft, low 'good-evening,' which we must confess rather astonished us. The salutation being eagerly returned by all present, one of the mediums, neither of whom moved from our side during the *séance*, asked the mysterious visitant whether she thought she should be able to leave the cabinet during the *séance*, when she replied, 'I will try.' This phase of the phenomena was what we most desired to witness. Nor were we kept long in suspense; for, in a very few minutes, the cabinet door opened slowly, and out stepped, in full view of us all, and just as she is represented in our illustration, the so-called spirit of the now famous Katie King! Although set down as a denizen of the other world, she seemed to us to be as objective a reality as ever trod this earth. She walked among us, permitted us to touch her hands, and her white robe; and spoke to us in good round modern English, which we considered somewhat extraordinary, seeing that she lived upwards of two hundred years ago, when the quaintness of Spencer overshadowed her native tongue. This and some kindred circumstances, which had previously come to our knowledge, we did not pause to analyze at the moment, for we felt that she was a very mysterious being, at least, and we were engaged in scrutinizing her person with all the coolness and vigour at our command. She was exceedingly handsome, and appeared to us to be about nineteen years of age, and of medium height. She wore a white robe of some singular fabric, and a light drab veil wound gracefully about her head. The folds of her dress concealed her feet, but her arms were bare, and, like her figure, exquisitely moulded. Her complexion was absolutely transparent, and her hair, instead of being dark as generally represented, was, in our opinion, auburn, with a golden tinge. She wore no ornaments, and after remaining with us four or five minutes, and making a few very commonplace observations, she re-entered the cabinet without closing the door. Here she stood facing us for a few seconds, when Mrs. Holmes asked her whether she could disappear before the visitors as she had done on previous occasions. To this interrogatory she made the same reply as she had to the other; and, surprising to relate, gradually faded away into thin air before us, until not a vestige of her was to be seen. Nor was this all, for a few moments subsequently, and outside the cabinet, within three or four feet of us, she began slowly to form again, until she stood before us in all her perfection once more. After this, she bade us a kind 'good-night,' and, re-entering the cabinet, she disappeared before the door was closed; and the *séance* was at an end."

After detailing the early manifestations, in which there was a showing of hands and faces, the *Adrian* account proceeds thus:—

"After this many others in the room, including the writer, were permitted to step to the cabinet, and receive touches from the hand of the mysterious personage. The reporter asked and received permission to shake hands with her, and received a very light pressure of the hand. Whether that hand was human or spiritual he does not pretend to say. Mrs. Holmes then asked the mysterious visitor whether she thought she would be able to leave the cabinet during the *séance*, and she replied, "I will try." During all this time there was singing by those present, or music by a violin and guitar. There was a short time of suspense, the only sound being the low, subdued sound of the violin; then the cabinet door opened slowly, and there stood, in full view of all in the room, the so-called spirit of the famous 'Katie King.' She was clad in the traditional white flowing robes of the 'Summer Land,' and appeared about nineteen years of age. Although said to belong to another world, she appeared as real as any being in the room, but with more of an ethereal look. Her white robe hung gracefully about her, while her head seemed enfolded in some kind of a veil. Upon her neck hung a beautiful cross, which glistened in the light. After a moment, she stepped back into the cabinet and closed the door. Soon afterward she appeared again in the open door. After standing an instant she stepped forward into the room some four or five feet, almost within touching distance of the writer. Here he had an excellent chance of observing her appearance. Her arms were bare, her feet were concealed by the folds of her dress, and her figure was finely moulded. Her complexion was almost transparent. After a little time she again returned to the cabinet. Mrs. Holmes then asked her if she should place a chair for her, and received an affirmative answer. A chair was placed near the cabinet and the door soon opened, and 'Katie' appeared again, walking out in the room as before, and then turning and sitting in the chair, where she remained a few moments, and again retired to the cabinet."

It will be readily granted, that the American, if not the same, equals the English Katie. In view of the facts before us, we claim, that all valid evidence of her being a spirit-visitant from "the undiscovered country" is utterly wanting. It is undeniable that no more mysterious facts are recorded of her than are known to result from exclusively mundane causes. This takes away absolutely all valid evidence of the genuineness of her spirit-pretensions. The hair cut from her head, and the garments she wears, are, as none will deny, of an exclusively mundane character. Such objects cannot be made, without miraculous interposition, to appear and disappear, as those belonging to Katie do, but by tricks of legerdemain. If by such means such objects may be made thus to appear and disappear, the same, undeniably, may be true of a human body to which such hair belongs, and is inside of such garments. The facts developed at Blissfield clearly evince her as a "false spirit" in the flesh. Why did not Katie King appear in the *séance* in the house on the evening when the man-Katie was caught outside of the house? Why did Mr. Holmes send a special messenger ten miles to Adrian, to replace the cane which the man-Katie had broken over the back of her captor? Why does Katie now, after having found that she "gained strength" through the presence of an individual in that bed-room—other avenues of access to her cabinet being then left unguarded—and after all the arrangements for a test *séance* have been agreed upon (one specific item of the agreement being that a man shall be in that bed-room while the *séance* is being held)—why does Katie now refuse to appear at all, unless that contiguous and convenient room shall be left for her exclusive occupancy? If she is a spirit, as she affirms herself to be, why does she not suffer herself to be caught and held fast, and then vanish from the sight, and touch, and grasp of those who hold her?

Permit us, before closing our observations on these *séances*, to refer to two or three facts which have come to our knowledge during our short stay in London. A personal friend of ours, a gentleman of high intelligence and integrity, a graduate of Cambridge University, was invited to attend a *séance* in a family whose reputation was such as to induce—if any such pretensions could—absolute confidence in the integrity of the whole exhibition. He, with several other friends, having paid the large admission fees required, took their places among other spectators. After the preliminaries were gone through with, a lady-medium having been put into a mesmeric sleep, and seated within the box, various spirit-faces appeared at the window, and communicated with the audience,—individuals being permitted to touch the hands and clothing of the spirits. At length a face partly covered appeared, and, with the sweetest smiles, bowed to our friend. As he looked at that countenance, he became fully convinced that there was before him the veritable face of a sister who had died a few years previous. Of course, he was deeply moved; and affirmed to his parents, on returning home, that he had that evening seen the spirit-face of their departed daughter.

At a *séance* subsequently attended by our friend, a man was the medium placed within the box. In this case a male ghost appeared, and a very vulgar one too, his manner and language being very gruff and uncouth. The ghost, however, freely conversed with the audience, and gave to all who approached him a cordial shake of the hand. On taking his hand, our friend perceived that it had the warmth of a human hand, those who had taken it before having affirmed it to have been ghostly cold. Our friend remarked to the ghost that his hand was then warm, and not cold, as it had been when touched by others, and asked him if he could not render his hand cold as it before had been. This the ghost promised to do. While the cooling process, which was quite long-continued, was going on, our friend put some paint, having prepared this beforehand, on the inside of his middle finger. The hand, on being taken a second time, was found to be still warm, but damp,—it evidently having been held in cold water. That hand was consequently in the proper state to receive and retain the paint put upon it. Immediately after this the *séance* was broken up. As the medium came out of the cabinet, however, the paint was visible on the back of his hand. A spiritualist gave this explanation of this fact: "Whatever you do to the spirit," he remarked, "you do to the medium,"—a statement which held literally true in the case before us. Such an explanation may satisfy a spiritualist; but what will be its impression upon all truly sane minds? Our friend, however, has, since this last disclosure, had no desire to visit the *séances* in search of ghosts. We have full permission to employ our friend's name, when we have occasion to do it.

The papers gave an account, some weeks since, of light being suddenly thrown on one of the circles of a dark *séance*, in this country, and there stood revealed before the audience the medium manipulating the faces of the simpletons in the circle with spirit-hands. The indignation of the audience turned, not upon their deceiver, but upon the individual who revealed to them the fact that they were being humbugged. By special invitation of a friend, we attended one of the so-called most wonderful of these *séances*. The thought that any rational being could infer the evidence of spirit-presence and agency from what was exhibited there, has led us to repeat an exclamation which we recal from our child's spelling-book, namely, "Oh, the folly of sinners!" What was pronounced by the manager as the leading wonder of the whole exhibition was the following: The medium, a young woman, being placed in the cabinet, and bound with cords, as is usual in such cases, a large bucket was placed in her lap, with this announcement, that after the doors had been closed for a little time, and then re-opened, that bucket would be found to have been taken from her lap, and placed over her head. On re-opening the cabinet, the bucket was, in fact, found as promised. What power on earth could perpetrate such a feat as that but "the spirits"? If we continue to reason thus, shall we not be compelled to conclude that our ancestors must have been monkeys?

Since writing the above, and after my manuscript was fully completed, news has come from America, intelligence of facts, which have closed up the occupation of ghost-exhibitions in that country. The *dêbut* of Katie King was, for a time, a great success in Philadelphia,—so great, that she was becoming an object of worship with spiritualists. The following is a stanza from one of the hymns which were being sung in her praise:—

"Oh, gather round, and let us sing
The praises of sweet Katie King,
Who, from her bright and happy sphere,
Comes smiling to us mortals here.

Chorus:
Then with sweet voices let all sing
The praises of sweet Katie King."

In their adoration of the heavenly visitant, ladies took off their jewelry and choicest ornaments, and gave them to the ghost, who promised to take such gifts with her, as keepsakes, to the celestial spheres. Her standing indorsers were the celebrated Robert Dale Owen, and Henry T. Child, M.D., of Philadelphia. In a late number of the *Atlantic Monthly*, Mr. Owen gives to the world a history of the facts which he had personally witnessed in respect to Katie, in the *séances* of Mr. and Mrs. Holmes. The facts, as he affirms, lead us to one or the other of these conclusions, namely, Katie King is a veritable spirit from "the undiscovered country," or "human bodies, without leaving a trace behind them, can freely pass through brick walls of the thickness of two or three feet." The fact, admitted by Mr. Owen, that when Katie disappeared, the solid jewelry, which she took with her, disappeared also, did not in the least stagger his faith in the validity of his logic. A gentleman of the city, however, in shaking hands with the ghost, perceived that "the sweet Katie King" had a very foul breath,—a fact of a seeming mundane character. This gentleman then determined to search out the whole matter. Keeping his eyes open as he was walking the streets of the city, he soon discovered a woman who was putting up in a certain house—a woman who was in all respects "the image and likeness" of the ghost Katie. This woman, as he found, always visited the Holmses prior to the holding of the *séances*, accompanied them to the room where the exhibitions were held, and, without leaving the place, was never visible in the audience. Having furnished the ghost with jewelry which he would recognise as soon as he should find the articles again, he now sought with much care a personal acquaintance with the woman referred to, and succeeded to his full satisfaction. In the course of their interviews the woman exhibited, for the entertainment of her new acquaintance, the mass of jewelry of which she was possessed. Among the articles exhibited, the gentleman selected those which he had himself furnished, and then confronted the woman with the charge, that she was the veritable Katie King. At first the charge was stoutly denied. When the proof was presented, however, she made a full confession, restored the jewelry to those from whom she had received it, and has since, under oath, given in the public papers a full account of the manner in which her deceptions had been perpetrated.

The individual who drew from Katie the confession

of her impositions was, at first, at a loss to determine how to make his discovery known, and to do it in a manner which would secure public confidence. He finally determined to lay the facts before Dr. Childs and Mr. Owen, and let them be the first to undeceive the people. This they promptly did, each, in a card published in *The Banner of Light*, the organ, as stated before, of Spiritualism in the United States, recanting his indorsements of the *séances* of Mr. and Mrs. Holmes. Mr. Owen, in the meantime, sent to the conductors of the *Atlantic Monthly* an agonising request that his article which he had furnished them, demonstrating the ghostship of "the sweet Katie King," with a foul breath, should not appear in their columns. The request came too late, however, and our friend was compelled to appear before the world in a very unpleasant predicament indeed—a predicament of which the *New York Tribune* thus very properly speaks:—"A man who is too strong-minded to believe in Christianity, and yet who finds no difficulty in believing that spirits come out of a closet, and dance breakdowns on a platform, and spin mosquito-netting out of the air, is scarcely a promising subject for argument. To say he disbelieves the Bible because he cannot understand it, and believes in Katie King because he has seen her, simply shows that he is as vain of the feebleness of his understanding as he is of the blindness of his eyes."

As the deceptions perpetrated by the young and beautiful widow with one child, Mrs. Frances, or Eliza, White, "the material spirit of Katie King," were of a legally criminal character, she was informed that it was right and proper for her to make a full exposure of the whole concern with which she had been connected. This she at length did as above stated, detailing, at full length, the manner in which she would seemingly vanish and reappear before audiences, her manner and places of concealment, when her hiding-places, the bed-room and others, were searched both before and after the *séances*, and all the other deceptions of herself and Mr. and Mrs. Holmes. The following account which Mrs. White gives of the manner in which their *séances* were brought to a close in Blissfield will interest the reader:—

"An evening was set for a party who were to come from Adrian. The inner circle was formed by Mr. and Mrs. Holmes, the family who lived in the house, and a Mr. B., a merchant of Blissfield, and two or three more friends of the family. The Adrian people were kept in the rear, and scattered about the room. I was playing the part of Katie, as usual, in the cabinet, and was in the act where Katie was disappearing and reappearing. I had faded away, and was just rising up to full stature, the cabinet door standing open, when Mr. Brown sprang forward and caught me in his arms. I had presence of mind enough not to scream. Mr. Holmes immediately grabbed Mr. B. by the heels, which threw him down. In the struggle I escaped. Mrs. Holmes immediately darted into Mr. B.'s arms, calling for someone to turn on the lights. When the lights were turned on, Mr. B. was lying in a horizontal position, with his heels outside the cabinet and his head inside, and Mrs. Holmes in his arms. I had escaped from the cabinet into the back room, taking with me the black cloth I held over me when I disappeared, and the stool I had been standing on. Mrs. Holmes declared that Mr. B. had grabbed at the spirit and caught her. Of course the excitement for a few minutes was very great. Mr. Holmes then shut the cabinet door. I returned into the cabinet and commenced imitating 'Dick,' telling the audience how foolish it was for anyone to attempt to catch a spirit; that Katie was very indignant at the gentleman grabbing her medium."

Mr. B. affirmed, however, that, contrary to his will, the ghost forced herself, at the time of his fall, from his arms, and that afterwards Mrs. Holmes, who was sitting in her chair, as all knew, at the time when the ghost was caught, forced herself into his arms. So the public believed, and, as Mrs. W. states, no more *séances* were held at the west, and all parties returned to Philadelphia, where the disclosures above presented were made. On these disclosures I make the following remarks: 1. The identity of this Mrs. White with the supposed ghost, Katie King, is an absolutely verified fact, which no candid person will dispute. 2. If we compare the accounts given by Mr. Owen and other credible witnesses, of the facts presented by the Katie King of Philadelphia, with those recorded by credible witnesses of the doings of the Katie King of London, the former will be found to be quite as mysterious, and of as difficult explanation, as the latter; and the fact, that the former stand revealed to the world as demonstrated impositions, takes away wholly all evidence that the latter are not of the same character. 3. As the Katie King manifestations are more mysterious and of more difficult explanation than any and all others ever presented in any *séances* in Christendom, all evidence that ghosts have appeared in any of these *séances* is utterly annihilated. Hence it is that, as we have said, the occupation of ghost-exhibitors is gone, as far as the United States are concerned. It remains to be determined, however, which portion of the Anglo-Saxon race, that on the east or west side of the Atlantic, has the strongest propensity for being humbugged.

The test applied at Blissfield may appear to some rather rude. We will propose one against which no such objection, or any objection of any kind, can be made. Let the city authorities of London, or the Faculties of Oxford or Cambridge, designate four or six ladies, and as many gentlemen, of known reputation for integrity and intelligence. Let these individuals attend the ghost *séances*, and if a female ghost appears, let the ladies, and if a male ghost shows itself, let the gentlemen, encircle, and lay, not a violent, but a firm, grasp upon the person appearing. If said person shall vanish from sight and touch, then all the world will admit that a veritable ghost has appeared among us. If, on the other hand, the person grasped turns out to be a human spirit in a human body, then all will know that these *séances* are base deceptions. Christ, as we know, did submit to an analogous test to prove that He was not a spirit. Why should not modern ghosts submit to a similar test, and thus demonstrate the fact that they are ghosts? Let the public universally demand such a test, and not another *séance* will ever be held in Christendom, and that for the reason that these ghosts and their exhibitors know absolutely that their *séances* are vile deceptions, and that such tests will demonstrate them to be such.

While such disclosures were being made in the city of Philadelphia, others of about equal importance were made in the cities of New York and Boston. An individual in the former city, being determined to know the truth on the subject, went to the noted

Andrew Jackson Davis, who now keeps the great spiritualistic book-store in that city, and asked him if he could designate, among the quite one hundred individuals who were known to be holding *séances* in the city, one or more whose integrity could, in his judgment, be relied on. Knowing, as he did, that the question was put for the simple purpose of correct information, Mr. Davis refused, not only to designate such persons, but to express an opinion that there was one individual among them who was not habitually dealing in fraud and deception. When three of the most distinguished of all the others were designated and inquired about, Mr. Davis refused to express an opinion favourable to their integrity. His only reply to all such inquiries was, "You must, as I do, find out the facts for yourself." The inquirer then visited the three mediums referred to, and detected them in the grossest attempts at deception conceivable. No candid mind can read the disclosures which this man has made through the columns of the *New York Herald*, and not infer that the trade of those mediums is "lying wonders." The mediums to which I now refer, do not make revelations, as Mrs. Fish and the Fox girls did,—that is, by means of real facts of nature which require explanation, and which we shall hereafter attempt to explain,—but by means of slight-of-hand tricks which have been invented and connected with Spiritualism since its origin. The following article from the *Boston Globe* will, notwithstanding its length, be regarded as worthy of a place in our pages.

"A young man lives within five miles of the state house who has made a study of all the tricks and illusions of modern legerdemain, and is an accomplished performer therein, whose interest has been excited upon the subject of Spiritualism. Some of his friends had become devout believers in Spiritualism, and he, feeling assured in his own mind that they were the victims of fraud, went to work to investigate and expose what had been to them the strongest evidence of spirit-presence. After three visits to the *séances* of Mrs. Hardy, in this city, he became convinced that he was master of the whole subject, at least so far as the dark-circle manifestations were concerned, and could give a successful *séance* of his own, without the help of spirits. Accordingly he arranged for the sitting at his own home, and it took place last evening. The same representative of the *Globe* who made a visit to Mrs. Hardy and gave an account of what he saw, as it appeared to him, was among the persons invited.

"A company of seventeen persons, all specially invited to see an *exposé* of the dark-circle manifestations, gathered at this house. When they had all come together, they were taken to a room in which chairs were arranged in the usual way for a circle.

They took their places, the chairs being drawn close together, making a ring of ten or twelve feet in diameter. The amateur "medium" took a chair in the middle of the circle, simply imposing the same conditions upon the company as are exacted by the professionals. The feet of one of the visitors were placed upon his to make sure that he did not move from his place, and he patted his hands together with a distinctly audible sound all the time, to show that they were not occupied in producing the manifestations. The hands of the persons in the circle were clasped together in the usual way. The light was then turned out, and, after the momentary pause usual in such cases, the raps were heard which announced the presence of the powers of darkness. The patting of hands continued without intermission, and presently a fan was seized from one of the party, and fanned the faces of the sitters all around the circle. Hands were shaken and patted, knees were slapped and faces touched by invisible beings. A watch was taken from one person and given to another on the opposite side of the circle. One man's cravat was taken off and given to another, and afterwards placed on the head of the owner. A music-box which had been placed in the hands of one person with the key in that of another was taken away and given to another in another part of the circle. The key was taken and the box wound up, and it could be heard tinkling through the air, above the head of the performer; and all the other demonstrations usual in these circles were produced with all the effect of the genuine spiritual *séance*. Finally, there was a cessation for a moment; raps were heard, indicating that the performance was over for the time being, a light was struck, and our amateur 'medium' was discovered in precisely the position he occupied when the gas was turned out, quietly clapping his hands; and the person who held his feet testified that he had not moved. After a little rest, he took a new position, with a different person holding his feet, and substantially the same performance was repeated. All the persons present, several of whom had been believers in Spiritualism, declared that the manifestations were every way as perfect and satisfactory as any that they had ever experienced.

"The young man then tried an experiment with perfect success, which he said he had seen Mrs. Hardy try three times, but without success, because, as she claimed, the conditions were not right for a proper working of the spirits. He was tied to a chair with a cord, the lower and upper part of his body, and had his wrists tied together with a handkerchief, in such a way that one would suppose that he would be unable to do anything. His feet were secured, as usual, a glass of water placed on the floor some feet from his chair, and the lights turned out. Instantly the clapping began, and similar demonstrations to those already described were kept up for a few minutes, and then a light struck, when the performer was revealed in the same position as before, with the cords and handkerchiefs securely tied, and the glass of water standing on his head. Yet another feat, more remarkable than this, followed. An ordinary padlock, which closed with a spring, was locked, and the key given into the keeping of a young lady. A cord was passed through the clasp and tied together with one hard knot after another, until more than a foot of knots was produced. This was thrown upon the floor. Then an euchre pack of cards was taken, including all the suits from the ten to the ace, and enough thrown out to reduce the number to seventeen, the number of persons in the circle. After due instructions had been given, the circle was formed in the usual way, with the medium in the customary position, clapping his hands. The lights were again turned out. The cards were taken from the box and shuffled by one person and passed to his left-hand neighbour, who shuffled them again, and so on around the circle. The person who began the shuffling then took the top card, and passed the pack along, each person taking off the top card in like manner, thus using up the entire pack. Then the first person interrogated the medium as to the card which the said person held. 'Is it a heart?' 'Is it a diamond?' 'Is it a spade?' 'Is it a club?' At the mention of some one of the suit, distinct raps were heard, indicating that that was the one. 'Is it the ten?' 'Is it the jack?' 'Is it the queen?' etc., was then asked, and when the right denomination was named the raps were repeated. So it went on around the entire circle, each person, meantime, having the card in his or her pocket, and being warned to remember what it was, according to the information of the raps. This process being completed, the light was struck. The 'medium' was bound up and tied to his chair with the cord that had been fastened so securely upon the lock, his hands were tied together with a handkerchief, and he was securely blindfolded with another handkerchief, and the lock was clasped into the button-hole of a gentleman's coat. Moreover, every person, without exception, found that he held the card designated in the dark by the raps.

"Now, of course, everybody was anxious to know how it was done. It was as mystifying as anything accomplished in the dark by professional mediums. The young man volunteered to give the first manifestations with the gas burning. The circle was formed in the approved way, the raps were made with his knuckles on the chair without perceptibly interrupting the clapping, to indicate that the conditions were right. In an instant he slipped off his coat, and his arms were bare to the shoulders. While he kept clapping with one hand, sometimes on the upper part of his arm, sometimes on the face, he stretched out the other hand, seized a fan, and fanned the faces all around. With one hand and then the other he clapped knees, shook hands, patted faces, and did everything done before in the dark without any intermission of the clapping, any moving of the feet, or any audible movement of the body. The whole thing was as simple as 'rolling off a log.' The coat was put on, one arm at a time, while the other hand kept up the patting sound on the performer's cheek, and the raps were given telling that the show was over. A woman with loose sleeves, furnished with a bit of elastic, would not have to take off or put on any garment. The other and more puzzling tricks were not explained, but everybody believed the assurance which they received, that they were tricks, and nothing more. The young man claims to have learned the art from his visit to Mrs. Hardy's circle, and to have obtained indubitable evidence that it was performed as he had shown. What the evidence was he stated, and it certainly seemed to be beyond question."

Mr. and Mrs. Holmes, it is well known, made quite a sensation in London before they opened rooms in Philadelphia. Mrs. White—this is not her real name, it being, at her earnest entreaty, kept from the public—was persuaded to furnish the letters which she had received from Mr. and Mrs. Holmes. We give one of these, as an example of the rest, that the public may understand by what kind of persons sensible people are being humbugged. Of the individuals who practise these deceptions, those that I have met with are uniformly of a low order of mind, with two exceptions—a bold and fearless impudence (like that with which a vile louse was once seen walking over the silk dress of a fair lady), and a sly cunning, which makes them perfect adepts in the arts of deception. Those who originated, and carried to the highest perfection, the ghost-*séances* of the United States, were wholly from the lower strata of society. Mrs. Holmes was accustomed to call her Katie, Frank, and Frankie. Of the authenticity of the following letter, and others of a kindred character, the Philadelphia *Enquirer* affirms that there can be no doubt. We feel humiliated when we read it, to think that sensible people will consent to be humbugged by such minds.

"BLISSFIELD, *August* 24, 1874.

"DEAR FRANK:—I wish I could see you to day it is very dull here in this little town, Nelson is ritten too and I expect he will rite ali the news to you you need not bee afraid of our not dooing the fair thing with you for we shall. I have been quite cick and am not able to set up now but thought I must rite a few lines to you I got dispointed in gitting the money that I told you I expected I found my brother in poor circumstances so he could not pay me eney thing but Nelson says he will send you fifty dollars next week then you had better cum as soon as you get this how is Sam getin along let me know. A kiss for you, from

"JENNIE HOLMES."

"exkuse this for I am cick to day love to Sam I must tell you something good Nelson and I have been very good to each other we have not had a cross werd since we left home that makes me feel glad and you will sympathise with me wont you dear Frank."

PHOTOGRAPHY AND SPIRITUALISM.

The main reliance of Spiritualism, at the present time, as I have recently been informed by a very intelligent spiritualist in this city, is upon spirit-phenomena connected with the art of photography. Spirits now disturb photographers (of the spiritualistic class) by causing their own likenesses to appear on the background on the plates on which the likenesses of individuals are being taken. In regard to this new wonder of Spiritualism, I would say, in all sincerity, that any man who is as well acquainted with past wonders of the system as the author of this treatise is, and does not choose to be humbugged, will be in the same attitude of mind in respect to this new wonder that a Dutch justice of the peace in America was towards an individual who was being tried before the former for theft. When the indictment was read, the prisoner confessed his guilt. The justice, however, called for witnesses to prove the charge. "Why," said the attorney for the prosecution, "the man confesses his crime." "I know that," replied the justice, "but the fellow is such an infernal liar, that he is not to be believed, let him say what he will." Every solitary wonder which Spiritualism has added to the kind of facts originally presented by Mrs. Fish and the Fox girls, has turned out to be a deception. We should, therefore, dementate ourselves, if we should run after any new wonder the system may present. In the case before us, however, the art by which just such spirit-faces as are shown in this city can be produced, is well known in America, and also, as I suppose, in this country; and just as many such likenesses can be furnished to order as those who wish to be humbugged will consent to pay for. The likenesses, also, which we have seen, are of such a low and mundane character, that any sensible man would blush with inward shame to admit that they are spirit-representations. These likenesses, also, present demonstrative proof that they are wholly deceptive. If a spirit were present for the purpose of having his likeness appear, he would be there as an invisible and intangible presence, and the light from the objects behind the spirit would be passing through it as freely as if it were not there. Those objects, consequently, by the laws of light, must appear in the background, and the spirit-face, if it should appear at all, would, by no possibility, appear but as a thin veil before said objects. When a veiled countenance is taken, for example, the countenance and the veil both appear, with the latter as before the former. So of the spirit-face. If it should appear at all, it must appear with the objects behind distinctly seen through it. The spirit-faces, in all the cases in which they are shown, as completely hide, on the other hand, the objects behind, as do the countenances of individuals who are sitting for the purpose of having said likenesses taken. Here, then, Spiritualism demands that our credulity shall be infinite; that is, that we admit the occurrence of facts through natural laws—facts, the occurrence of which, without miraculous interposition, the known laws of nature render impossible.

To the above, spiritualists present this reply: the spirit, when present, draws to itself all the electricity existing in all the bodies present, and then produces its own image, not through common, but through electric, light. Here we have a mere assumption, unsustained by the remotest degree of evidence whatever. Besides, as electric differs from common light, so must the appearance of the countenances which they respectively produce, differ from one another. No such differences, however, do appear. We have all the evidence, on the other hand, that we possibly can have, that all images which appear upon the plate were originated there by the same identical kind of light. Nor, I remark finally, does the electricity which the spirit may gather to itself prevent the common light from passing, with absolute fulness and freedom, from the objects behind the spirit to the place where they must image their own forms. Every aspect in which the subject can be viewed, renders the photographic pretensions of Spiritualism, like its other "lying wonders," intentional deceptions. I have been gravely assured but a few days since, and that in the city of London, that spirit-likenesses are actually taken in total darkness. "Give me light," exclaimed the ancient Grecian hero, "and Ajax asks no more." "Give me darkness," exclaims Spiritualism, "and if creatures are disposed to be humbugged, I can deceive the universe." That is all the reply that such a pretension demands of any sensible person.

I have been told that, in America, photographs are taken in which the objects behind the spirit are also seen through it. The art of producing just such phenomena, and that without the aid of spirits, is well known in that country. We do, also, a great many strange things in America, and seem to be endowed with special gifts for humbugging sensible people on this side of the Atlantic. I give it as my opinion, that no object absolutely invisible and intangible can be photographed at all. Any object to be photographed must possess sufficient solidity to receive, stop, and reflect light, and that in sufficient quantity to make an image; and such object must be visible. If the art under consideration has verified anything, I think it has done this, that light reflected from any object cannot form an image more visible than is the object which reflects the light.

LEVITATION.

Much is said in the papers, at the present time, on the subject of levitation, the ascent of human and other bodies from the earth, and that from no visible cause. In the progress of this treatise, facts of this character will be undeniably verified. Such facts, however, as will also appear, have no more connexion with the claims of Spiritualism, one way or the other, than they have with the transit of Venus. Suppose that a human or any other heavy body should rise up before us, and we cannot tell the reason why. What infinite fools we should make of ourselves, if we should leap to the conclusion, that intangible, impalpable, and unearthly spirits laid hold of that object, and lifted it from the earth. Let us not, in our reasonings upon this and other subjects, permit our intelligence to fly to "brutish beasts."

CONCLUDING REMARKS, AND PLAN OF THE TREATISE.

Thus far, as has been rendered sufficiently evident, the proofs adduced in favour of Spiritualism—proofs drawn from visible and tangible manifestations of spirit-presence—have been palpable failures, and have turned out to the dishonour of not a few of its advocates. At the basis of the system, however, there have, in all ages and countries (for the system is about as old as the race),—there have been at the basis of the system, we say, real facts of an intellectual and physical character, which demand a careful examination of all who would understand the world within and the world without them, as they are. It will readily be admitted by all candid minds, that if the classes of facts now under consideration shall be fully explained, and evinced as resulting from exclusively mundane causes, the residuum may be left for future investigation and discovery, and thus left with the assurance that science will discover for these a similar exposition. In prosecuting our investigations, we shall consider the subject in the following order:—

I. Electricity, Magnetism, and Animal Magnetism distinguished.—Effects of Animal Magnetism upon the Human System.

II. The Odylic or Psychic Force—Its Properties—Its Relations to Spirit-manifestations, and to the Phenomena of Mesmerism and Clairvoyance.

III. Physical and Intellectual Manifestations Elucidated.

IV. Proof that all these Manifestations have an Exclusively Mundane Origin.

V. Tendency of Spiritualism.

VI. Miscellaneous Topics.

CHAPTER I.

ELECTRICITY, MAGNETISM, AND ANIMAL MAGNETISM DISTINGUISHED.

In accomplishing the object immediately before us, we would remark, that philosophers have unitedly affirmed, and the public generally are now fully aware of the truth of that affirmation, the existence and action of the three following distinct powers or forces in nature, namely, *Electricity*, *Magnetism*, and *Animal Magnetism.* While they all have many characteristics in common, each is distinguished from the others by properties altogether special and peculiar. They all have in common *polarity*, and with it the power of strongly attracting and repelling certain bodies. The points of agreement and distinction between electricity and magnetism are thus set forth by Professor Olmsted : " Electricity and magnetism agree in the following particulars. 1. Each consists of two species, the vitreous and resinous electricities, and the austral and boreal magnetisms. 2. In both cases, those of the same name repel, and those of opposite names attract, each other. 3. The laws of induction in both are very analogous. 4. The force, in each, varies inversely as the square of the distance. 5. The power, in both cases, resides at the surface of bodies, and is independent of their mass.

"But electricity and magnetism are as remarkably unlike in the following particulars. 1. Electricity is capable of being excited in all bodies, and of being imparted to all; magnetism resides almost exclusively in iron in its different forms, and, with a few exceptions, cannot be excited in any but ferruginous bodies. 2. Electricity may be *transferred* from one body to another; magnetism is incapable of such transference; magnets communicate their properties merely by *induction*, a process in which no portion of fluid is withdrawn from the magnetizing body. 3. When a body of an elongated figure is electrified by induction, on being divided in the middle, the two parts possess respectively the kind of electricity only which each had before the separation; but when a bar of steel or a needle magnetized by induction is broken into any number of parts, each part has both polarities, and becomes a perfect magnet. 4. The directive properties and the various consequences that result from it, the declination, annual and diurnal variations, the dip, the different intensities in different parts of the earth, are all peculiar to the magnet, and do not appertain to electrified bodies."

Animal magnetism has, in common with the two forces above named, as we have said, *polarity*, and consequently the property of attraction and repulsion. This statement is verified by an experiment with which all who have seen persons in a magnetic or mesmeric sleep are familiar. When the ends of the fingers of the magnetizer, for example, are brought near those of the magnetized, the latter being perfectly blindfolded, so as not at all to be aware of what is being done, the hand of the person magnetized will instantly be attracted towards that of the magnetizer, and will follow it in any direction, just as the loadstone, and evidently for the same reason, draws after itself the needle, or any object in respect to which it has attractive power. Here stands revealed the *polarity*, and consequently the attractive force of this mysterious power in nature. Its essential dissimilarity from electricity, is equally manifest in the fact, that *living* bodies can be charged with the former in circumstances in which they cannot be with the latter, that is, in the presence of electric conductors. The human body, for example, can be charged with the electric fluid, only by being placed upon glass, or some other non-conductor. In direct and immediate contact with such non-conductors, the same body may be most fully charged with animal magnetism. From magnetism it is distinguished with equal manifestness, by the fact, that it may be excited, in all its force, in *animal* bodies, while the former is developed, in force, only in *iron* and kindred substances. We might refer to other characteristics, in which this substance, or force in nature, is distinguished from electricity on the one hand, and from magnetism on the other. The above, however, are sufficient for our present purpose. It remains to specify some of the peculiar characteristics of this power, as developed in animal bodies—the human body we now refer to. Among these we would specify the following, to which very special attention is invited, as they will hereafter be seen to have a fundamental bearing upon our present inquiries.

EFFECTS OF ANIMAL MAGNETISM UPON THE HUMAN SYSTEM.

1. It operates with immense power upon the muscular system, imparting to the limbs a rigidity and inflexibility which render any motion at the joints almost as impossible as at any other parts. We will give a single fact in illustration, a fact which occurred some years since in the city of Cleveland, Ohio. The subject was a young woman who laboured as a domestic in the family where the fact occurred. After putting the individual into a magnetic sleep, and while she was sitting in a chair,

6

the magnetizer extended her right arm in a horizontal direction, and having made a few passes of his hand from the shoulder to the hand of the subject, he requested the pastor of the First Presbyterian Church of that city, who was present by invitation, to bring that arm down from the position referred to. Taking hold of the hand and wrist of the subject, and pressing downward with much weight, he expressed the fear that he should break the arm, should he add to the pressure. On being assured by the magnetizer that he had no reason for apprehension on that subject, Dr. Aikin affirms that he laid out all the strength he could command, without being able to move the limb downwards. It seemed to possess the inflexibility of a rod of steel. The above fact comes from a source which will command universal belief, and is but one among numberless others of a similar nature that might be cited. With what astonishing power must this force act upon the muscular system to produce such results!

2. Such also is the effect of this substance, or force, upon the physical system generally, that the mind is thereby, in many instances, wholly insulated from any communication with the external world, through any of the senses, and, in instances not a few, rendered equally insensible to any effects produced upon the physical organization itself. A

limb may be amputated, for example, and the subject experience no pain, nor any conscious sensation whatever, from the operation. The senses also are all locked up from any communications with the world around but through those with whom, and in respect to objects with which, they are in mesmeric communication. Facts falling under this class are too well authenticated to be denied, and too well known to need illustration, or explanation by the citation of particular examples.

3. In some instances, under the influence of this same substance, the perceptive faculties are greatly quickened, so that the mind perceives objects which lie wholly beyond, and at a great remove from, the reach of the senses, when the mental and physical powers are in a normal state. That perceptions of this character are to be numbered among real facts of clairvoyance, there can rest upon no candid mind, which has made adequate investigations, any doubt whatever. "However astonishing," says Sir William Hamilton, "it is now proved beyond all rational doubt, that in certain abnormal states of the nervous organism, perceptions are possible through other than the ordinary channels of the senses." "It has been, I believe," says Dr. Wayland, "proved beyond dispute, that persons under this influence have submitted to the most distressing operations without consciousness of pain; that other persons have

cognized events at a great distance, and have related them correctly at the time; and that persons totally blind, when in a state of mesmeric consciousness, have enjoyed for the time the power of perceiving external objects." As we wish to have very special attention directed to this class of facts, on account of their bearings upon our subsequent inquiries, we will confirm the truth of the above statement of Dr. Wayland, by the following extract from a letter addressed to him by J. M. Brooke, Esq., of the United States Navy, and contained in the work from which the above is taken, namely, "Wayland's Intellectual Philosophy."

"WASHINGTON, *Oct.* 27, 1851.

"SIR,—It affords me pleasure to comply with your request, made through my brother William, relative to some experiments performed on board the United States steamer 'Princeton,' in the latter part of the year 1847; she being then on a cruise in the Mediterranean. Nathaniel Bishop, the subject of the experiments, was a mulatto, about twenty-six years of age, in good health, but of an excitable disposition. The first experiment was of the magnetic or mesmeric sleep, which overpowered him in thirty minutes from the commencement of the passes made in the ordinary way, accompanied with a steadfast gaze and effort of will that he should sleep.

"In this state he was insensible to all voices but mine, unless I directed or willed him to hear others; he was also insensible to such amount of pain as one might inflict without injury, that is, what would have been pain to another. He would obey my directions to whistle, dance, or sing. When aroused from this sleep he had no recollection of what occurred while in it. That such an influence could be exerted, I was already aware, having previously witnessed satisfactory experiments. Of clairvoyance I had never been convinced; indeed, considered it nothing but a sort of dreaming produced by the will of the operator. I became aware of its truth rather through accident than design.

"It happened, one day, that some of my brother officers asked a question which the others could not answer. Bishop, who had been a few moments before in a mesmeric sleep, gave the desired information, speaking with confidence and apparent accuracy. As the information related to something which it seemed almost impossible to know without seeing, we were very much surprised. It struck me that he might be clairvoyant; and I at once asked him to tell me the time by a watch kept in the binnacle, on the spar or upper deck, we being on the berth or lower deck. He answered correctly, as I found upon looking at the watch, allowing eight or nine seconds for time occupied in getting on deck. I then asked him many questions with regard to objects at a distance, which he answered, and, as far as I could ascertain, correctly.

"For example, one evening, while at anchor in the port of Genoa, the captain was on shore. I asked Bishop, in the presence of several officers, where the captain then was. He replied, 'At the opera with Mr. Lester, the consul.' 'What does he say?' I inquired. Bishop appeared to listen, and in a moment replied, 'The captain tells Mr. Lester, that he was much pleased with the port of Xavia; that the authorities treated him with much consideration.' Upon this, one of the officers laughed, and said that when the captain returned he would ask him. He did so, saying, "Captain, we have been listening to your conversation while on shore.' 'Very well,' remarked the captain, 'what did I say?' expecting some jest. Then the officer repeated what the captain had said of Xavia and its authorities. 'Ah,' said the captain, 'who was at the opera? I did not see any of the officers there.' The lieutenant then explained the matter. The captain confirmed its truth, and seemed much surprised, as there had been no other communication with the shore during the evening. I may remark that we touched at several ports between Xavia and Genoa.

"On another occasion, an officer being on shore, I directed Bishop to examine his pockets; he made several motions with his hands, as if actually drawing something from the officer's pockets, saying, 'Here is a handkerchief and a box; what a curious thing! full of little white sticks with blue ends. What are they, Mr. Brooke?' I replied, 'Perhaps they are matches.' 'So they are!' he exclaimed. My companion, expecting the officer mentioned, went on deck, and meeting him at the gangway, asked, 'What have you in your pockets?' 'Nothing,' he replied. 'But have you not a box of matches?' 'Oh! yes!' said he. 'How did you know it? I bought them just before I came on board. The matches are peculiar, made of white wax with blue ends.'

"The surgeons of the 'Princeton' ridiculed these experiments, upon which I requested one of them (Farquharson) to test for himself, which he consented to do. With some care he placed Bishop and myself in one corner of the apartment, and then took a position some ten feet distant, concealing between his hands a watch, the long hand of which traversed the dial. He first asked for a description of the watch. To which Bishop replied, ''Tis a funny watch, the second hand jumps.'

"The doctor then asked him to tell the minute and second, which he did; directly afterwards exclaiming, 'The second hand has stopped!' which was the case; Dr. Farquharson having stopped it. 'Well,' said the doctor, 'to what second does it point, and to what hour, and what minute is it now?' Bishop answered correctly, adding, ''Tis going again.' He then told twice in succession the minute and second.

"The doctor was convinced, saying that it was contrary to reason, but he must believe. I then proposed that the doctor should mark; and directed Bishop to look in his mother's house, in Lancaster, Pa. (where he had never been), for a clock; he said there was one, and told the time by it; one of the officers calculated the difference in time for the longitudes of Lancaster and Genoa, and the clock was found to agree within five minutes of the watch time."

4. The relations existing between the magnetized, when in the magnetic state, and the magnetizer or other persons in mesmeric communication with the person magnetized, next claim our special attention. Among these relations the following may be specified as having a special bearing upon our present investigations. (1.) Any *sensations* induced by any cause in the magnetizer are instantly reproduced in the individual magnetized, and that when it is impossible to induce any such feelings by any effects directly produced upon the physical organization of the latter. If the magnetizer tastes, smells, or touches any particular object, the person magnetized instantly experiences the same sensations. Any sensation *unexpectedly* induced in the former, by secretly

twitching his hair, pinching his body, or pricking it with a needle or pin, and when this is done in a manner and form which preclude the possibility of any knowledge of what is done, on the part of the latter,—any sensations, we say, even thus induced in the magnetizer, will be instantly reproduced in the person magnetized, each individual, in almost all instances, being affected in the same part of the physical system. A gentleman of our acquaintance, to remove all doubt from his own mind in regard to the question of collusion, called a magnetizer aside, and while speaking to him, put a vial of hartshorn to his nose, the vial having just before been sent for from a distance: "Do take that from my nose," instantly exclaimed the subject who was in a magnetic state. The world is full of facts of a precisely similar nature wherever the mesmeric phenomena have been witnessed.

The *law* which obtains in these circumstances seems to be this. This mysterious power acts with such force upon the sensitivity of the individual under its influence (the person magnetized), that it can, for the time, be affected but through this one power. Any feeling or sensation induced in the magnetizer acts upon this power, and through it upon the sensitivity of the person magnetized, reproducing there the same feelings which had previously been induced in the magnetizer.

(2.) In a similar manner, the *thoughts* of the magnetizer are reproduced in the mind of the individual magnetized, especially when the former wills it. This holds true, not only in regard to common conceptions, but equally of all acts of the imagination. A very intelligent and pious lady, a member of the Baptist church in Poughkeepsie, N. Y., while upon her death-bed, made the following statement to her pastor, from whom we received the same: "When you come to investigate the facts of mesmerism," she remarked, "you will find this to be true, that the clairvoyant, when in mesmeric communication with you, *can speak your thoughts.* I was once present when A. J. Davis, then a lad, was in this state, and was requested to touch his forehead with my own. I did so, and found that he would instantly speak out any thought that came into my mind."

A scientific gentleman from the interior of New England, while in the city of New York, some years ago, called upon, and was put into mesmeric communication with, a clairvoyant whom he had never seen before. The latter mentally accompanied the former to his (the inquirer's) father's residence, describing the facts of the journey, the external and internal appearance of the house and the surrounding scenery just in accordance with his recollections and conceptions at the time. He then *imagined* a meeting-house standing before the front door of that residence (no such object existing), and asked the clairvoyant, "What do you see now?" "A meeting-house," was the answer. The object was then described in exact accordance with the image pre-existing in the inquirer's mind, both in regard to location, form, size, colour, etc.

(3.) A control equally perfect can the magnetizer exercise over the *muscular* system of the individual in a magnetic state. By simply willing it, with no external motions whatever, the latter can render the whole body, or any given member of the same, perfectly stiff and motionless, and hold it in any given position for any given length of time. This power often continues for a period subsequent to the time when the subject has come out of a mesmeric state. Take as an illustration and confirmation of this statement, the following additional extract from the letter of J. M. Brooke, Esq.: "The power which I acquired by putting him to sleep remained after he woke, and was increased by its exercise. If not exerted for several days, it decreased, sometimes rendering it necessary to repeat the passes, and again put him to sleep. While awake, and under my influence, I made many experiments, such as arresting his arm when raising food to his mouth, or fixing him motionless in the attitude of drinking. On one occasion I willed that he should continue pouring tea into a cup already filled, which he did, notwithstanding the exclamations of those who were scalded in the operation. These influences were exerted without a word or change of position on my part."

(4.) Hence I remark, in the last place, that the entire mental and physical activity of the magnetized is, in many instances, under the complete control of the magnetizer, while the mesmeric relation between them continues—a relation which, as we have seen, often continues for a period, longer or shorter, after the subject has come out of a mesmeric sleep. The wildest imaginings of the latter are thus reproduced in the mind of the former, the objects of those imaginings appearing as objects of real external perception. The magnetizer puts his handkerchief, for example, into the hands of his magnetic subject, and it becomes, to that subject, a flower of surpassing beauty, a kitten, lap-dog, an infant, or a serpent, just as the magnetizer secretly wills. Mr. Brooke says still further of his subject: "He remembered or forgot what he saw when clairvoyant, as I willed, of which I satisfied myself by experiment. All his senses were under control, so completely indeed, that had I willed him to stop breathing I believe that he would." A magnetizer agreed with a friend of ours, a gentleman of the most unquestionable veracity, to induce his magnetic subject to sing, she being a beautiful singer, and to stop the singing the instant our friend raised his finger. As the singing proceeded, and while the singer was uttering a long note, our friend raised his finger, and the voice instantly ceased, with that note half finished. The magnetizer willed the singing to proceed again, and that note, a thing impossible to a person in a normal condition, was finished, and with it the remainder of the stanza. This was done while the subject was deeply blindfolded, and the magnetizer stood several feet from her, with his eyes fixed intently upon our friend, waiting for the raising of his finger. No collusion therefore was possible.

Facts of the most authentic character, and bearing with equal force upon the same conclusion, might be multiplied to any extent. These, however, are abundantly sufficient. From all the facts above adduced, pertaining to the action of this mysterious power in nature, the following conclusions are undeniable :—

1. There is in nature a medium of communication between mind and mind, other than that by which communications are had, through the ordinary channels of the senses.

2. Through this same force, one mind may, when the proper conditions are fulfilled, control the action of the mental and physical powers of another mind.

3. The action of this force upon the physical system, and through it upon the mind of the mag-

netized, is as the feelings, thoughts, and purposes of the magnetizer.

4. Through this same power, the mind of the person magnetized, when he happens to be in mesmeric communication (rapport) with any object, however distant, and however removed from the reach of the senses, will have a direct and immediate cognition of the same.

5. The action of this force, when certain conditions are fulfilled, is determined, in many important particulars, by mental states and acts, and accords with the same, and here its nature and relations to mind stand revealed; a fact of fundamental importance, but which seems not, hitherto, to have been distinctly and generally recognised by philosophers. Mesmeric facts have demonstrated the existence of this power in nature, and thereby laid the foundation for the explanation of many facts around us which have, to this time, appeared to be totally inexplicable.

CHAPTER II.

THE ODYLIC, ODIC, OR PSYCHIC FORCE.

To prepare the way still further for the full and distinct elucidation of the subject before us, we will now advance to a consideration of a peculiar force in nature, a force the existence, properties, and laws of which philosophers had developed and verified, by the most careful and decisive experiments, years prior to the appearance of these so-called spirit-manifestations, and which they had denominated the Odylic Force. This force, which indeed pervades all bodies in nature, has many properties in common with electricity and magnetism—*polarity*, and with it the property of *attracting* and *repelling* other bodies, for example. At the same time, it differs from these forces in particulars equally fundamental, being, for example, undeniably transmissible through magnetic and electric non-conductors. The physical organisms of individuals of peculiar physical temperaments, become, in some instances, in certain localities, permanently and very strongly charged with this force. The following may be enumerated, as among the more important phenomena which characterize its developments under such circumstances.

1. It acts upon other objects, and is reacted upon by them, as a very strong *attractive* and *repulsive* power; objects, in many instances, even without visible contact, being drawn towards or driven from such individuals, and in other particulars acted upon in a very singular and unaccountable manner.

2. Upon the walls, floor, and ceiling of rooms occupied by such individuals, rapping sounds, very much like those produced by striking against such objects with the knuckles, or with a mallet, are not unfrequently heard; such phenomena being also occasionally attended with a sensible jarring of surrounding objects, and sometimes with rumbling sounds, resembling the roaring of distant thunder.

3. The physical systems of such individuals are very powerfully affected, so powerfully as, in many instances, to derange totally the action of the mental powers.

4. In the mental developments thus induced, we have, without exception, all the mesmeric and clairvoyant phenomena, as above presented.

5. This force, when developed in the human organism, has generally a special location in some of the *nerve centres.* When such centre is not immediately connected with the brain, then the action of this force, like that of magnetism, is simply that of a repulsive

and attractive power, without the characteristics of intelligence. When that centre is the brain, then the *direction* of the action of this power bears, in many important particulars, the characteristics of intelligence, the action of the force, in such cases, being not only in accordance with, but evidently directed by, mental states.

In illustration of the above statements, and in verification of the same, we will now present a few well-authenticated facts. We cite only such facts as have a direct and immediate bearing upon our present inquiries. Those who would understand the science of the Odylic Force, are referred to the fundamental works upon the subject which are now before the public.

With facts which really and truly indicate the existence and action of such a force in nature, so far especially as its attractive and repulsive properties are concerned, almost every one is, no doubt, familiar, though these facts, as generally witnessed, having nothing of a startling character about them, have, for the most part, escaped any special notice. Who has not witnessed, for example, in passing his hand over the head of another, the evidence of an attraction between the hand and the hair upon the head of such individual, an attraction sufficient to disarrange the hair, and cause the ends of it to rise from the head? Such facts clearly indicate the existence of the attractive force of which we are speaking. Some months since, as we called upon an aged clergyman who was just recovering from sickness, he related to us a somewhat interesting fact which had just occurred in his own experience. While engaged, a day or two previous, in adjusting some papers for the purpose of putting them on file, on withdrawing his hand from the paper which he had placed upon the top of others, that object followed his hand, being evidently attracted by it. After repeated attempts, he found it impossible to adjust that paper, because it would follow his hand when he would withdraw it. His attention being thus attracted, he was led to make some special experiments. On placing the ends of his fingers upon the paper, and raising them up, the object adhered to them, and remained, for some time, suspended, just as a needle and other objects are raised and suspended by the magnet. On trial, he found that no such attraction existed, at the time, between his hand and any other paper before him, for the obvious reason that this attractive force, the presence of which is here undeniably evinced, was not thus relatively developed between his hand and any other paper, as between it and this one. We have only to suppose this same force developed between the organism of this individual and some heavy object, such as the table, and developed to a certain degree of strength and intensity, and for the same reason that this paper was attracted by his hand so as to be raised from the table, the table itself would be drawn after him all around the room, or thus driven from him, if the polarity of this force, as developed in his organism and the object, were different or opposite from what we have supposed it to be. The table itself, also, attracted by the hand of the individual just as the paper referred to was, might, like that object, be lifted from the floor, and for the same reason. Suppose, further, that this force should happen to be developed at the same time, and in the same form, in the table and the floor beneath it. In that case, on the known principle that, with all forces having polarity, opposite poles attract, while the same ones repel each other, the table would be spontaneously lifted from the floor, and, for a time, held, as by an invisible power, suspended in the atmosphere. If the same force was developed at the time, in some object near, but with opposite polarity, then the table would be drawn towards such object, whirled over, and thrown, it might be, with much violence upon the floor. Thus alternately attracted by some objects, and repelled by others, it would now be driven forcibly against some individuals, and fly from others with seeming terror, and tumbled strangely about the room, till all present were convinced that it must be bewitched, while all these terrifying phenomena are the exclusive result of the natural and necessary action of a peculiar force existing in nature all around us, a force which, like electricity in a thunderstorm, happens, at this time, to be developed with special power, in this particular locality, and in connexion with the objects referred to, and when these *now* strange and unaccountable phenomena lose all their power to astonish and to terrify, as soon as the existence and properties of the force from which they result come to be recognised and understood.

A lady attempts to spread out upon a table a silk dress, for the purpose of ironing it. The article adheres to her hand, winding all around it, so that she finds it very difficult or impossible to adjust the article so as to accomplish her object. We state a case which actually occurred in our own family, some years since. Another individual adjusts the same article without any difficulty, no such attraction appearing between her hands and the object referred to. In the case of the first individual, this force happened to be, at the time, developed in such relations between her hands and the object, the dress, as to occasion the singular phenomena under consideration. Such facts, which are of almost every-day occurrence in the world around us, render manifest the existence, in the human organism, and in external nature, of the force of which we are speaking, and when wisely considered, prepare us to look with scientific scrutiny, and with less wonder, incredulity, and scepticism, upon authentic cases in which this same power is developed in the organism of individuals to such a degree as to produce the phenomena which astonish mankind. To a few of these cases, all of which, we believe, have all the marks of credibility that we can, with any show of reason, demand, very special attention is now invited.

The first case that we adduce is that of Angelique Cottin, of which we have two well-authenticated accounts, one of which is given by Catherine Crowe, in the "Night-side of Nature," and the other in the "Courier des Etats Unis," of Paris. Both of these accounts are combined in the following extract from "Rogers' Philosophy of Mysterious Rappings," to which we are indebted for other important facts hereafter to be cited.

"Angelique Cottin was a native of La Perriere, aged fourteen, when, on the 15th of January, 1846, at eight o'clock in the evening, while weaving silk gloves at an oaken frame, in company with other girls, the frame began to jerk, and they could not by any efforts keep it steady. It seemed as if it were alive; and, becoming alarmed, they called in the neighbours, who would not believe them, but desired them to sit down and go on with their work. Being timid, they went one by one, and the frame remained still till Angelique approached, when it recommenced its movements, while she was also attracted by the frame. Thinking she was bewitched or possessed, her parents took her to the presbytery, that the spirit might be exorcised. The curate, however, being a sensible man, refused to do it, but set himself, on the contrary, to observe the phenomenon; and, being perfectly satisfied of the fact, he bade them take her to a physician.

"Meanwhile, the intensity of the influence, whatever it was, augmented; not only articles made of oak, but all sorts of things, were acted upon by it, and reacted upon her; while persons who were near her, even without contact, frequently felt sudden shocks. The effects, which were diminished when she was on a carpet or a waxed cloth, were most remarkable when she was on the bare earth. They sometimes entirely ceased for three days, and then recommenced. Metals were not affected. Anything touching her apron or dress would fly off, although a person held it; and Monsieur Herbert, while seated on a heavy tub or trough, was raised up with it. In short, the only place she could repose on was a stone covered with cork; they also kept her still by isolating her. When she was fatigued, the effects diminished.

A needle, suspended horizontally, oscillated rapidly with the motion of her arm, without contact; or remained fixed while deviating from the magnetic direction. Great numbers of enlightened medical and scientific men witnessed these phenomena, and investigated them with every precaution to prevent imposition. She was often hurt by the violent involuntary movements she was thrown into, and was evidently afflicted by chorea,"* or St. Vitus' dance.

The French paper mentions the circumstance that, while Angelique was at work in the factory, "the cylinder which was turning was suddenly thrown at a considerable distance without any visible cause; that this was repeated several times; that all the young girls in the factory, terrified, fled from the factory, ran to the curate to have him exorcise the young girl, believing she had a devil." After the priest had consigned her to the physician's care, the *Courier des Etats Unis* goes on to say: "The physician, with the father and mother, brought Angelique to Paris. M. Arago received her, and took her to the observatory, and in the presence of MM. Laugier and Goujon made the following observations, which were reported to the Paris Academy of Sciences.

"1. It is the left side of the body which appears

* See "Night-side of Nature."

to acquire this sometimes attractive, but more frequently repulsive, property. A sheet of paper, a pen, or any other light body, being placed upon a table, if the young girl approaches her left hand, even before she touches it, the object is driven to a distance, as by a gust of wind. The table itself is thrown the moment it is touched by her hand, or even by a thread which she may hold in it.

"2. This causes instantaneously a strong commotion in her side, which draws her towards the table; but it is in the region of the pelvis that this singular repulsive force appears to concentrate itself.

"3. As had been observed the first day, if she attempted to sit, the seat was thrown far from her, with such force that any person occupying it was carried away with it.

"4. One day a chest, upon which three men were seated, was moved in the same manner. Another day, although the chair was held by two very strong men, it was broken between their hands.

"5. These phenomena are not produced in a continued manner. They manifest themselves in a greater or less degree, and from time to time during the day; but they show themselves in their intensity in the evening, from seven to nine o'clock.

"6. Then the girl is obliged to continue standing, and is in great agitation.

"7. She can touch no object without breaking it or throwing it upon the ground.

"8. All the articles of furniture which her garments touch are displaced and overthrown.

"9. At that moment many persons have felt, by coming in contact with her, a true electrical shock.

"10. During the entire duration of the paroxysms, the left side of the body is warmer than the right side.

"11. It is affected by jerks, unusual movements, and a kind of trembling, which seems to communicate itself to the hand which touches it.

"12. This young person presents, moreover, a peculiar sensibility to the action of the magnet.

"When she approaches the north pole of the magnet she feels a violent shock, while the south pole produces no effect; so that if the experimenter changes the poles, but without her knowledge, she always discovers it by the difference of sensations which she experiences.

"13. M. Arago wished to see if the approach of this young girl would cause a deviation of the needle of the compass. The diviation which had been foretold was not produced. The general health of Angelique Cottin is very good. The extraordinary movements, however, and the paroxysms observed every evening, resemble what one observes in some nervous maladies.

"The great fact demonstrated in this case, is,

"That, under *peculiar conditions*, the human organism gives forth a physical power which, *without visible instruments*, lifts heavy bodies, attracts or repels them, according to a law of polarity,—overturns them, and produces the phenomena of sound."

The case which we next cite is so well authenticated, as to remove all reasonable doubt, to say the least, of its actual occurrence. The facts occurred in the family of Mr. Joseph Barron, of Woodbridge, New Jersey, in the year 1834. We give the account as published, at the time, in the *Newark Daily Advertiser*.

"The first sounds were those of a loud thumping, apparently against the side of a house, which commenced one evening when the family had retired, and continued at short intervals until daylight, when it ceased.

"The next evening it commenced at nightfall, when it was ascertained to be mysteriously connected with the movements of a servant girl in the family,—a white girl, about fourteen years of age. While passing a window on the stairs, for example, a sudden jar, accompanied with an explosive sound, broke a pane of glass, the girl at the same time being seized with a violent spasm. This, of course, very much alarmed her; and the physician, Dr. Drake, was sent for, came, and bled her. The bleeding, however, produced no apparent effect. The noise still continued, as before, at intervals, wherever the girl went, each sound producing more or less of a spasm; and the physician, with all the family, remained up during the night. At daylight the thumping ceased again. In the evening the same thing was repeated, commencing a little earlier than before; and so every evening since, continuing each night until morning, and commencing each night a little earlier than before, until yesterday, when the thumping began about twelve o'clock at noon. The circumstances were soon generally spread through the neighbourhood, and have produced so much excitement that the house has been filled and surrounded from sunrise to sunset for nearly a week. Every imaginable means have been resorted to, in order to unravel the phenomenon. At one time the girl would be removed from one apartment to another, but without effect. Wherever she was placed, at certain intervals the thumping noise would be heard in the room. She was taken to a neighbouring house. The same result followed. When carried out of doors, however, no noise is heard. Dr. Drake, who has been constant in his attendance during the whole period, occasionally aided by other scientific observers, was with us last evening for two hours, when we were politely allowed a variety of experiments with the girl, in addition to those heretofore tried, to satisfy ourselves that there is no imposition in the case, and, if possible, to discover the secret agent of the mystery. The girl was in an upper room, with a part of the family, when we reached the house. The noise then resembled that which would be produced by a person violently thumping the upper floor with the head of an axe five or six times in succession, jarring the house, ceasing a few minutes and then resuming as before. We were soon introduced into the apartment, and permitted to observe for ourselves. The girl appeared to be in perfect health, cheerful and free from the spasms felt at first, and entirely relieved from everything like the fear or apprehension which she manifested for some days. The invisible noise, however, continued to occur as before, though somewhat diminished in frequency, while we were in the room. In order to ascertain more satisfactorily that she did not produce it voluntarily, among other experiments we placed her on a chair on a blanket in the centre of the room, bandaged the chair with a cloth, fastening her feet on the front round, and confining her hands together on her lap. No change, however, was produced. The thumping continued as before, except that it was not quite so loud; the noise resembling that which would be produced by stamping on the floor with a heavy heel;

yet she did not move a limb or muscle, that we could discover. She remained in this position long enough to satisfy all in the room that the girl exercised, voluntarily, no sort of agency in producing the noise. It was observed that the noise became greater the farther she was removed from any other person. We placed her in the doorway of a closet in the room, the door being ajar to allow her to stand in the passage. In less than one minute the door flew open as if violently struck with a mallet, accompanied by precisely such a noise as such a thump would produce. This was repeated several times, with the same effect. In short, in whatever position she was placed, whether in or out of the room, similar results, varied a little perhaps by circumstances, were produced. There is certainly no deception in the case. . . . The noise was heard at least one hundred yards from the house."

In this case also, as well as in those previously cited, there is no ground for the least suspicion of the action of any other than an exclusively physical cause.

"In the year 1835, a suit was brought before the sheriff of Edinburgh, Scotland, for the recovery of damages suffered in a certain house owned by Mr. Webster. Captain Molesworth was the defendant at the trial.* The following facts were developed: Mr.

* See "Night-side of Nature," p. 400.

Molesworth had seriously damaged the house, both as to substance and reputation,

"1. By sundry holes which he cut in the walls, tearing up of the floors, etc., to discover the cause of certain noises which tormented himself and family.

"2. By the bad name he had given the house, stating that it was haunted. Witnesses for the defendant were sheriff's officers, justices of the peace, and officers of the regiment quartered near by; all of whom had been at the said house sundry times to aid Captain M. detect the invisible cause of so much disturbance."

The important facts bearing upon our subject were the following: —

"1. The disturbance consisted in certain noises, such as knockings, pounding, scratching sounds, rustlings in different parts of a particular room,— sometimes, however, in other parts of the house.

"2. Certain boards of the floor would seem to be at times most infected with the noises. Then certain points in the walls (at which Mr. M. would discharge his gun, or cut into with an axe, all to no purpose, however).

"3. The bed whereon a young girl, aged thirteen years, had been confined by disease, would very often be raised above the floor, as if a sudden force was applied beneath it; which would greatly alarm her and the whole family, and cause the greatest perplexity.

"4. This force was soon discovered to be in some strange way connected with this invalid.

"5. The concussions which it often produced on the walls would cause them visibly to tremble.

"6. Wherever the young invalid was moved, this force accompanied her."

How perfectly similar the above occurrences are to those which happened in the family of Rev. Dr. Phelps,* of Stamford, Ct., occurrences which consisted of rapping sounds, moving of tables, etc., and which commenced March 10, 1850. Of these singular events the Doctor makes, among many others, the following statements:—

"The phenomena consisted in the moving of articles of furniture in a manner that could not be accounted for. Knives, forks, spoons, nails, blocks of wood, etc., were thrown in different directions about the house. They were seen to move from places and in directions which made it certain that no visible power existed by which the motion could be produced. For days and weeks together, I watched these strange movements with all the care and caution and close attention which I could bestow. I witnessed them hundreds and hundreds of times,

* Dr. Phelps, we would say, is personally well known to us, and related to us the leading facts, as they occurred in his house.

and I know that in hundreds of instances they took place when there was no visible power by which the motion could have been produced. Scores of persons, of the first standing in the community, whose education, general intelligence, candour, veracity, and sound judgment none will question, were requested to witness the phenomena, and, if possible, help us to a solution of the mystery. But as yet no solution has been obtained. The idea that the whole was a 'trick of the children,'—an idea which some of the papers have endeavoured, with great zeal, to promulgate,—is to everyone who is acquainted with the facts as stupid as it is false and injurious. The statement, too, which some of the papers have reiterated so often, that 'the mystery was found out,' is, I regret to say, untrue. With the most thorough investigation which I have been able to bestow upon it, aided by gentlemen of the best talents, intelligence, and sound judgment, in this and in many neighbouring towns, the cause of these strange phenomena remains yet undiscovered."

A writer in the *New Haven Journal and Courier* relates the following facts, of which he was an eyewitness.

"While we were there," says he, "the contents of the pantry were emptied into the kitchen, and bags of salt, tin ware, and heavier culinary articles, were thrown in a promiscuous heap upon the floor, with a loud and startling noise. Loaves of delicious cake were scattered about the house. The large knocker of the outside door would thunder its fearful tones through the loud-resounding hall, unmindful of the vain but rigid scrutiny to which it was subjected by incredulous and curious men. Chairs would deliberately move across the room, unimpelled by any visible agency. Heavy marble-top tables would poise themselves upon two legs, and then fall with their contents to the floor, no human being within six feet of them."

According to the statements of Dr. Phelps, the following are some of the circumstances attending these manifestations:—"1. They were most violent when the whole family were together," "less frequent and feebler when but one of the two children (belonging to Mrs. Phelps, she being the Doctor's second wife) were in the house," and "more frequent in connexion with a lad (one of the above children) of about eleven" years of age. "2. These children had been frequently mesmerized into the trance and clairvoyant state by their father," and one was subject to "spontaneous trance, and was found, at one time, in the barn, in a cataleptic state." 3. "When these children, with their mother, removed to Pennsylvania, the phenomena did not follow them." No facts can more clearly indicate the presence and action of an invisible, but purely physical, cause—a cause connected with the organism of particular individuals—than these.

The following letter, which has been kindly furnished us by Rev. E. N. Kirk, will be read with interest, and the facts stated will not be doubted by our readers :—

"REV. A. MAHAN :—

"Dear Brother,—By your request, I commit to paper the following narrative :—

"In the course of my residence in Albany, as pastor of the Fourth Presbyterian Church, somewhere about the year 1834 (I have no means at present of recalling the precise year), I was witness to phenomena at that time totally beyond the sphere of all former experience, and, by me, utterly inexplicable.

"I had been preaching three times on a Sunday, and was lying on the sofa in my house, at about ten o'clock, when a gentleman entered the parlour in a highly excited state of mind. He spoke very hurriedly, saying, 'A young woman is possessed of the devil, and wishes you to come and pray with her.' Without waiting for further explanations, I hastened to follow him. On entering the house I saw a girl of about twenty years of age, lying quietly on a large bed, surrounded by a few persons. They described her as seeing frightful spirits, who threatened to carry her off; and their approaches to her were always indicated to the spectators by a convulsive action of her whole frame, an earnest entreaty to be saved from them, and a peculiarly sudden, sharp knocking. I at once suspected some collusion, and made as thorough an examination of the premises as I could; but nothing appeared which could furnish any explanation of the sounds they described. I then treated her as I would any other person in sickness calling for the counsel and prayers of a clergyman. At about midnight I concluded that my presence was no longer needed, and that my curiosity was not to be gratified by witnessing anything marvellous. I accordingly went to the bed and leaned upon the high footboard (the bedstead being of the French pattern). As I looked earnestly into her face, she suddenly started from her reclining posture, screaming and staring wildly; and, at the same instant, three distinct, sharp raps, as if made with the knuckles of the fist, upon the very board on which I was leaning, startled me. I examined if her feet were touching the board; or if any visible connexion existed between the board and the floor, except that of the bedposts. Nothing of the kind was visible. I then requested her friends to lay the bed on the floor on the opposite side of the room, and furnish me a lamp, that I might go into the room beneath, and watch the floor (for the room was directly over the cellar). After watching there for half an hour, the rappings were repeated, but with no visible cause. I then left the house. On the next day, as I was informed, President Nott, of Union College, went to see the girl; but no knockings occurred after I saw her.

"When this case occurred, I remember a gentleman stating that something similar had been witnessed in Poughkeepsie, many years ago, of which I now speak, only to put you on the track of inquiry, if you wish to accumulate evidence of these phenomena having occurred long before the present day.

"Wishing you Divine guidance, and great success in rescuing our fellow men from hurtful delusions,

"I remain, cordially yours,

"EDW. N. KIRK.

"BOSTON, *June* 26, 1855."

Similar facts occurred in the family of Cotton Mather, in the case of some children whom he had taken under his care, in consequence of their being supposed to have been bewitched. These children would repeat the secret thoughts of those who came into communication with them. Even when passages from the Hebrew or Greek Scriptures were read to them, they would give the correct interpretation, that is, the meaning which the *reader* attached to said passages. Where passages were read in the Indian language, however—a language of course not understood by the reader—the interpretation could not be given. Any thought in the inquirer's mind was instantly reproduced in that of the child, precisely in accordance with what occurs in the mesmeric relations. Cases of this kind were commonly accompanied with physical manifestations in accordance with those which we have above noticed. Our fathers were as familiar with the rapping sounds, the movement of articles of furniture, etc., as we are. They, in their ignorance, attributed these manifestations to satanic agency. We, in our wisdom, have attributed them to the interposition of departed spirits.

However mysterious the facts above cited may appear, the following conclusions pertaining to them are too manifest to be denied, to wit: 1. The *cause* of these strange phenomena is exclusively mundane and physical. Nothing can be more unphilosophical than to attribute such phenomena to the interposition of disembodied spirits. 2. This power, when developed in the human system in connexion with the brain, as its nerve centre, accords in its action, in certain respects, with the mental states of such individuals, and is determined in its action by such states. 3. When other individuals come into certain relations to such persons, the mental states of the former are, in many instances, by means of this force, reproduced in the minds of the latter, and this precisely in accordance with what occurs in the mesmeric relations. 4. Individuals under the influence of this same force often present all the peculiar perceptions and other phenomena which characterize what is called independent clairvoyance. They have perceptions by other means than the organs of sense, and of objects located totally beyond the reach of the senses. 5. With the terrible mental and physical effects induced in such individuals by this force, it operates in their physical systems as a very strong polar force, attracting and repelling other bodies in accordance with the peculiar phenomena of electricity and magnetism. 6. Other bodies in contact with such persons, or in their immediate vicinity, often become charged with the same force, so as to be strongly attracted towards, or repelled from, each other. The force which produces these effects is called the Odylic, or Odic, and sometimes the Psychic, Force. To us, the name is of no account. The reality and character of the force itself is what we are concerned about. Its properties have been most carefully investigated by such philosophers as Richenbach, Metteuccyi, Thelorier, Lafontaine, and Ashburner, in Europe, and the validity of their experiments has been indorsed by the highest authorities of both continents.

This force, we would now remark, may be, and is everywhere being, developed by means *voluntarily* resorted to by individuals for the purpose of ascertaining its character. Of cases of this kind, cases which are constantly occurring in all spirit-circles, we would invite special attention to the following.

Physical Manifestations.

As an example of the physical manifestations, we will adduce the following case, which is so well attested as to remove from every candid mind all rational doubt in regard to its actual occurrence. Among the signers of this document, which originally appeared in the *Springfield Republican*, we have the names of such men as Professor Wells of the Cambridge Laboratory, and other individuals of such character for intelligence and integrity as to demand the credence of the public. The document is entitled, "*The modern wonder—a manifesto.*"

"The undersigned, from a sense of justice to the parties referred to, very cordially bear testimony to the occurrence of the following facts, which we severally witnessed at the house of Rufus Elmer, in Springfield, on the evening of the fifth of April:—

"1. The table was moved in every possible direction, and with great force, when we could not perceive any cause of motion.

"2. It (the table) was forced against each one of

us so powerfully as to remove us from our positions, together with the chairs we occupied,—in all, several feet.

"3. Mr. Wells and Mr. Edwards took hold of the table in such a manner as to exert their strength to the best advantage; but found the invisible power, exercised in the opposite direction, to be quite equal to their utmost efforts.

"4. In two instances, at least, while the hands of all the members of the circle were placed on the top of the table, and while no visible power was employed to raise the table, or otherwise move it from its position, *it was seen to rise clear of the floor, and to float in the atmosphere for several seconds,* as if sustained by a denser medium than the air.

"5. Mr. Wells seated himself on the table, which was rocked to and fro with great violence; and at length it poised itself on two legs, and remained in this position for some thirty seconds, *when no other person was in contact with the table.*

"6. Three persons, Messrs. Wells, Bliss, and Edwards, assumed positions on the table at the same time, and while thus seated, the table was moved in various directions.

"7. Occasionally we were made conscious of the occurrence of a powerful shock, which produced a vibratory motion of the floor of the apartment. It seemed like the motion occasioned by distant thunder, or the firing of ordnance far away,—causing the tables, chairs, and other inanimate objects, and all of us, to tremble in such a manner that the effect was both seen and felt.

"8. In the whole exhibition, which was far more diversified than the foregoing specification would indicate, we were constrained to admit that there was an almost constant manifestation of some intelligence which seemed, at least, to be independent of the circle.

"9. In conclusion, we may observe that D. D. Hume, the medium, frequently urged us to hold his hands and feet. During these occurrences the room was well lighted, the lamp was frequently placed on and under the table, and every possible opportunity was afforded us for the closest inspection, and we submit this one emphatic declaration: *We know that we are not imposed upon nor deceived.*

DAVID A. WELLS, WM. BRYANT,
B. K. BLISS, WM. EDWARDS."

To present the whole subject at one view, we now adduce the following extract from "Rogers' Philosophy of the Mysterious Rappings." The authority by which the occurrence of the facts stated is verified, is of such a character as to place those facts out of the circle of rational doubt.

"The following, also, were developed at the house of Rev. Dr. Griswold, New York. Among the persons present were Mr. J. F. Cooper, George Bancroft, Rev. Dr. Haws, Dr. J. W. Francis, Dr. Marcy, Mr. N. P. Willis, William Bryant, Mr. Bigelow of the *Evening Post*, Mr. R. B. Kimball, Mr. H. Tuckerman, and General Lyman.

"The mediums present were the members of the Fox family.

"Only Mr. Cooper, Dr. Francis, and Mr. Tuckerman, seemed to come into close rapport with the psychological and nerve-centres of the mediums. The others, according to the account, could develop few or no intelligent characteristics, and could obtain a development of the physical force alone;—thus giving us a plain hint of the distinction we are to observe between the physical phenomena and the psychological characteristics which frequently accompany them.

"The physical force stands alone *as* a physical force. It bears no characteristics in its action but that of itself, unless some other is made to impress its characteristics upon it, as the intelligent will do in the movement of the arm. But the physical force may move the arm without intelligence, as in spasms, etc.

"The following peculiar physical phenomena were developed during the evening:—

"'One little peculiarity, hitherto unremarked,*

* Taken from Willis' *Home Journal.*

came to our notice. The questioner's seat (to give him access to paper and pencil) was on one side of the table; and, chancing to occupy the place between him and the ladies (mediums), we [Mr. Willis] had accidentally thrown our arm over the back of his chair. Whenever the knockings occurred, we observed that his chair was shaken, though our own intermediate chair and the two standing immediately behind were unmoved. We called attention to it, and it was corroborated by the other gentlemen.

"'With such heavy weight in the chair as Mr. Cooper's or Dr. Francis', it would have taken a blow with a heavy hammer to have produced so much vibration.' The table was not moved, though requested.

"An experiment was tried as to what would be the effect with one of the ladies alone, or with two without the third, or with a gentleman and one or two of the ladies. The strongest knockings were on the floor when the widow and her two sisters stood anywhere together. With two of them the knockings were fainter. 'We placed ourself between the widow and one of the young ladies,' says Mr. Willis, 'and *no* sounds were produced as a consequence. With *one* of the mediums alone, there were no phenomena.'

"These peculiar characteristics of the conditions

are worthy of careful consideration. We have found several cases where no decided physical phenomena could be evolved without the presence of two persons, both in a palpable abnormal state; and we shall give one case, in a future chapter, where three clairvoyants were required.

"All such conditions clearly indicate the physical agency to belong to the physical organism. These characteristics will be considered in a more fitting place. We would simply direct attention to them here. The most important phenomena of this character, however, have not been sufficiently observed to develop their laws.

"But to return. An experiment was tried of another kind, in this circle at Dr. Griswold's. Three gentlemen placed themselves on the outside of the door, and three on the inside, and watched it closely, when suddenly it was knocked with great violence, without any visible instrument. 'We witnessed this,' says Mr. Willis, 'with one hand upon the panels; and what can it be but the exercise of a power beyond anything of which we have hitherto known the laws? That it is subject to human control,' he continues, 'seems probable, for it acts at present in a certain obedience to human orders [not of the medium, however], and is most obedient to those who have used it longest.'

"Mr. Ripley, of the *Tribune*, in speaking of the

same sitting says: 'The ladies were at such a distance from the door as to lend no countenance to the idea that the sounds were produced by any direct communication with them. . . . Other sounds were made which caused sensible vibrations of the sofa, and apparently coming from a thick hearth-rug before the fireplace, as well as from other quarters of the room.'"

Rev. H. Snow, in his work entitled "Spirit Intercourse," gives an apparently well-authenticated case, in which a medium was himself "raised entirely from the floor, and held in a suspended position by the same kind of invisible power." For ourselves, we have no disposition to question such a statement, knowing, as we do, that cases perfectly similar and analogous are attested by evidence which we are compelled to regard as valid.

That musical instruments have given forth musical sounds, in these circles, when no persons were touching such instruments, we also freely admit, and admit for the reason that the facts of the case are affirmed by authority which we cannot, with the consciousness of moral integrity, call in question. A very intelligent Christian lady, an utter disbeliever in Spiritualism, for example, told us that in her presence a guitar was once placed in the middle of the room; that when no one was within several feet of it, musical sounds proceeded from it; that when she extended her hand toward it, it was instantly raised up and attracted to her hand, just as the appropriate objects are drawn towards the magnet when it is placed near them ; and that when she laid hold of the instrument, it was, by a force which she could not control, wrested from her hand, just as objects charged with electricity are wrested from our hands when we grasp them. Facts affirmed by such testimony we regard ourselves as bound to admit.

Some time prior to the year 1853, Count Agenor De Gasparin organized a circle in Paris for the specific purpose of investigating (by experiments about which there could be no mistake) the phenomena under consideration. A careful record of their experiments after the 20th of September of the year referred to, was kept, and was afterwards published, with discussions of the facts developed, in two volumes. In their varied sessions, to which intelligent visitants had free access, all the physical manifestations known to Spiritualism, together with most of the others, were fully developed. We venture to affirm, that no candid mind can read the facts contained in the work under consideration, without a full conviction that the Odylic or Psychic force in nature is a verified truth in science. Every member of this circle, we must bear in mind, utterly repudiated the deductions of spiritualists. The object of the author in publishing his work, which is entitled " Science against

Modern Spiritualism," is to disprove the doctrines of that system. "Thus the fact," he says, "is established. Multiplied experiments, various irresistible proofs, mutually supporting each other, give to fluid action an entire certainty." . . . "It is not our fault if the results have been more and more conclusive, if they have reciprocally confirmed each other, if they have finally taken on the form, and acquired the character, of perfect evidence. To study, to compare, to begin, and begin again, to exclude, in short, everything that remained in any degree contestable—this was our duty. We have tried not to fail therein. I affirm nothing here that I have not verified several times; I have scrupulously abstained from admitting that which appears to me probable, not certain—that which has often, but not always, succeeded."

What Gasparin and the advocates of the mundane theory deny, is, not the material facts presented by spiritualists,—these we admit and affirm,—but the *deductions* they base upon these facts.

We now give an extract from a report of a sub-committee of a committee of the London Dialectical Society, a committee of learned men appointed to investigate and report upon these phenomena:—"Of the members of your sub-committee about *four-fifths* entered upon the investigation wholly sceptical as to the reality of the alleged phenomena, firmly believing them to be the result of *imposture*, or *delusion*, or of *involuntary muscular action*. It was only by irresistible evidence, under conditions that precluded the possibility of either of these solutions, and after trial and test many times repeated, that the most sceptical of your sub-committee were slowly and reluctantly convinced that the phenomena exhibited in the course of their experiments were veritable facts.

"The result of their long-continued and carefully-conducted experiments, after trial by every detective test they could devise, has been to establish conclusively:—

"First: That under certain bodily or mental conditions of one or more of the persons present, a force is exhibited sufficient to set in motion heavy substances, without the employment of any muscular force, without contact or material connexion of any kind between such substances and the body of any person present.

"Second: That this force can cause sounds to proceed, distinctly audible to all present, from solid substances not in contact with, nor having any visible connexion with, the body of any present; which sounds are proved to proceed from substances by the vibrations which are distinctly felt when they are touched.

"Third: That this force is frequently directed by intelligence.

"At *thirty-four* out of forty meetings of your committee some of these phenomena occurred.

"A description of one experiment, and the manner of conducting it, will best show the care and caution with which your committee have pursued their investigations.

"So long as there was contact, or even the possibility of contact, by the hands or feet, or even by the clothes, of any person present in the room, with the substance moved or sounded, there could be no perfect assurance that the motions and sounds were not produced by the person so in contact. The following experiment was therefore tried:—

"On one occasion, when eleven members of your sub-committee had been sitting round one of the dining-tables above described, for forty minutes, and various motions and sounds had occurred, they, by way of test, turned the backs of their chairs to the table, at about nine inches from it. They all knelt upon their chairs, placing their arms upon the backs thereof. In this position, their feet were of course turned away from the table, and by no possibility could be placed under it, or touch the floor. The hands of each person were extended over the table at about four inches from the surface. Contact, therefore, with any part of the table could not take place without detection.

"In less than a minute the table, untouched, moved

four times; at first about *five* inches to one side, then about twelve inches to the opposite side, and then, in like manner, four inches and six inches respectively.

"The hands of all present were next placed on the backs of the chairs, and about a foot from the table, which again moved, as before, *five* times, over spaces varying from four to six inches. Then all the chairs were removed twelve inches from the table, and each person knelt on his chair as before, this time, however, folding his hands behind his back, his body being thus about eighteen inches from the table, and having the back of the chair between him and the table. The table again moved four times, in various directions.

"The table was then carefully examined, turned upside down and taken to pieces, but nothing was discovered to account for the phenomena. The experiment was conducted throughout in the full light of gas above the table."

As the reader progresses in this treatise, he will meet with similar experiments made in the city of Boston and other parts of the United States—experiments made by men of the highest intelligence and prudence, men who have no faith in Spiritualism, and whose only motive is to know facts as they are. If anything can be discovered by experiment, and verified by testimony, the existence of the Odylic, Odic, or Psychic Force in nature, a force possessed of the properties attributed to it, is a verified truth of science.

THE ODLYIC FORCE IDENTICAL WITH THAT WHICH IS THE IMMEDIATE CAUSE OF THE SPIRIT-MANIFESTATIONS.

We now enter upon a very important department of our investigations. Spiritualists themselves admit, as we have already said, that spirits do not cause these manifestations directly, but *mediately*, that is, through the instrumentality of a certain force of some kind pre-existing in nature, a force which they have learned to control. The agency of the spirits is manifest, if at all, not in the existence or properties of this force, but in the *direction* of its action. The mere fact that sounds are heard and objects moved in these circles, no one has the folly to adduce as proof of an *ab extra* spirit-interposition of any kind. Such interposition, on the other hand, is inferred from the accordance of these phenomena with intelligence, and other considerations of a kindred nature. This force, also, spiritualists, as well as others, admit to be exclusively *physical* in its nature. So far, no difference of opinion, as far as our knowledge extends, exists between them and their opponents. The question which here arises, and to which a specific answer is here demanded, is, What is the nature of this mundane, physical force which is the immediate cause of these so-called spirit-manifestations? We answer, *It is identical with the Odylic Force,* which we have above developed. This we argue from the following considerations:—

1. The relation of these causes to certain specific localities is a very decisive proof, in connexion with other facts, of their absolute identity. In Boston, for example, the centre of the phenomena of witchcraft, and where the odylic phenomena have ever manifested themselves, mediums were developed as soon as the circles were constituted. In Philadelphia, on the other hand, where the odylic phenomena had hardly, if ever, appeared, months elapsed before any of the so-called spirit-manifestations appeared, though the most careful and persevering efforts were made to induce them. It is also known, and published by spiritualists themselves, that individuals who were good mediums in one locality have utterly lost the power by simple change of locality. The origin of "the Rochester Rappings" should not be overlooked in this connexion. All agree that these phenomena first made their appearance in a certain house occupied by Mr. Michael Weekman, of the village of Hydesville, in the town of Arcadia, Wayne county, New York. Of the facts which occurred when he was a resident of the house, we have the following account.

"Mr. W. resided in this house for about eighteen months, and left sometime in the year 1847.* Mr. Weekman makes the statement in substance as follows: That one evening, about the time of retiring, he heard a rapping on the outside door, and, what was rather unusual for him, instead of familiarly bidding them 'come in,' stepped to the door and opened it. He had no doubt of finding some one who wished to come in, but, to his surprise, found no one there. He went back and proceeded to undress, when, just before getting into bed, he heard another rap at the door, loud and distinct. He stepped to the door quickly and opened it, but, as before, found no one there. He stepped out and looked around, supposing that some one was imposing upon him. He could discover no one, and went back into the house. After a short time he heard the rapping again, and he stepped (it being often repeated) and held on to the latch, so that he might ascertain if anyone had taken that means to annoy him. The rapping was repeated, the door opened instantly, but no one was to be seen! He states that he could feel the jar of the door very plainly when the rapping was heard. As he opened the door, he sprang out and went around the house, but no one was in sight. His family were fearful to have him go out, lest some one intended to harm him.

* See "History of the Mysterious Communications with Spirits," Capron and Barron, p. 10.

It always remained a mystery to him, and finally, as the rapping did not at that time continue, passed from his mind, except when something of the same nature occurred to revive it."

The Weekman family at length left the house, and in December, 1847, the Fox family entered it. In the following March, the mysterious sounds were heard again. "It seemed," they say, "to be in one of the bedrooms, and sounded to them as though some one was knocking on the floor, moving chairs, etc. Four or five members of the family were at home, and they all got up to ascertain the cause of the noise. Every part of the house was searched, yet nothing could be discovered. A perceptible jar was felt by putting the hand on the bedsteads and chairs; a jar was also experienced while standing on the floor. The noise was continued that night as long as any-one was awake in the house. The following evening it was heard as before, and on the evening of the 31st of March the neighbours were called in for the first time."

The following is Mrs. Fox's statement of these strange occurrences:—

"On Friday night we concluded to go to bed early, and not let it disturb us; if it came, we thought we would not mind it, but try and get a good night's rest. My husband was here on all these occasions, heard the noise, and helped search. It was very early when we went to bed on this night,—hardly dark. We went to bed early because we had been broken so much of our rest that I was almost sick.

"My husband had not gone to bed when we first heard the noise on this evening. I had just lain down. It commenced as usual. I knew it from all other noises I had ever heard in the house. The girls, who slept in the other bed in the room, heard the noise, and tried to make a similar noise by snapping their fingers. The youngest girl is about twelve years old; she is the one who made her hand go. As fast as she made the noise with her hands or fingers, the sound was followed up in the room. It did not sound any different at that time, only it made the same number of noises that the girl did. When she stopped, the sound itself stopped for a short time.

"The other girl, who is in her fifteenth year, then spoke in sport, and said, 'Now do just as I do. Count one, two, three, four,' etc., striking one hand in the other at the same time. The blows which she made were repeated as before. It appeared to answer her by repeating every blow that she made. She only did so once. She then began to be startled; and then I spoke, and said to the noise, 'Count ten,' and it made ten strokes or noises. Then I asked the ages of my different children successively, and it gave a number of raps corresponding to the ages of my children.

"I then asked if it was a human being that was making the noise; and, if it was, to manifest it by the same noise. There was no noise. I then asked if it was a spirit; and, if it was, to manifest it by two sounds. I heard two sounds as soon as the words were spoken." *

"These 'manifestations' caused great excitement in the village, and many persons called at the house of Mr. Fox to hear the noises. Many questions were asked and answered by *raps* correctly. Sounds were only made when an affirmative answer was the correct one to a question, or when numbers were to be designated. When the alphabet was called over, there was rapping at particular letters.† Soon the experiment was carried still further, and, by request, entire names and sentences of considerable length were spelled out. A signal for the alphabet was soon understood to be five raps in quick succession.

"In a few months after the manifestations were first heard by the Fox family, several of the members removed from Hydesville to Rochester, and resided with a married sister, Mrs. Fish. The sounds were here heard in the presence of Margaretta Fox and Mrs. Fish. They were talked about, and elicited general attention,—got into the newspapers, and were

* See Account by D. M. Dewey, Rochester, N. Y. Also, History of the same, by Capron and Barron, p. 14.

† See Account by E. E. Lewis, Canandaigua, N. Y.

immediately speculated upon in all parts of the Union. The third town in which the *raps* were heard was Auburn, N. Y. Catharine, the youngest daughter of Mr. Fox, visited this place, and the sounds were made at the houses she visited. In Rochester the *raps* have not been confined to the Fox family. Since the 'manifestations' in Auburn, they have been communicated with in Greece, Monroe county, N. Y., in Sennett, Cayuga county, N. Y., in New York city, on Long Island, at Troy, N. Y., at Boston and Springfield, Mass., and a number of other towns and cities."

Who can doubt that the immediate cause of these phenomena was a physical one, a cause developed in the physical organisms of those individuals, in consequence of a residence in that particular locality? Equally manifest is the fact that that cause is identical with the Odylic Force, as developed in the cases above cited. How perfectly do the facts above given correspond with those connected with Frederica Hauffe and others; and how manifest is the identity of causation in these cases.

2. The absolute identity of the physical phenomena of these two forces, as physical causes, presents, in their action upon surrounding objects, the most decisive proof of their identity. In both cases the rapping sounds have the same relations to the organism of individuals. The rapping and other sounds

are precisely similar in their nature, and are frequently attended with the same *jarring* of surrounding objects, and each alike is occasionally attended with the same rumbling noises, as of the rolling of distant thunder. The same manifestations of an attractive and repulsive power between the physical organism and surrounding objects, appear in both cases. What facts can reveal an identity of causation, if these do not? We might with the same propriety affirm that each clap of thunder is occasioned by a new and before undeveloped force in nature, and that such phenomenon is proof of the fact, as to refer the two classes of phenomena under consideration to different and opposite causes.

3. A similar identity of *effects upon the physical organism*, on the one hand, and upon the *mental powers*, on the other, argues, with equal absoluteness, the perfect identity of these two causes. "Catalepsy, trance, clairvoyance, and various involuntary muscular, nervous, and mental activity in mediums," are among the effects enumerated by Mr. Ballou as accompanying the action of this force in connexion with the so-called spirit-manifestations. Precisely similar phenomena mark the action of the Odylic Force, in all cases like those which we have enumerated. Every mental and physical phenomenon which characterizes the manifestations of the one power, is equally characteristic of those of the other.

Is "speaking, writing, preaching, lecturing, philosophizing, prophesying," etc., attendant on the action of this force, in one instance? They are equally so in the other. The same holds equally true in all other instances. We have no right to reason at all from phenomena to the nature of the substances to which they pertain, or to attempt to identify causes by arguing their nature from their peculiar effects if we may not infer the identity of the causes under consideration, from the phenomena which they everywhere exhibit.

4. There is a peculiar effect which individuals often experience on approaching mediums, on the one hand, and those who are under the influence of the Odylic Force, on the other—an effect which renders the identity of the two forces under consideration undeniable. Those who approached Angelique Cottin, for example, were often affected with what they denominated an electric shock. Spiritualists themselves, in their own writings, often speak of having experienced in themselves precisely similar effects when approaching mediums; similar phenomena also occurring in the presence of those who are in a mesmeric state. It would be a violation of all the laws of science not to admit an identity of cause, in the presence of effects bearing such undeniable characteristics of absolute similarity.

On this point we need not enlarge, as the proposition under consideration, we may safely assume,. will not be disputed by intelligent spiritualists anywhere, it being, as far as our knowledge extends, admitted by them that spirits produce these manifestations, if at all, by controlling this very force.

THE IMMEDIATE CAUSE OF THESE MANIFESTATIONS IDENTICAL WITH THAT FROM WHICH RESULT ALL THE PHENOMENA OF MESMERISM AND CLAIRVOYANCE.

We now advance to another very important proposition. It is this: *The immediate cause of these manifestations is identical, not only with the Odylic Force, on the one hand, but with that from which the phenomena of mesmerism and clairvoyance result, on the other.* The truth of this proposition is rendered undeniably evident from the following facts and considerations, the most if not all of which are proclaimed by spiritualists themselves, in their own writings.

1. Mesmeric subjects, and those who have become clairvoyants through mesmeric influence, have, to a very great extent, become mediums, and of all other persons most readily become such. This is a fact which no one will deny.

2. Mesmerizing and pathetizing are among the common means proclaimed by spiritualists of developing mediums. When individuals desire to render some persons in their circles mediums, persons who

have been accustomed to be pathetized are first put into a mesmeric state, and then, as the persons thus affected sit with others around the table, they become mediums, thus showing that the two states are the results of the same force developed in different degrees.

3. But a fact still more decisive of this question is this: in these circles, as spiritualists themselves affirm, some individuals become mediums, while others, under precisely the same influence, not unfrequently become clairvoyant. Under the same cause, and in the same circumstances, the mesmeric phenomena, on the one hand, and the so-called spirit-manifestations, on the other, appear, thus indicating that the immediate cause of these two classes of phenomena are, in all instances, one and the same.

4. Individuals who have had experience of the mesmeric force, recognise themselves at once as subject to the action of the same cause, when sitting in the "spirit" circles; the effects which they experience in both cases being so perfectly identical, that they feel that they cannot be mistaken in regard to the nature of the causes themselves.

5. In approaching mesmeric subjects, on the one hand, and mediums, on the other, the same electric shocks are, as before observed, not unfrequently experienced, indicating that the two classes of individuals are charged with the same force.

6. The perfect identity of the conditions of entering these two states, and of the disturbing causes common to both, present a very strong evidence of the perfect identity of the immediate causes of the two classes of phenomena. To enter the mesmeric state, on the one hand, and to become mediums, on the other, one and the same condition is requisite in both instances, namely, a state of *mental passivity*. It is a fact also equally well known, that no mesmerizer can pathetize his subject when a stronger mesmerizer is by who internally resolves that that effect shall not be induced. It is a fact equally notorious and undeniable, that the same class of individuals, when sitting in the spirit-circles, can, by internally and strongly willing it, and that when no one is aware of their mental states, render it impossible for the circles to obtain any responses whatever. Who can doubt, in the presence of such facts, the absolute identity of the immediate causes of these two classes of phenomena? A very strong mesmerizer, for example, was once sitting in a spirit-circle by the side of an invalid, who was there for the purpose of being operated upon by the spirits, for the restoration of her health. None of the usual effects produced upon her appeared, till this gentleman took hold of her hand, when the desired results appeared, and appeared with much greater power, the spiritualists present remarked, than they had ever witnessed before. The gentleman left the circle, and

all the supposed spirit-phenomena instantly disappeared. The cause of the effects which then appeared cannot be doubted. They differed, however, only in degree from what had been witnessed on previous occasions, showing that the same cause had been operating in all instances alike.

CHAPTER III.

PHYSICAL AND INTELLECTUAL MANIFESTATIONS ELUCIDATED.

TWO classes of facts, as we have seen, demand our special attention in our present inquiries—the merely *physical* facts, on the one hand, and intellectual communications, on the other. As preparatory to a direct consideration of the question at issue between the advocates of the mundane and spirit theories, some remarks are deemed requisite in elucidation of the character of the phenomena under consideration. We will first consider

THE EXCLUSIVELY PHYSICAL PHENOMENA.

A moment's reflection will convince any candid mind that we have, in this class of facts, no evidence whatever of the presence or angency of disembodied spirits. The facts to be accounted for are purely physical effects arising in the presence of the action of physical causes. To refer such effects to causes *ab extra* is simply to convict ourselves of palpable ignorance of the first principles of scientific induction and deduction. A company of individuals seat themselves around a table, and placing their hands upon its surface, await the physical results which may follow. Any mere physical results which may arise under such circumstances, present no more evidence of the presence and action of disembodied spirits than would the warmth which these persons would experience were they all to place their hands near a heated body. An individual is engaged in adjusting his papers. He finds that one of these, and only that one, will adhere to his fingers, so that he cannot adjust it as he desires. Does it not throw a wonderful degree of light upon such a phenomenon, to conclude that a spirit from the upper spheres is causing this paper to play such antics? Articles of furniture in a certain house begin, from no visible cause, to move towards each other, while raps are heard in diverse places. We should make fools of ourselves if we should conclude that nothing but extra-mundane spirit-agency can produce such results. A company of individuals seat themselves around a table under the full belief that, if the object shall move under their touch, "the spirits" must cause such movements. Another company try the same experiment, in utter disbelief that "the spirits" will have anything to do in originating any results which may arise. A third company try precisely the same experiment, and, at the same time, challenge "the spirits" to prevent the expected movements. Under all these diverse mental and identical physical conditions, exactly the same results arise. What must we think of the intelligence and motives of "the spirits" in thus proving and disproving their presence and agency? What must we think of the intelligence of men who, in the presence of such facts, infer the presence and agency of "the spirits"? Undeniably, all mere physical phenomena must be set aside as having no bearing, in any direction, upon our inquiries. Extra-mundane spirit-presence can be evinced but through extra-mundane facts—facts of an intellectual character especially. Look now at the facts above cited, as occurring at the house of Dr. Griswold of New York. The three mediums of the Fox family were present, a widow and her two unmarried sisters. "An experiment was tried," we are informed, "as to what would be the effect with one of the ladies alone, or with two without the third, or with a gentleman and one or two of the ladies. The strongest knockings were on the floor beneath, when the widow and her two sisters stood anywhere together. With two of them the knockings were fainter. 'We placed ourself between her and one of the young ladies,' says Mr. Willis, 'and *no* sounds were produced as a consequence. With *one* of the mediums alone, there were no phenomena.'

"These peculiar characteristics of the conditions are worthy of careful consideration. We have found several cases where no decided physical phenomena could be evolved without the presence of two persons, both in a palpably abnormal state; and we shall give one case, in a future chapter, where three clairvoyants were required. All such conditions clearly indicate the physical agency to belong to the physical organism." No other evidence can be required to evince absolutely that all mere physical manifestations are to be left wholly out of the account in determining the question under consideration. Spiritualism must find its proofs, if it has any, among *intellectual* phenomena exclusively, and nowhere else. When we find these movements of physical objects to accord with mental states, and these sounds to respond to thoughts in our minds, then we find the evidence of mental control in what we see and hear, and inquire for the mental cause of the facts before us. This leads us to a consideration of the only form of real evidence which can be adduced in favour of the claims of Spiritualism. We refer, of course, to its

AFFIRMED INTELLECTUAL COMMUNICATIONS.

Before we can legitimately argue from such facts

(the reality of which we freely grant) the truth of the Spirit-theory, or adduce them as presenting any form or degree of evidence of its truth, it must be shown, as we have already said, and as none will deny, that such communications can, in fact, be obtained from no exclusively mundane causes, and from no other source but the specific one assigned, to wit, revelations from disembodied spirits. If precisely the same or similar communications can be obtained from minds in the body, and uncontrolled by spirits from other spheres, then these same revelations can never, without a flagrant violation of all the principles of rational and scientific deduction, be adduced as having any real bearing in favour of this theory. If we can go still further, and prove undeniably, not only that similar phenomena do result from exclusively mundane causes, but that a very large and fundamental part of these so-called spirit-communications do, in fact, result from such causes, and from nothing higher, we shall have subverted utterly the foundation on which the system rests. We here find ourselves in the presence of facts which spiritualists and the public appear not to have duly considered. Suppose that it could be rendered undeniably evident that, granting all the affirmed supernatural facts recorded in the Bible did occur, and occur as related, precisely similar facts do result from exclusively mundane causes, and that the most important of these, the raising of Lazarus from the dead and the resurrection of Christ, were the exclusive results of mundane causes,—then, according to the express admission of our Saviour Himself, no individual on earth would be bound to admit that He came out from God. No individual who has any respect for truth, will object to the subjection of the claims of Spiritualism to this infallible test. What are the facts of the case?

THE THREE CLASSES OF MEDIUMS.

Before proceeding to argue this question, a few remarks are deemed requisite, pertaining to the manner in which these manifestations are produced, through the action of the force under consideration, as developed in different classes of mediums. In three important particulars, there is a perfect agreement between us and spiritualists, as we suppose, on this subject, namely, that these manifestations are produced, directly and immediately, through the instrumentality of this or some kindred force existing in nature around us; that this force is directed, in the production of the class of phenomena under consideration, by some *intelligent* cause; and finally, that this controlling cause is the minds constituting the circles, or disembodied spirits out of the circles. So far, and that for the most obvious and conclusive reasons, no difference of opinion obtains. But how, it may be asked, can the thoughts, feelings, and mental determinations of the minds constituting these circles, unconsciously, as must be the case in most instances, control this force, so as to produce these manifestations, and that through rapping sounds, writing, and speaking? The mystery, it should be borne in mind, and here lies the grand mistake of spiritualists, is not at all removed by supposing that the same force is controlled, in the production of the same phenomena, by the thoughts, feelings, and mental determinations of disembodied spirits out of these circles, this being the only way in which such spirits ever control the action of this power, if they do it at all. Suppose that a given thought exists in a mind in a circle, and in that of a disembodied spirit out of it. That thought becomes embodied in one of these so-called spirit-communications. We affirm that it is much more reasonable to suppose that the thought lying in the mind in the organism in which this force is developed, guided its action, in the production of this phenomenon, than to suppose that the same idea existing in the mind of a disembodied spirit out of the circle, and sustaining no known relations to any mundane cause whatever, guided the action of the same force, in the production of the same phenomenon. This statement we hold to be self-evidently true.

Still a mystery hangs around the question pertaining to the *manner* in which mental states, whether pertaining to minds in the body or out of it, act upon this force, in the production of these phenomena. In regard to this subject we would observe, that there are three distinct classes of mediums through whom such communications are obtained—the rapping, writing, and speaking mediums. In the last two classes the action of this force is attended with convulsions, and very great agitation of the physical system. In the first, such phenomena very seldom, we believe, appear. The reason is obvious. In the first class, this force, owing to peculiarities of physical condition in the subject, passes off, when excited to a certain degree, to some odylic conductor, causing, when striking the object to which it passes, the rapping sounds under consideration. In the former cases, it remains in the physical organism as a disturbing force, and thus causes the convulsions referred to. As the direction of the action of this force, in the organisms of such persons, and that from its nature and relations to mind, accords with, and is controlled by, the mental states of minds in odylic rapport with such mediums, the direction of their hands, or vocal organs, will be determined by such states, just as the mental states of the mesmerizer are reproduced in the minds of mesmeric subjects. So far the facts themselves, and their manner of occurrence, perfectly accord with those which occur in the mesmeric relations, and no *ab extra* spirit-agency is even apparently demanded, to account for the embodiment of any thought pre-existing in these circles, in communications thus given forth. So obvious is this accordance, that to us it has been a matter of surprise that such phenomena have been referred to spirits out of these circles.

The case of rapping mediums is not so obvious, at first thought, to say the least. A moment's reflection however, will show that this class of phenomena is equally explicable with the others. The physical systems of the individuals in these circles may be compared to a galvanic battery which is continuously, but more especially on occasions of the least extra excitement, developing this force. As soon as it is developed to a certain degree in the organism of the rapping medium, it passes off to some object near—a chair, table, the ceiling, or floor, as the case may be—and produces, in passing into the object, the raps which have astonished the world so much. The presence of a particular thought, in any mind, the putting of a question, any such occurrence, is sufficient to occasion the excitement necessary to develop this force to the degree requisite to produce the raps, in the manner explained. An inquirer, for example, asks if a spirit is present that will communicate with him? The putting of the question excites him, and through him the medium, sufficiently to develop the force to that degree that occasions the number of raps understood as implying an affirmative answer. He now asks the name of the spirit, his own mind being fixed upon some individual. As the letters of the alphabet are called, the moment the first letter of the name of that person is pronounced, the mind of the inquirer is sufficiently excited to occasion, in the manner described, a rap. So also as each subsequent letter of that name is pronounced, till the whole is given. On principles precisely similar, answers to questions proposed may be obtained. Suppose, on the other hand that the inquirer has no particular name in his mind. When the first letter of the name of a certain individual is pronounced, the law of unconscious association may produce the excitement requisite to occasion the rap, and thus the name may be given. These suggestions, together with the fact, most abundantly established, that this power acts in many important particulars in accordance with mental states, and is determined in the direction of its activity by the same, will, we think, satisfy the reader, as far as any inquiries may arise in his mind, in regard to the *manner* in which these rapping sounds are produced.

We will now proceed to argue the questions, whether

phenomena of the identical character of these so-called spirit-communications are obtained through exclusively mundane causes, and whether a large and essential portion of these communications are not themselves obtained through such sources. To such questions we answer, *precisely similar communications have been obtained through exclusively mundane sources.*

1. The identical communications which are obtained in these circles can, we remark, and that without exception, be obtained in circumstances and relations in which there is the highest evidence of the total absence of all *ab extra* spirit interposition. We enter a spirit-circle in which we are total strangers, and where our visit was wholly unexpected. We put our questions pertaining to every subject on which spirits are ever questioned there, and receive every form of answer which is ever reported, as coming from spirits. We then go into the presence of an individual rendered clairvoyant by mesmeric influences, an individual to whom we sustain the precise relations above specified. We here put the identical questions we did before, and receive in return the identical communications which we then and there obtained. We then repeat the same experiment, with precisely the same results, in the presence of other individuals similarly related to us,—individuals rendered more permanently clair-

voyant by the influence of drugs, or a residence in certain localities. In the two instances last named, our communications are undeniably obtained in the total absence of the agency of disembodied spirits. If any individual, to save the doctrine of Spiritualism, should assert the contrary, he would not only be guilty of denying what the world knows to be true, and he himself has hitherto admitted as self-evident, but would betray a degree of ignorance and moral obtuseness which would render him unworthy of being reasoned with at all. We may as reasonably affirm that all our mental perceptions of every kind are from spirits, and are caused exclusively by their interposition, as to affirm that the mental perceptions of clairvoyants are thus induced. Yet we obtain, through these individuals, all the responses, with all their peculiar characteristics, which are obtained, or can be obtained, through spirit-mediums. Do we obtain *intelligent* communications through the latter? So we do through the former. Do we obtain, through the latter, correct responses to questions pertaining to subjects of which they are profoundly ignorant? So we do through the former. Do we obtain, through the latter, responses to purely mental questions? So we do through the former. Do we, in some instances, through the latter, obtain correct responses to inquiries pertaining to subjects of which ourselves, and all present, are ignorant? So we do through the former. Do our communications, through the latter, come *as* from spirits? So, by simply willing it, the same communications may come to us, through the former, *as* from spirits, the same spirits, too, invoked through the latter. There is not a single communication, or characteristic of any communication, which is obtained, or can be obtained, through the mediums, which are not and may not be obtained through clairvoyants, when under the exclusive influence of purely mundane causes, the identical causes by which all these so-called spirit-communications are immediately originated. How can the claims of Spiritualism be sustained by an appeal to such communications—communications perfectly identical with those which proceed from exclusively mundane causes? The system falls to pieces upon its own fundamental facts. It has adduced, and can adduce, not a solitary fact, physical or mental, whose occurrence and total characteristics may not be and are not accounted for by a reference to exclusively mundane causes. None but purely mundane facts are adduced. How can we argue from these the presence and interposition of *ab extra* mundane causes? Nothing can be more illogical than any such deductions.

2. As we said of the physical manifestations, so we now affirm of those under consideration, nothing but

precisely these or similar communications could have been anticipated from a careful induction and classification of all the facts pertaining to the action of this force in relations and circumstances where no spirit agency is to be supposed, the very force through which these manifestations are immediately induced. We have, in these circles, the same power operating, and operating upon individuals in precisely similar relations to each other as in clairvoyance. The circles are to the mediums what the magnetizers, and others in magnetic communications with the magnetized, are to such individuals. If similar phenomena were not developed in the spirit-circles to those which do appear, supposing no disembodied spirits were ever present in them, such a fact would be an anomaly in the history of the action of this force when developed in the human organism; a fact just as wonderful and unaccountable on any other supposition than some *ab extra* mundane agency to prevent their occurrence, as their occurrence now appears to those who are ignorant of the peculiar properties of this mysterious force in nature. Their non-occurrence in these circles would be a much higher proof of the presence and interposition of spirits than is their actual occurrence now.

If we should recur to the most important and decisive communications ever obtained through the spirit-mediums, we should find even those more than paralleled by precisely similar communications about which "the spirits" undeniably have nothing to do. In these circles, in instances very few and far between, as compared with the multitudinous errors there made in respect to the subjects of which we are now speaking, correct answers are obtained to questions about which all present are profoundly ignorant—visions of objects occur far removed from the observation and even the thoughts of such persons, and coming events are foreshadowed. If we should compare the number of the correct with the false communications thus obtained, we should have little, very little, occasion to suppose the presence in the circles of much higher sources of information than what does, in fact, characterize common guessing. When one is true, ninety-nine false ones are undeniably obtained of the class under consideration. The correct ones, on the other hand, are more than paralleled by dreams and clairvoyant visions, in respect to which no aid from the spirits is to be supposed.

Of dream-visions, take the following fact stated by Dr. Bushnel in his great work entitled "Nature and the Supernatural." We condense the account referred to, an account of the validity of which none will doubt who will read Dr. Bushnel's statements. A wealthy planter in California had a vision in his sleep of a company of emigrants blocked in by the snow in a mountain pass between the eastern and the

Pacific coast. He observed and remembered accurately the scenery around, and the countenances of individuals of the company. This man had never visited or heard of that scenery, having emigrated by the Panama rout. The vision was regarded as nothing but a singular dream-fancy. Immediately after, some hunters spent a night with the planter. While they were recounting their adventures, he told them of his singular dream-vision. As he described the scenery, the hunters assured him that he had given an exact description of a certain pass which they named, a pass which lay on the emigrant rout, they having frequently visited the place. The planter, amid the ridicule of his neighbours, gathered provisions, and placing them upon mules, started with a company of hired men for the place referred to. On his arrival, he found the emigrants as he had seen them in his vision, and at once recognised the countenances of the leading individuals.

The public papers of the city of Cincinnati, Ohio, fully vouch for the truth of the following statements. A young woman of that city had a brother in the gold regions of California. In her sleep, one night, she had the following dream-vision in respect to her brother. She saw him rise very carefully from his bed in his log hut, and after getting his bowie knife, stand, holding his weapon in a striking position, by the side of the bed. Soon she saw a hand, holding a dagger, pass in through the opening between the logs at the head of the bed. As the hand passed near the spot where her brother had lain, there was a violent stab. Her brother, with a single blow with his heavy weapon, severed the arm of the would-be assassin from his body. A fearful shriek, and the report of a pistol was heard on the outside of the hut. The brother ran out and brought in the body of the dying man, who had shot himself with his remaining hand, after the other had been cut off. The sister told the vision to the family and neighbours, and it was much spoken of as merely a very singular dream. The next letter received from the brother gave a detailed statement of events in exact accordance with all the particulars of the dream, events which occurred on the very night of the dream. The would-be assassin was a Mexican, who had become offended with the brother. Are dream-visions revelations of "the spirits"? Yet the former are sometimes as true and strange, and always as reliable, as are the latter, when they relate to events distant and unknown.

How accurate in some instances, and yet how generally unreliable, are ordinary clairvoyant visions, visions with which none suppose "the spirits" have anything to do. We need only refer here to those already cited from the works of President Wayland. Spiritualists can boast of not one of their mediums through whom communications in respect to unknown and distant objects and events are obtained, at all comparable in reliability with those obtained through the mesmerized individual referred to. The same holds true in numberless other cases. We will here specify one which occurred in the family of our own daughter. Her husband, a member of the legal profession in the city of Cleveland, Ohio, U.S., was accustomed to spend, in company with several other gentlemen, two or more weeks prior to the setting in of winter each year, in hunting in the northern part of the state of Michigan, the object being health and pleasure. On one occasion, he had gone in company with seven associates. All that our daughter knew of their whereabouts was that they were somewhere in the northern regions of the state referred to, several hundred miles from home. After she had retired to her bed one night, being, for quite a long period, on account of nervousness, unable to sleep, she had, when perfectly awake, the following distinct vision of that company of hunters. While they were all lying in profound sleep, in pairs, in different parts of a single room, a small and deformed female, holding in her hand a lighted tallow candle, passed very carefully through that room. When near its centre, she stopped for a moment to look around her. This gave our daughter an opportunity to take a distinct view of the woman, the room, and of the specific locality of each man in the room. On the return of her husband she gave him the particulars of that vision. "Well," he replied, "you have given an exact account of the appearance of the woman, of the room, and of the specific locality of everyone in it. But of the passage of the woman through the room I know nothing." "Of course you know nothing of that fact," our daughter replied, "because you were all sound asleep at the time."

A friend of ours, a gentleman of known intelligence and integrity, gave us an account of an aged friend of his, a lady, who had long been the subject of similar visions. One winter evening, when the family were sitting around their fire, she started up with the announcement that, in such a locality, a quite distant one, a man had become bewildered and lost, and was perishing in the snow. A company, with a dog and lights, went to the place designated, and found the man as stated. Such facts lie all around us, in the history of the race. The law which obtains in such cases is obviously this. When the proper conditions, the conditions of ordinary vision, are fulfilled, we have a direct and immediate perception of objects around us. When certain psychic conditions obtain between us and any objects, however remote from and unknown to us, we then have a preception, equally direct and immediate, of such objects, and this whether those relations are fulfilled in our sleeping or waking moments. To say that such preceptions sometimes occur in the spirit-circles simply evinces the presence and action of the odylic force there; and this force being present, it would be a mystery if this kind of communications did not sometimes occur there.

Certain individuals, also, of a peculiar temperament, have, at times, a singular pre-impression of coming events. Some one or two years since, one of the most calamitous accidents known in the history of railroads occurred on the road between Cleveland, Ohio, and Buffalo, New York. The statement went the rounds of the papers that one of our distinguished Baptist clergymen had lost his life in that catastrophe. Soon after, an authenticated statement to this effect appeared. On the arrival of the train prior to the one under consideration, at Cleveland, that clergyman left the depôt, with his baggage, and had his name registered at one of the hotels. This he did with the fixed purpose of remaining over until morning, and then taking the train in which the accident occurred. As he was about to retire to his room, a very distinct and strong impression was made upon his mind that he should instantly hasten to the depôt and take the train he had left. This he did, and escaped the death he would otherwise have suffered. The next morning an entire family, well known in that city, a family consisting of an aged mother, her daughter, son-in-law, and children, were prevented taking that train by the following circumstance. When the entire family were dressed for the journey, the carriages being at the door, and the trunks being put on board, that aged mother suddenly stated that she could not go in that train. On being very strongly expostulated with, she remarked that the rest might go on, but she must tarry until the next train. The whole company accordingly tarried, and the lives of that entire family were saved. Dr. Walker, the author of "The Philosophy of the Plan of Salvation," and his wife, they having no children of their own, adopted two orphan sisters. These children had, from time to time, singular premonitions of coming events. When spending a season in their family, Mrs. Walker, in the presence of her husband, made to us this statement. When her husband was absent, and was not at all expected home short of one or two days, one of the children said, "Mamma, father will come home at such an hour to-day: he will enter that door,"—a door which he was not accustomed to enter when coming home from abroad,—"and he will place his umbrella in that corner." At the exact time specified he did enter that door, and set his umbrella in the place designated. The return of Dr. Walker, as he informed me, was unexpected to himself, and he could give no reason for the fact that he entered his house and did as the child had predicted. We could readily fill a volume of well-authenticated facts of this character—facts in the origination of which "the spirits" undeniably have nothing whatever to do. Unless Spiritualism, which is impossible, can show higher facts than these, facts, too, entirely diverse in character from these, it cannot present even presumptive evidence that "the spirits" originate even its highest known phenomena.

Nor should the wonders of common guessing be overlooked in this connexion. We once, in a discussion of the claims of Spiritualism, made before a great congregation in Cleveland, Ohio, the following statement. The leading spiritualist in the city, a former graduate of Yale College, had missed an important paper, and searched in vain for it in every part of his house where he even conjectured it might be found. On mentioning the fact to a gentleman of the city, the latter said: "Let me see now, if I cannot tell you just where that paper can be found." After thinking a moment he continued: "Go into the south-east chamber of the second story of your house; go to the bureau which stands on the north side of that room, open such a drawer, and in the north-east corner of that drawer you will find that paper." Following those directions, Mr. S. found his papers in the very spot designated. Yet the man who gave the directions afterwards affirmed, and I so stated in the presence of Mr. S., who admitted the facts, that every one of those directions was a mere guess in the dark. The man had never been in that chamber, and did not know that there was a bureau in it.

All the classes of facts above stated undeniably owe their origin to exclusively mundane causes, causes over which "the spirits" have no control. Yet, if we add to the ordinary mesmeric communications all the above classes of facts, we have perfectly paralleled all the ordinary and extraordinary intellectual phenomena of which Spiritualism can boast, and have thus utterly annihilated all reasons for attributing said phenomena to the agency of "the spirits."

A LARGE AND ESSENTIAL PORTION OF THESE AFFIRMED SPIRIT-COMMUNICATIONS HAVE AN EXCLUSIVELY MUNDANE ORIGIN.

When called upon to determine the cause of a given class of facts, all having the same essential characteristics, all that is requisite is to render it undeniably evident that an *essential* portion of them are the exclusive result of a specific cause. It is, then, to be presumed that all the remainder are the results of the action of the same cause. How is it in respect to the question before us? Let us, in the first place, listen to the views and testimony of spiritualists themselves—spiritualists of the highest standing known among them. According to the admissions of the most intelligent and influential individuals among them—indeed, of the whole sect, so far as our knowledge extends—*all* these communications are more or less determined, in their characteristics, by the mediums themselves; and many of them are *wholly* caused, not at all by disembodied spirits, but by the mediums, or by individuals in the spirit-circles. "The medium," says Mr. Ballou, and we have yet to hear of the first spiritualist who dissents from this view, "is a sort of amanuensis, a translator or interpreter of the spirit's leading ideas. In this character media will exhibit, in various degrees, the defects of their own respective rhetoric." Again, he says, "It is amazing to see the unreasonableness and pertinacity of our opponents. They have taken the ground that *none* of these manifestations, *none* of these communications are from departed spirits. We have taken the position that *some* of them *are* from departed spirits, and others *not*." The italics are our author's. In another place still, we have the following very important statements:—

"I have now to treat of cases under Class Second; *i.e.*, 'those in which some of the important demonstrations were probably caused or greatly affected by *un*departed spirits.' I mean by *un*departed spirits, persons in the flesh who by their *will* or psychological power, control the agency which gives forth sounds, motions, etc. I refer not to *impostors*, playing off *counterfeits*. I am treating of phenomena caused by mental power alone, coacting with the mysterious agency under consideration.

"I have cases such as the following:—

"1. In which the bias, prejudice, predilection, or will of the medium evidently governed and characterized the *demonstrations*. In these cases the answers given to questions, the doctrines taught, and the peculiar leanings of communications spelled out, were so obviously fashioned by the medium's own mind, as to leave no doubt of the fact.

"In absolute confirmation of this, questions have been written out and presented to the medium, with a request that the answers should, if possible, be given *thus* and *so*. And they were given by *raps* accordingly. I myself gave questions in this way to a certain medium, and found that answers could be obtained in the affirmative or negative, or in flat contradiction to previous answers, if the medium would but agree to *will* it. At the same time, I made myself certain that this medium could not procure the *rapping* agency at will. It *came, stayed*, and *went* as it would; and in *that* respect was uncontrollable. But when it chanced to be *present*, it could be overruled, biased, and perverted more or less by the medium.

"2. In other cases there has been an overruling psychological influence exerted by some powerful mind or minds present in the room with the medium. In such cases this powerful influence, *with* or without the consciousness of the medium, has elicited answers just such as had been wished or willed by the managing mind. And these answers have alternately contradicted each other in the plainest manner, during the same half-hour's demonstration.

"In one instance a strong-willed man resolved to reverse certain disagreeable predictions frequently repeated through two *tipping* media who often sat in conjunction. The result was, he could overrule *one* of them sitting *alone*, and get a response to suit himself. But both of them together over-matched his psychological powers. I might give names, places, dates, and details in this connexion; but it is unnecessary. There can be no reasonable doubt of the facts just stated. It may be set down as *certain* that there are cases wherein some of the important demonstrations are caused or greatly affected by *un*departed spirits. How far influences of this sort extend and characterize spirit-manifestations, remains to be ascertained. We can positively identify them in many cases.

"In some, they are known to the parties concerned, and acknowledged to have been consciously and intentionally exerted. In others they may be justly suspected, where no consciousness of them is felt by the medium, or by any dominant mind."

"I do not, of course, mean," says Rev. H. Snow, "that I believe in *all* the claims that have been advanced, of this character; on the contrary, I am of opinion that much which purports to come from unseen beings does in reality come, either partly or wholly, from minds in the body."

If the validity of the above admissions and statements were denied, undeniable facts affirming their validity are so multitudinous, and decisive in their bearing, as to induce the most unwavering conviction in all candid minds. So conscious do mediums become of the control which they can exercise over the action of this force, when developed, that they no doubt often direct its action for the purpose of deceiving the circles in which they are holding forth. We will give, in illustration, a fact which occurred some years since, when a medium was entertaining circles in Cleveland, at the house of the distinguished spiritualist, Joel Tiffany, Esq. We do not hold him responsible at all for the acts of the medium. The case was this. A gentleman, a member of the bar in that city, on his first introduction to the spirit-circles, was strongly inclined, to say the least, to embrace, in full, the doctrine of Spiritualism, so inexplicable, on any other theory, did the undeniable facts presented appear. Subsequently, however, he became fully convinced that while the rappings were a reality, and no imposition, the force which produced them was, sometimes consciously, but more generally unconsciously, controlled by spirits in and not out of the body. He, accordingly, having gained the confidence of the medium, one of the best that ever appeared among us, united with her in deceiving temporarily, for his own amusement, some of his friends, who visited these circles. On one occasion, he remarked to those present that none of the tests which they had applied were, or ought to be, fully satisfactory; because that, in all instances, they had to depend upon the testimony of individuals in regard to the question whether their inquiries were or were not correctly answered. He would propose a test about which there could be no mistake, and of the character of which they could all alike judge for themselves. He would retire from the circle, and write down seven questions, and having returned, he would put them in succession mentally, no one, as they could all testify, seeing the paper but himself. The answers, as rapped out, they should take down, and when completed, he would read each question in order, and they should read the answer, and see for themselves how they corresponded, each to each. Seven questions were accordingly written out, and put as suggested, and seven answers were rapped out. When compared it was found that each question had been specifically and correctly answered. We will give three of them as examples of the rest, namely, the first two, and the last. "Question. How many days are there in a week? Ans. Seven. Ques. Who performs these wonders? (This was put in Latin.) Ans. The spirits. Ques. What do the spirits think of any in this circle who are not now convinced? Ans. If an angel from heaven should speak to them, they would not believe." All who understood not the facts as they were, were astounded and convinced, of course. The gentleman subsequently informed his wondering friends that he had, prior to that meeting, put all those answers in writing into the hands of the medium, informing her that corresponding questions would be put in the form stated, and that she must prepare herself accordingly. The answers, as he affirms, were given, word for word, as he wrote them. The *spelling*, however, was hers, she being a poor speller. Yet the rappings, he further adds, were no imposition, and remain to this day, to his mind, a deep mystery. The deception lay exclusively in persuading the persons present that spirits out of the circle, and not the minds in it, controlled the action of the force by which the answers were given forth.

In this case, no one can doubt that the cause of the manifestations was exclusively mundane. The fact, then, that many of these communications are wholly from the minds in the circles, and in no form from spirits out of them, is not only admitted by spiritualists, but is too manifest to be doubted or denied, for a single moment. Now these facts and admissions are far more sweeping in their necessary consequences, than spiritualists appear to have ever imagined. All evidence of the truth of their theory, derived from all their several classes of facts but the last, the fact that events are sometimes correctly reported in these circles, events of which all present were previously ignorant, is utterly annihilated. If *one* thought existing in these circles may become embodied in these communications, without the agency of disembodied spirits, any other and all others may be. If one question, whether put verbally or mentally, pertaining to any subject of which the inquirer or anyone present is informed, may be correctly answered, without the interposition of spirits, any other such question may be thus answered, and all evidence of the truth of Spiritualism, derived from such communications, is utterly annihilated. Yet upon precisely such facts, the claims of this theory have hitherto been mainly based. We obtain, in these circles, it is argued, *intelligent* communications, thus evincing the fact that they originate from an intelligent cause. Responses are obtained to questions pertaining to subjects about which the mediums and all present, but the inquirers, were profoundly ignorant. Purely mental questions, also, are thus answered. All this is freely granted. We must bear in mind, however, that answers to precisely such questions, every class of them, are obtained, in the total absence of any control or agency of disembodied spirits; a fact so undeniable, that even spiritualists universally admit it. How can the truth of that theory, then, be argued from such communications? The entire evidence of its truth derived from any one of these classes of facts, or from all of them together, is utterly annihilated. All its claims, all the hopes of its abettors to sustain them, hang exclusively upon one solitary class, the simple fact that, in some instances, correct responses are obtained to inquiries where the true answer was not previously known to any persons in the circles at the time when the meeting commenced. When we shall have accounted satisfactorily for this one class of facts, we shall utterly have annihilated *all* the evidence of every kind of the truth of Spiritualism. To a careful consideration of this class, we will now advance. All that we have to do to gain our point, is to prove that there are existing and operating in these circles, purely mundane causes from which, without the interposition of disembodied spirits, this new information may have been brought into the circles, and thus have been embodied in the responses referred to. On this point, we have occasion to call attention merely to the following decisive considerations.

1. There are known to be present, and in active exercise, in these circles, three forms of mental activity, which are abundantly sufficient to account for this entire class of facts, on the supposition that disembodied spirits have no connexion with them whatever, namely, the Imagination, the principle of Conjecture or Guessing, and Clairvoyance. A question is proposed in one of these circles. The attention of every one is consequently fixed upon it, with the curiosity of all intensely excited. Each individual, of course, forms in his own mind, through the action of the imagination, some conception of what the answer should be, and among the possible answers which should be given, he will also of necessity conjecture or guess that some specific one is true. This act of the imagination on the one hand, or the conjecture on the other, becomes embodied in the response rapped, written, or spoken out through the medium. In some instances, of course, and the case could not be otherwise, when the guessing principle and the imagination are continuously, in myriads of circles, occasioning responses of this kind, the answer given forth will be right, and the perfect coincidence between it and the state of facts a matter of surprise. Now suppose, which is true and notoriously so among

spiritualists the world over, that all wrong answers are set aside as of no account, while every response which happens to be true is set down as certain proof of this theory. We should, in that case, find in the works with which the community is being flooded from the spirit-presses, the same wonderful facts adduced in favour of the claims of Spiritualism that we now have. Now we record it as our solemn conviction, and we speak advisedly in what we utter, that there is not one in a hundred of the well-authenticated cases of this kind that has ever occurred in these circles that cannot be accounted for on the principles under consideration, and that would not be just what it is, supposing spirits to have no connexion whatever with these communications. Then to account for the very few facts which perhaps should not be referred to these principles, we need only refer to what is known and affirmed by spiritualists themselves to be true, the occasional occurrence of states of clairvoyance in these circles. Suppose that when a question is put, the medium, or some other individual, is in a state of clairvoyance, and happens, at the instant, to come into rapport with the real facts inquired after. The perceptions thus obtained would, of course, be embodied in the response given forth, and thus, without the interposition of spirits, we should have the wonderful revelations which are now being spread before the world as coming from spirits, and as proof of their presence and interposition. All this might occur, and the clairvoyant not be distinctly conscious of what had happened, just as individuals, as spiritualists themselves admit, often produce responses when honestly supposing that spirits do it. Now, on the supposition that no disembodied spirit was ever present in any of these circles, we could not fail to have, from the action of the three causes under consideration, all the wonderful revelations, just as they occur, which spiritualists are holding before the public mind as proof of their theory. We have no occasion to refer to an *ab extra* spirit-agency to account for any real revelation that has ever been given forth in any circle in the wide world, and consequently nothing can be more absurd than such reference. Facts which could not but occur, with all their peculiarities as they are, if no disembodied spirits were present, cannot, without a flagrant violation of all the laws of scientific and common sense procedure, be adduced as proof of their presence and agency. No other facts ever have been or can be adduced in favour of the claims of Spiritualism.

2. These revelations bear all possible characteristics of an origination from the very causes to which we have referred them, and none which they would bear did they come from spirits, and especially from *the* spirits to whom they are referred. Did they originate

from these three causes exclusively, then the responses pertaining to subjects of which all in the circles were ignorant, would be, in instances very "few and far between," right, and strikingly so, and in all others wrong. Now this undeniably is the precise character of all these professed spirit-revelations pertaining to such subjects. If, on the other hand, they came from intelligent spirits, good or bad, who did not wish to stand revealed to the world as superlative liars and deceivers, we should find, what we do not now find, that these responses are generally, to say the least, correct, and only in instances "few and far between," wrong. Spirits of common prudence, such as is possessed by men in the flesh, and not utterly reckless of their character for truth and veracity, would be exceedingly careful about the answers which they should give forth to such inquiries. On no other principle could they distinguish their responses from those originating from the causes above named, and thus give evidence of their own agency in these revelations. Yet these so-called, par excellence, spirit-revelations have none of the characteristics which they certainly would have did they come from spirits, and all and none others that they would have did they originate from the causes to which we have assigned them. The validity of these statements cannot be shaken, and spiritualists, we think, will not attempt to do it. Yet here lies an immovable rock, namely, facts which cannot be denied, upon which this system must fall to pieces. Their facts, the only facts on which they can rely, are just such as would not come from spirits, good or bad, and just such as could not but originate from the very mundane causes to which we have assigned them.

3. The very principle on which the entire claims of Spiritualism rest, would, if its validity were admitted, affirm with equal absoluteness the most false and absurd claims of the grossest impostors that ever existed. A devoted spiritualist, for example, made an inquiry in a spirit-circle, in reference to a subject of which he was ignorant, and wished to be informed, and accompanied the inquiry with this statement: "If the answer obtained turns out to be wrong, it will not shake my confidence in Spiritualism itself, in the least." A very influential and devoted spiritualist, in conversation with us, years ago, referred to certain startling predictions which "the spirits" had just uttered in regard to the affairs of Europe, predictions which were to be fulfilled by the middle of February 1854, predictions not one of which has been verified, but all proved false. The reference was accompanied with this remark: "If these predictions turn out to be true, very well; if not, they go for nothing." This is the precise principle everywhere assumed by spiritualists, in arguing for the truth of their theory; and in doing so, they sell themselves to

be deceived. Take a case in illustration. A friend of ours, a clergyman, when on the way to visit a family belonging to his congregation, some time since, forecast in his own mind whom of the family, and whom of the neighbours, he should find in the parlour on his arrival, and where each should be seated, etc. On his arrival, he found that these fore-imaginings were, in almost every particular, correct. Suppose, now, that he had wished to impose himself upon his people as a divinely-inspired prophet; that for this end he should begin to give public utterance to numberless foreshadowings of a similar kind, one in a hundred or a thousand of which could not, of course, fail to be true; that he had also occasional revelations by means of clairvoyance, and that these should be mingled with the other professed revelations; and that his people should receive every prediction and utterance which happened to be fulfilled as a proof of his assumed claims, while, by universal consent, they should pass by all false ones as having no bearing, one way or the other, upon the subject. Who does not see that such an individual, through such a principle, would soon stand revealed to the people as a divinely-inspired and authorized prophet, with as high claims as Isaiah or Elijah, and with an authority as absolute as Jesus Christ, though he were one of the darkest impostors that ever existed? No other result could arise from such a principle of judging, and upon this very principle exclusively the entire claims of Spiritualism are based. Predictions and communications which happen to be true, are trumpeted through the world as demonstrating its claims, while the hundred or thousand false ones, to one that turns out to be true, are dropped, as having no bearing either way. Were they to present to the world a true record of the false responses continuously given forth, in their own circles, with the true ones standing here and there in their midst, solitary and alone, the world would turn in utter disgust from the spectacle, and spiritualists themselves would blush with shame, to intimate a spirit-origin for such monstrosities.

4. The nature of many of these communications, also, render it demonstrably evident that they must have an exclusively mundane origin and cause. When the celebrated medium, Mrs. Fish, had, as was supposed, finished the sessions of one of the circles, on an evening in Cleveland, Ohio, loud raps were unexpectedly heard, indicating that "the spirits" had something special to reveal. The alphabet was taken, and the following revelation was rapped out: "The spirits direct that Mr. ——," our informant, "now go down to the saloon, and taking the medium with him, get some oysters." As we shall see hereafter, a spirit affirmed to have come down from the upper sphere, rapped out, in answer to mental questions, put in a

high circle in the city of Boston, Mass., his own name as "Miserable Humbug," and affirmed that, in that highest of all the spheres, "the spirits live on pork and beans." Will any man in his senses attribute such communications to "the spirits"?

The spirit of a certain lad was affirmed to have told, some time after his death, where a pen-knife which he had lost might be found, and it was found accordingly. In each of two public debates held, at intervals of several years from each other, at Cleveland, Ohio, that fact was adduced by the same speaker, one of the leading spiritualists in America, and introduced, in both instances, as one of the main pillars of his high argument.

We have carefully examined the revelations of "the spirits" from the first up to the present time, and found them all, with very few exceptions, to be similar to the above, and those next presented. We took up, for example, the late works of the famous R. D. Owen, in the expectation of finding recorded therein fact which would rise at least somewhat above common-place. We found very little, however, which rose much higher than that which pertains to the pen-knife. Take as examples of these revelations pertaining to the unknown, the following:—

An individual who has a husband in California, who has learned, by experience, that it is not only not good for *man*, but for woman also, "to be alone," and who, in her loneliness, has come so far within the attractive influence of one who is not her husband, as to make "a local habitation and a name" with him an object of strong desire, enters a spirit-circle, and is there accosted, very unexpectedly, it is affirmed, by the spirit of her husband, from whom she had failed to obtain information at the time expected. With the tenderest expressions of affection, he informs her that he is no longer in the body, but an inhabitant of the "spirit land." There was one thing, and only one, requisite to the completion of his happiness there—her *immediate* union, in marriage, with the individual above referred to. The ceremony must be performed the very next evening—we think that was the time—at such an hour, and in such a room, which was to be darkened, where he would be present, and himself, as a rapping revelator, preside over and conduct the exercises. Of course the mourning widow was not "disobedient to the heavenly vision," and the desired union was consummated accordingly. After the lapse of a few weeks, however, a letter arrived from the California husband, bearing date some days subsequent to the ceremony in the dark room. So strong was the sympathy of "the spirits" for human woe, in this instance, that they were willing to become reckless liars for its relief. New but false information was here conveyed. Such are some of the credibly reported doings and new revelations of the spirits in the state of Ohio.

In another instance, a husband went to California under the belief, as his friends affirm, of infidelity to him on the part of his wife, who subsequently, in appearance, as they further affirm, drawn by a new attachment, was making efforts to obtain a divorce from "her liege lord." But while the law was "dragging its slow length along," behind the "hot haste" of human desire, the spirit of that husband addressed the wife, through a medium, in a spirit-circle, and informed her that she was now "loosed from the law of her husband," "and would not be an adulteress, though she should be married to another man." Subsequent intelligence confirmed, in this case, the revelation of the spirits, though there are yet among his friends doubters of the fact of the death of the individual referred to. This is one among the cases on which the claims of Spiritualism are based.

We need not argue this question any further. A fact which is openly admitted by spiritualists themselves, and which is evinced by real proof too obvious to be questioned by any class of candid thinkers, may be assumed as a valid basis for future deductions.

We claim to have established, undeniably, two important facts in regard to these phenomena: that they are, in kind, the same, in every essential respect, as those which are known to result from exclusively mundane causes; and that a large and important portion of these so-called spirit-phenomena have no other but such causes. We are now prepared to consider the question whether they all, in common, have not the same origin and cause. In arguing this question, we do not commit ourselves against the doctrine that departed spirits have, in ages past, appeared, and do now, from time to time, appear, unto men in the flesh. We have now to do with facts of a peculiar and special character, and the question is, Have we valid evidence that this one class of facts has the spirit-origin that is claimed for it?

CHAPTER IV.

POSITIVE AND CONCLUSIVE PROOF THAT ALL THESE COMMUNICATIONS AND MANIFESTATIONS ARE THE EXCLUSIVE RESULT OF MUNDANE CAUSES, AND NOT OF THE AGENCY OF DISEMBODIED SPIRITS.

WE believe that we have fully established the propositions—that there is in the world around us purely mundane causes from which phenomena, in all respects similar and analogous to those adduced by spiritualists, do arise; that the former classes of phenomena are perfectly parallel and similar to the latter; that these so-called spirit-phenomena do occur in circumstances in which these mundane causes are known to exist and to act; that a large and essential portion of these very phenomena are the exclusive result of the action of such causes; and that, consequently, we have no occasion to go beyond these causes to account for these manifestations in their entireness. We have thus rendered it utterly impossible to prove the spiritualistic hypothesis. Our next proposition yet remains to be established, namely, *that from these exclusively mundane causes, and not from the agency of disembodied spirits, all these manifestations do, in fact, proceed.* When we shall have established this proposition, we shall have proved Spiritualism to be exclusively, as far as its claims to a spirit-origin are concerned, a system of error and delusion. This is what we propose to do. It may be important, in this connexion, to remind the reader of the precise points of agreement and disagreement between us and the spiritualists on this subject. On all hands it is agreed—that the *immediate* cause of these manifestations is some force, by whatever name it may be called, a force existing in the world around us; that this force is controlled in the production of these phenomena by some intelligent cause or causes; that the cause of a portion of these phenomena is the minds in the circles; that the controlling cause of the remaining phenomena is the minds in the circles, or disembodied spirits out of the same. The only difference of opinion which does or can obtain pertains exclusively to the *location* of the cause of the residuum of facts last referred to. We maintain that, in the production of these communications, this force is controlled consciously or unconsciously—for the most part unconsciously—by the mental states of the minds constituting these circles. Spiritualists, on the other hand, maintain that the same facts are determined by the mental states of disembodied spirits. Here only do we differ, as far as the question at issue in this department of our enquiries is concerned. We will now proceed to adduce the evidence in favour of the former, and against the latter, hypothesis. The facts and arguments which we have to present may be ranged under the following classes :—

I. THE ADMITTED FACT, THAT AN ESSENTIAL PART OF THESE PHENOMENA ARE UNDENIABLY ORIGINATED BY EXCLUSIVELY MUNDANE CAUSES, REQUIRES, WITHOUT ABSOLUTE PROOF TO THE CONTRARY, THAT THEY ALL BE REFERRED TO THE SAME CAUSES.

All the laws of scientific deduction require us, in view of the proposition already established, to regard as true the hypothesis we maintain, and the opposite one as false. Whenever an essential portion of a given class of facts, all bearing the same leading characteristics, are proved and admitted to have resulted from a given cause or causes, it is always assumed as positive proof that the remaining portion of said facts were produced by the same cause or causes, unless the most absolute proof to the contrary is adduced. Especially is this the case when it has been shown that, by a reference to this specific cause or causes, all the facts alike can be readily accounted for. In our preceding discussions, it has been proved (1) that *some* of these manifestations are produced exclusively by the minds in the circles, and not by spirits out of them; and (2) that this one cause, in the circumstances supposed, is all that is requisite to account for *all* these manifestations. It would, therefore, be a violation of all the laws of scientific deduction to attribute any of these phenomena to any other cause. This conclusion is undeniable.

II. No new, and none but exclusively mundane, truths are represented in these communications.

The great fact that we next adduce is, in our judgment, of the most absolutely decisive character conceivable—the undeniable fact, that no *new truths* or *principles* are found in these communications.* They come to us as affirmed revelations from the highest minds, among others, in the immortal spheres. Yet they are, in fact, no revelations at all. They are, on the other hand, a mere chaos of truth and error, with which the world was familiar before. We hazard nothing in affirming that amid all these manifestations there is not a solitary new truth, or new fundamental principle pertaining to the universe of matter or spirit, although "the spirits" present themselves as most

* We here distinguish, of course, between mere information pertaining to matters of fact, and important truths and principles. It is to the latter that we now refer.

benevolent, self-sacrificing, and indispensably-needed guides, in reference to both. They come to free men from error, and to "guide them into all truth," and then they simply re-affirm all forms of mere *human* opinions in reference to this world and the next, and that without revealing to us a solitary new truth, or presenting us with a solitary new principle by which we can distinguish truth from error. They come to enlarge the sphere of human science and discovery, and then, as far as they assert anything that is true, simply follow *iniquis pacibus*, in the track of human research and discovery. If there is anything that we can know *a priori* of such minds as Francis Bacon's, if they should, after dwelling for centuries amid the illuminations of eternity, descend to earth, as our guides and teachers, it is this, that they would not only impart to us new truths, but higher and more perfect forms of thinking than those with which all the world are perfectly familiar. Especially may we affirm, with absolute certainty, that such minds, instead of giving utterance to such truths and such thoughts, would not retail, as forms of the highest wisdom, the senseless gossip of every-day thinking among men. How self-evident is the truth of the saying of the forerunner of Christ: "He that is of the earth is earthly, and speaketh of the earth: he that cometh from heaven is above all." Now we have, in the spirit-manifestations, the professed teachings of the very class of heaven-descended minds referred to; and what have we in these revelations? All possible characteristics of an origin purely and exclusively earthly, and nothing else. We should, therefore, be guilty of the highest folly should we attribute them to any higher origin. Since the mission of "the spirits" commenced, great advance has been made in scientific research and discovery, in respect to very important principles and facts pertaining to the earth and the heavens, and that in reference to realities about which "the spirits" have largely discoursed, and about which it is absurd to suppose those who are affirmed to have come from heaven to teach us were ignorant. Yet they never have anticipated the advance of human research and discovery, but have very tamely followed it. The Poughkeepsie Seer, after being reminded of the fact that many new planets had been discovered since his "Divine revelations" were given forth—revelations in which he affirmed himself about to reveal every "visible and invisible existence," was asked why it was that he had not anticipated the march of human discovery by announcing beforehand the existence and location of these planets. The prophet was silent, of course. We put the same question in reference to "the spirits." If they are from heaven, why have they not anticipated the march of scientific research and discovery, which they professedly come to perfect and hasten? The reason, and the only reason, is, that these revelations are mere human thoughts unconsciously re-affirmed by spirits in the body, and not what they are by some supposed to be, revelations from spirits out of the body. The great and undeniable fact before us admits of no other explanation.

It remains with spiritualists to deny the statements above made, and to prove them false, by adducing the truths and principles whose reality is denied, or to account for the facts affirmed, and in that case admitted, consistently with the claims of their theory. The former we are quite sure they will not attempt to do; the latter we know absolutely is an impossibility. Whatever inexplicable facts may be connected with these manifestations, the total absence of any new truths or principles, and the undeniable presence in them of mere pre-existing human opinions only, render demonstrably evident their exclusively mundane origin. It is the height of folly to refer mere mundane facts to extra-mundane causes. A greater absurdity cannot be conceived of than to suppose that the great minds from the upper spheres have descended to earth, to retail as new and eternal verities old and hackneyed thoughts with which mankind have been familiar for ages.

III. ALL THESE COMMUNICATIONS TAKE SPECIFIC FORM FROM THE KNOWN SENTIMENTS OF THE PAR-

TICULAR CIRCLES IN WHICH SAID COMMUNICATIONS ORIGINATE.

Another fact equally decisive of the question of the origin of these manifestations is this: the opinions and sentiments revealed in them uniformly take *form from, and correspond with, those peculiar to the particular circles* in which they originate. In China, "the spirits"—for they have spirit-circles there—are all followers of Confucius. In Siam, they are equally devoted Buddhists. In Hindostan, they are worshippers of Juggernaut. In Christendom, they are Catholic or Protestant, Christian or Infidel, Churchmen or Dissenters, Orthodox or Heterodox, of all opinions and no opinions, just according to the peculiar complexion of the circles in which they appear. This is true, not only of different classes of spirits, but equally of the same identical spirits. Take any spirit that can be named, and introduce him into each circle on earth in succession, and he will affirm, as only true, the peculiarities of opinion existing in each circle, and as positively deny every opposite opinion, though he has, for thousands of times, asserted its truth before. This he will do with the most unblushing effrontery, boldly denying, in every circle, that he has ever, since he entered the spirit-land, changed his opinions, or at any time, or in any place, contradicted his present teachings. There is not a solitary form or shade of human belief, the denial of the existence of spirits excepted—a form of belief held by Christian, Turk, or Infidel—which has not been absolutely affirmed and denied by the same authority. "The spirits," and the same individuals among them too, take all sides of every question just as occasion requires, advocating, in succession, the peculiar doctrines of each circle that chances or chooses to call upon them. We have our orthodox circles, in which all the peculiarities of the evangelical faith are solemnly affirmed, without contradiction, by every spirit that appears among them. In one circle, in the city of Cleveland, we had all the physical and mental manifestations that can be obtained anywhere else. In the town of Madison, Geauga county, Ohio, during the progress of a revival of religion, the minister became a spiritualist. He found a medium of the same faith with himself. A perfectly orthodox circle was thus formed, into which the oldest and strongest Universalists and Infidels were introduced, and *as* from their own children, relatives, and friends, were assured that their sentiments were all wrong, and that under their influence they were descending, with infallible certainty, to the gulf of eternal death. The spirit of a Deacon Branch, who, for many years, had lived in the place, and had died there in the esteem and confidence of all, appeared in the circle. Between him and the unbelievers the most solemn communications, to the following import, passed:— Tell us, Deacon Branch, is what is affirmed in the Bible and by Christians, of heaven and hell, true? It is. Is hell as terrible a place as it is represented to be? Far more so. What must we do to escape it? You must "repent and believe on the Lord Jesus Christ." In that circle "the spirits" affirmed absolutely that all communications of an opposite character which had ever been given forth in any spirit-circles were exclusively from "the father of lies" and his agents, and were given forth for the fell purpose of deceiving men, to their eternal ruin. Yet in no circle in the wide world has there ever been given more conclusive evidence of the presence and teachings of disembodied spirits. A friend of ours, for example, entered that circle in company with his wife. They had buried two children, in different towns, in another state, and were perfectly certain that none present but themselves knew anything about those children. Yet their names, one or both having double names, the places of their birth and burial, their ages, even to the specific number of years, months, weeks, days, etc., were given forth with perfect correctness. At length "the spirits" found, in this place, another medium of different and opposite sentiments, and round her formed a circle of corresponding character. In this circle, they unitedly affirmed, the spirit of Deacon

Branch among the rest, that no spirits at all had, at any time, made any communications whatever in the orthodox circle. Deacon Branch, however, immediately reappeared in the circle last named, and solemnly affirmed, in a communication to his own son, in whose house the sceptical circle was meeting at the time referred to, that he had had no connexion at all with the communications which had thus been sent forth from the latter circle as from him. Such is the state of facts the world over. In the infidel and kindred circles, the spirits of orthodox ministers appear, and with expressions of the deepest regret, abjure their earthly teachings and ministrations. In the few orthodox circles,—and we could multiply them by thousands and tens of thousands ; yes, we could fill the world with spirit-voices if we chose,—Infidels and Universalists of every grade, as from the world of despair, affirm every article of the orthodox faith, and abjure their own earthly opinions, as being nothing else than "the doctrines of devils." Now what evidence can be conceived more conclusive of the truth of any proposition, than is here presented of the exclusive mundane origin of these communications, in the two undeniable facts before us, namely, that in these communications none but mundane opinions appear, and that the former vary as the latter do? No questions pertaining to this world, or the next, can be settled by any evidence whatever, if this question is not to be admitted as settled by the evidence before us.

We will, however, give one additional fact—a fact witnessed, as stated in the public prints, several years since, by an English gentleman while in New Zealand. The mediums were an old woman and her son, who were living together in a miserable flat-roofed hut. When the proper conditions were fulfilled, the mediums most earnestly called upon their god to manifest himself, and convince the stranger of the truth of their religion. At length the sound of footsteps was heard on the roof of the hut, and finally, in a manner unaccountable to the stranger, an inhuman voice proclaimed the presence of the god, and the truth of the religion of the mediums. The same undeniably obtains throughout the wide world. We can obtain from "the spirits," and from the same identical spirits, an absolute affirmation of the truth and falseness of every religion and form of belief known on earth; and these affirmations and denials will always accord with the beliefs or assumptions of the inquirers, or mediums, at the times in which such affirmations and denials are given forth.

IV. KNOWN EXCEPTIONS CONFIRM THE DEDUCTION UNDER CONSIDERATION.

We now present, as confirmatory of the views which we hold on this subject, a class of *apparent* exceptions to the facts above adduced. It is true that the answers obtained do not *always* correspond with the sentiments of those who make inquiry, nor with those of the majority of the persons present, on any given occasion, though this is generally the case. An individual, as stated in an extract given above from the work of Mr. Ballou, wished to have certain disagreeable communications which he had obtained, when two mediums were present, reversed. He could have his wish when one of them was absent, but not when both were present. "He could," in the language of the author, "overrule *one* of them, sitting *alone*, and get a response to suit himself. But both of them *together* overmatched his psychological powers." As is the *prevailing* psychological power, for the moment, such will be the character of the responses obtained; and this power, at times, may be with the mass in the circle, in opposition to that exerted by individuals, as in the orthodox circle above referred to, where sceptics were making inquiries; and in some occasional instances, owing to peculiar coincidences, it may be with individuals, in opposition to the sentiments of the majority. A medium, for example, on one occasion, was, in a circle in Leroy, N. Y.,—a circle which had met to obtain communications through her, and which was constituted almost, if not quite, exclusively of sceptics. As the so-called spirit-influence came upon her, this solemn affirmation came out, as from the spirits, "Ye must be born again." All were astounded, and none more so than the medium. Yet during the entire evening, nothing could be obtained from "the spirits," whatever questions were asked, and many were, but this one sentence, "Ye must be born again." How shall this fact be accounted for? The answer is plain. The medium was of orthodox sentiments, and had just come from another meeting, in which this and kindred truths had been very deeply fixed in her thoughts. This would account for the expression of that truth, in the first instance. Then its sudden and unexpected appearance in the circle would fix all minds most intently upon it, so intently, that no other thought could find an expression during that sitting. Just such facts as these would occasionally occur in these circles if our theory were true, and would not occur if that of Spiritualism were true. Such exceptions, therefore, confirm instead of contradict the conclusion deduced from the important facts included in the last two classes above presented.

V. THE CHARACTER OF THE AFFIRMED SPIRIT-THOUGHTS, AS CONTRASTED WITH THE KNOWN LIFE-THOUGHTS OF INDIVIDUALS, EVINCE THE FORMER AS HAVING NONE BUT A MUNDANE ORIGIN.

There is still another characteristic of many of these revelations which renders demonstrably evident the fact that they cannot come from the spirits to whom they are referred; and if they do not come from these, we are bound to suppose that they do not come from any spirits at all, and thus discredit the whole theory of spirit-manifestations. We have professed revelations from minds such as Bacon, who have been progressing for centuries in light and knowledge, amid the revelations of eternity. We have also the recorded ideas of the same minds upon the same themes, while they were in the body. We have, then, here a fair opportunity to compare their present and past mental condition and capacities. What is the conclusion to which any intelligent and candid mind must come, as the result of such careful comparison? It is this and no other—that if it is really and truly the author of the great Organon who is speaking in the work given forth as from him and other kindred spirits, by Judge Edmonds and his associates, that mind cannot but be in a state of absolute and hopeless idiotcy, before it has been among "the spirits" for two centuries longer. We made this remark some time since to a very intelligent lawyer, who had publicly defended, and that with great ability, the doctrine of the spirit-manifestations, and who had read with much interest the work referred to. "I must admit," his reply was, "that you are right there;" and no intelligent man who is acquainted with the writings of Bacon can come to any other conclusion. The posterity of that man, if any exist, ought to be able to obtain heavy damages in a suit for slander against these individuals, for attributing such thoughts to their great ancestor. We hazard little in affirming that it is about as reasonable to suppose that Michael the archangel is the author of the celebrated work entitled "The House that Jack Built," and that this is the highest production that he could originate, as to suppose that it is the spirit of the immortal Bacon that is communicating in the senseless production referred to. So, in other instances, we have seen essays from the spirit of the great Franklin, on electricity; essays given forth through the best of mediums, and which have all the evidence that he is their author, that any of these revelations do that they come from any spirits at all; essays commencing very much like the composition of a certain tyro on perseverance, namely, "Perseverance is the best thing that ever happened to man," and bearing throughout marks of corresponding perfection of thought and style. One fact is undeniable to any intelligent and unprejudiced mind, in regard to these manifestations, namely, "the spirits" are not speaking in them at all, or their progression is altogether in the direction of idiotcy, and nowhere else. Consider, as proof of these statements, what follows under the next class of facts adduced.

VI. REVELATIONS WHICH DO NOT, AS CONTRASTED WITH THOSE WHICH DO, ORIGINATE IN THESE CIRCLES, CONFIRM THE SAME CONCLUSION.

The information not, as contrasted with that which is, communicated in these professed revelations, presents another undoubted indication of the non-spirit-origin of these communications. According to the fundamental teachings of "the spirits," if such are the intelligences responding to our inquiries in these communications, we are all continuously surrounded with guardian spirits, who deeply sympathize with us in our joys and sorrows, our pleasures and sufferings mental and physical, and who are able to communicate to us, as they choose, through these mediums, any information which they may possess, and which might alleviate our sorrows or increase our joys, by being communicated to us. Now, if these communications do proceed from this source, such, we may safely conclude, would be their character, and we should find by experience that here is an *available* and *reliable* source of information on such subjects. Now, this is the precise kind of information which cannot be obtained through "the spirits." As a source of information, it is not an available one, on the one hand, nor a reliable one, on the other. Hundreds of thousands of families and individuals in England and France, for example, had their husbands, sons, brothers, and endeared relations in the Crimea, and were under the most agonizing apprehensions, of course, in regard to their condition, and that while all individual communications were for long periods suspended. In the greatest agony of apprehension, wives, parents, brothers, sisters, and "nearer and dearer ones," rushed to the spirit-circles, and entreated "the spirits" to relieve that agony by giving the information desired. What an opportunity was here presented in which "the spirits," in the presence of the world, could, by manifesting their sympathy with human suffering, and revealing themselves as reliable informants on subjects of vital importance, have established the claims of Spiritualism immovably in the high regard of mankind. What an opportunity, also, to reveal themselves to the heart of grateful nations, as being really and truly what their apostles affirm them to be, *the guardian spirits* of humanity. But no. To all appeals made to their compassion by agonizing sufferers, they stood revealed, exclusively, as "dumb dogs," from whom no responses could be obtained. This ominous silence indicates a total ignorance of what *guardian* spirits ought to have known, or a most barbarous, if not fiendish, indifference and callousness to human suffering. All the world are aware of the living death which Lady Franklin has been enduring these many years, and how deeply the great heart of England and of Christendom has sympathized with her mental agony. Why have not her guardian spirits sped to those northern regions, and brought back the intelligence which would relieve that mind from that heart-sickness which arises from "hope deferred"? Why has not the spirit of the lost one, if *alma lux*, the light of life, has departed, winged his way to the sufferer at home, and revealed his fate to her? Why, to say the least, did not some of his or of his associates' guardian spirits fly to her with the information which she so much desired? It would seem that they must have got fast frozen up in some of those ice mountains, or that they must carry hearts of ice in their bosoms. Where was the spirit or guardian spirits of Emma Moore, or those of her agonized friends, that from none of them were tidings brought to those friends during the interval between the time of her disappearance and the discovery of her body, of her untimely end? When the fell seducer, as a stealthy boa constrictor, is following the footsteps of unsuspecting innocence, why do not these guardian spirits, who can read even the secret thoughts and purposes of men, reveal to the intended victim the perils which encircle her? Years ago, a proclamation was professedly sent forth from the spirit-world, that if thieves and robbers and murderers and seducers did not cease their doings, the spirits, who had a full knowledge of human conduct, would reveal the authors and perpetrators of crime to the ministers of justice. All this these "guardian spirits" are professedly able to do. Why have they not done it? Such revelations have been made by means of clairvoyance, and even by dreams. Why do not "the spirits" show their love to the race by performing such promised offices? Why do not the spirits of murdered persons reveal facts, in these circles, which will lead to the detection of the murderers? The spirits appear to have no hearts for such forms of well-doing as these. As informants of facts to us unknown, the revelations of "the spirits" have very different and opposite characteristics. Let us consider a few of these revelations.

The following wondrous facts we take from the *Spiritual Telegraph,* the leading organ of the sect in the city of New York. We give the statements as quoted from that paper in the *Evening Post,* with the introductory remarks of the editor of the latter paper.

"The believers in rappings and communications from the 'land of spirits' are increasing in this city. Private families, in circles of from six to a dozen persons, nightly indulge in the 'grave amusement.' A regular organization meets every

Sunday at Dodworth's Hall, in Broadway, next to Grace Church, where anyone is allowed to give his views on the subject.

"Conferences are also held during the day and evening each week at the head-quarters of the spiritualists in Broadway, near Prince Street. At the assemblies many 'tough yarns' are told. The *Spiritual Telegraph*, the organ of the 'faith' in this city, gives us some samples of recent occurrence. It says:—

"'A gentleman from New Haven related the following: A Mr. Fairfield, a medium, was some weeks ago sent from Springfield, Mass., to the house of a Mr. Barnes, another medium, in Fairhaven (a village near New Haven), Conn. He knew not the purpose of his mission, and when he got to the house of Mr. Barnes, found he had not money enough left in his purse to pay his fare home. On the evening of the same day he and Mr. Barnes were both simultaneously entranced, when they put on their overcoats and went out. Our informant, who was present, followed them. They went up the road some distance and stopped, when Mr. Barnes began to scratch in the snow, which was about three inches deep, as if in search for something.

"'Presently he grasped something in his hand, and they both returned to the house, where, on opening his hand to the light, it was found to contain two quarter eagles, which, in obedience to the spiritual impulse, were divided equally between the two mediums. They went out again, our informant following them as before; and when they came directly in front of a certain church, they began to grope in the snow again, and digging out a board which had been covered up, they threw it aside. They then commenced a search where the board had lain; as the hand of one of them was passing to a particular spot, the narrator distinctly saw a small object lying there, which on being picked up proved to be a silver coin—a quarter of a dollar, if we remember.

"'They then went and scratched in the snow and dirt on the steps of the Odd Fellows' hall, and found another coin.'"

There is a medium in the state of Ohio, of whom it is affirmed, in illustration of the *new* things revealed by "the spirits," that at times, when under their inspiration, he will walk for miles with his eyes shut, passing, in the mean time, over fences and through forests, till he arrives at a particular place, when he will order, in the name of "the spirits," those who have accompanied him to dig down at a certain spot which he designates. They do so, and find at length some dry bones, an Indian hatchet, and other pieces of old iron of equal value.

A very intelligent spiritualist told us that he had been present and witnessed these very wonders.

Such are "the spirits" as informants of facts which we do not know. We do not affirm that no higher facts are ever revealed in these communications. These, however, are fair examples of what we do obtain, spiritualists themselves giving the record. If these revelations are from disembodied spirits, judging from what they do and what they do not reveal, we affirm, without fear of contradiction, that they are, almost without exception, beings of the most debased morality and demented intelligence, and that to regard such communications as coming from the inhabitants of the immortal spheres, tends to produce nothing in us but corresponding debasement and dementation.

Before closing our remarks on the class of facts now under consideration, we should make the following undeniable statement in regard to them, a statement which has a very important and decisive bearing upon the question of their origin. The statement is this: most of the cases of this kind reported to the public have been, and are, found, on careful inquiry, to have either no foundation in fact, or to be characterized by very great exaggerations, while the well-authenticated cases are very few, much fewer than we should expect from the myriads of sources from which these manifestations proceed, even supposing them not to be given forth by disembodied spirits at all. In listening to the popular lecturers on Spiritualism, we find, as they approach this class of facts, that they uniformly begin by telling their hearers that they could spend the whole night in relating cases which they themselves have witnessed personally, and then out will come the old pen-knife story, and other hackneyed facts of a similar character. How few are the cases related by Mr. Ballou, and other great defenders of this new faith, and how far do they have to travel to collect even these! To us, after having investigated the nature of the power by which these manifestations are produced, there is but one matter of surprise, namely, that this class of manifestations are not, in the spirit-circles, of more frequent occurrence than they are.

VII. THE GENERAL INTELLECTUAL CHARACTER OF THESE COMMUNICATIONS DEMONSTRATE THEIR NON-SPIRIT ORIGIN.

The general character of these communications, considered in a mere *intellectual* point of view, in comparison with the productions of minds in the body, precludes wholly the supposition that they are from disembodied spirits. Communications coming from the high spheres above, we cannot but know, as we have already observed, would move upon a level altogether above the highest forms of thinking among men in the flesh. We cannot but be mentally and morally degraded ourselves to entertain any other ideas of a future state. Suppose that we have masses and floods of communications professedly descending to us from those high spheres, communications which, while they contain nothing new, not only never rise above the higher forms of mundane thinking, but almost, if not quite, invariably fall incomparably below them; very seldom, indeed, rising above mere commonplace, and more frequently embodying the most senseless puerilities conceivable. What higher evidence can we have of an exclusively mundane origin, than is thus presented? When we will consent to receive such forms of thinking as from spirits, spirits, too, from the higher celestial spheres, as these are generally affirmed to come, we consent to our own mental and moral degradation, and voluntarily subject ourselves to influences of all others most efficient to produce that result. We will cite a few passages as examples of "spirit-wisdom." Our citations are exclusively from books advertised in the *Spiritual Telegraph* of New York, as among the standard spiritual productions which are kept for sale at that office, books embraced in the catalogue, to all of which the "reader's attention is particularly invited." In a communication of upwards of forty pages from George Washington, a communication contained in a book entitled "Love and Wisdom from the Spirit World," we find the following important announcement: "If men were governed by love, truth, wisdom, and harmony, then they would be under one grand, universal government of peace and harmony." No one can fail, we think, to understand the important principle here affirmed by the father of our country, and it is certainly just as true as the momentous proposition that an oyster is an oyster. Further on we are told that in order that mankind may "become acquainted with the natural and spiritual laws which govern their own being," knowledge requisite to "enjoy peace, harmony, and happiness," "it is necessary that they obtain light on these important subjects." The meaning of the last part of the following sentence is not to us quite so plain as the foregoing: "These glorious realities," the blessings of one universal brotherhood among men, "cannot be enjoyed until there is a general reformation in all governments, laws, institutions, and modes of teaching the generation together with the present." At the head of the address, presenting throughout corresponding perfection of thought and style, we have a likeness of the author, a likeness at the bottom of which we find a scrap of poetry, made by Washington himself, as we are given to understand, for the express purpose of accompanying that likeness. The poetry reads as follows:—

"When the likeness of this portrait you see,
Remember that it is to represent the likeness of me;
But the spirit in its brightness you cannot see,
For that is far above the likeness of thee.
G. WASHINGTON."

The likeness of Franklin, which stands, in the book above named, at the head of a long essay from him on "Progression of the Mineral, Vegetable, Animal, and Spiritual Kingdoms," is also accompanied by the following lines, composed by that great mind, in his "angel's home."

"The likeness of this portrait is to represent
The likeness of man when he dwelt here below,
But the likeness of the spirit you would like to know,
And this would be no more than I would like to show;
But the mind is not prepared the likeness for to see
Of the spirit in his angel's home as bright as we.
B. FRANKLIN."

"The elevated spirits" communicating in this book affirm, we are told, that they "impressed every word and sentence" found in it upon the medium's mind before it was written. We have then here, it would seem, an infallible criterion by which we can judge of the progression of these minds in "love and wisdom" during their residence in the celestial spheres. From another work, entitled "Light from the Spirit World," we take the following specimens of spirit-thinking and composition. An essay on Wisdom commences thus:—

"Wisdom is what is wise, and what is wise is wisdom. Wisdom is not folly, and folly is not wisdom. Wisdom is not selfishness, and selfishness is not wisdom. Wisdom is not evil, and evil is not wisdom." Again: "Wisdom is wisdom. All is not wisdom. All is not folly." Further on we are told that if we would get wisdom, those of us who have it not, we must "get it where it is to be found." For ourselves, much as we value this priceless treasure, we feel very little inclined to resort to "the spirits" to get it, though we can obtain from them the great truth that, "Men are what they are," together with the momentous information that, "Change is alteration," and although they assure us that they come to us, "in wisdom which is from heaven," "with glad tidings on their tongues, with the rainbow of promise over their heads, with the cup of salvation in their hands, with the wine of consolation to the mourner, and the balm of healing to the sorrow-stricken and despondent." We must give one additional quotation. The essay "On Works" thus commences: "Works are the doings of a worker. Indolence is not work. Industry is work. Industry, accompanied with wisdom, works a wise work. Wisdom works wisely, and the works of wisdom are not works of vanity." The medium through whom these great thoughts are communicated to us assures us that "the spirits" express themselves, after reviewing what they have here communicated, well satisfied with their work. In a work entitled "Discourses from the Spirit World, dictated by Steven Olin, through Rev. R. P. Wilson, writing medium," we have the following somewhat original definition of the phrase "the kingdom of God:"—

"By the phrase 'kingdom of God' is meant, 1. The most internal essence, or the love, wisdom, and will principles. 2. The subordinate principles of expansion, attraction, and circulation. 3. The agencies of heat, light, and electricity. These principles and agencies constitute the realm of this kingdom, with reference to its internal nature and relations." So much for the theological lore of "the spirits," for their wondrous insight into the secrets of spiritual wisdom and knowledge.

We shall not multiply quotations further. We contend that what we have presented is not an unfair representation of the real wisdom of "the spirits." For ourselves, we have searched in vain among these communications, and we have examined the works commended to our regard by the best informed spiritualists in the country, as among the fundamental and standard spirit-productions; we have searched in vain, we say, among all these productions for a *new* or a *great* thought. We have found, almost without exception, forms of thinking far below those which appear in the ordinary productions of men in the flesh, and which do not shock all our hallowed sentiments, and debase all our conceptions, in regard to immortality, when received as from spirits inhabiting the celestial spheres. A friend of ours, Hon. George Bradburn, as he has affirmed before the public, has read upwards of six thousand pages of these productions, and has turned from them with the identical impressions above stated. They have absolutely none of the characteristics which we cannot but know they would have did they come to us from spirits standing amid the high revelations of eternity. On the other hand, they have all the marks, and none other, of an origin purely and exclusively mundane. For example: 1. None but *mundane thoughts* are here embodied, thoughts which vary in their forms with the opinions of the circles in which they originate. 2. These communications present the precise *kinds* of thinking which we know would proceed from the surface of minds in the very passive and unthinking state in which mediums affirm themselves to be, when they suppose themselves under the inspiration of the spirits; and which can proceed from no other source. We find just such thoughts as these in these communications, and little else. 3. All the peculiarities of style and manner which characterize the mediums, and those who are around them, when communicating, are embodied in these communications. No spirit, from any sphere, can spell correctly, speak grammatically, or utter anything but senseless puerilities, when communicating through certain mediums. 4. We find all the peculiarities of sentiment, forms of expression, and mere ignorance of the mediums and spirit-circles reflected in these productions. We find, for example, in a communication given forth as from the spirits, through Mrs. Fish, when in Cleveland, such expressions as the following: "Go, sit under the teachings of that orthodox D.D., who says that all these rappings and other physical manifestations are humbugs," etc. Again: "This conclusion that all these spiritual manifestations are a humbug, because spirits cannot have power to make such manifestations, strikes their own pretended faith flat in the face." There is one fact which has struck our minds with peculiar interest, in reading these works. Whenever the inquirer asks questions of the spirits, pertaining to subjects which real spirits must be acquainted with, but of which he is ignorant, and about which he is perplexed, we always find that the spirits here responding not only do not know anything more than he does, but that his ignorance and perplexity are reflected in the responses which he obtains; thus indicating most decisively that the inquirer, and he only, is answering his own questions. The following we give, as examples, from Rev. H. Snow's work entitled "Spirit Intercourse":—

"Can you give any idea of the manner in which spirits converse?

"You had better not attempt to penetrate so deeply into our affairs, for it can be of no use to you. There is, however, with us a common and universal method of holding intercourse, but of which you can form no just idea until you are permitted to make use of it.

"Are there any evil-disposed or mischievous spirits that have it in their power to approach and communicate with us?

"You cannot fully understand what you wish to know upon this subject either. It is not in our power to enlighten you much in this respect.

"Can it be explained, without implying deception on the part of spirits, how great men are said to be present, and to communicate, when what is communicated shows plainly that the great men are not present?

"You must not think that we can give you all the satisfaction you wish on this point. It may be said, however, that it is not *necessary* to suppose deception, as there are other ways of accounting for such facts. You cannot understand the matter fully," etc.

Thus it is that every peculiarity in the state of the inquirer's mind is perfectly reflected back upon him, in the responses which he obtains. If he understands, is ignorant of, or perplexed about, the subject about which he inquires, his own knowledge, ignorance, or perplexity, and nothing else, will be presented in the answer obtained. 5. Finally, how great soever the number, and diverse the character and relations of spirits which communicate through one and the same medium, the style of each will be one and the same with that of all the others, thus showing that they are the product of one and not of many minds. What perfect identity of style, for example, characterizes the various productions of different minds, professedly communicating their thoughts to the world, in the two volumes published by Judge Edmonds. We must repudiate all the laws of criticism, and ignore the entire dictates of common sense, before we can admit that different minds are here communicating. So in regard to all of these works. The same spirits, communicating through different mediums, are wholly unlike themselves, in style and manner, and forms of thinking. All minds, on the other hand, communicating through the same channel, present a perfect unity in these respects.

There is an apparent exception to the above statements, an exception which, instead of contradicting, really and truly confirms the principle which we have assumed. When the medium, or some one present, knows the style of the individual whose spirit is professedly communicating, such style will sometimes be in some degree copied, though almost without exception very imperfectly. So also when an imaginary character is communicating, such as a news-boy, forms of expression which that class of persons are known to use, will sometimes be embodied in the communications obtained. In all other cases, we believe, and we think we cannot be mistaken, the principle under consideration fully obtains. No one spirit has anything like a fixed style by which he can be identified, as he appears in different circles and communicates through different mediums. All spirits, on the other hand, with the exceptions above named, when communicating in the same circles, and through the same mediums, have a perfect identity of style ; a style, too, which varies as the character of the circles and mediums varies. We noticed, for example, some years since, several communications purporting to have come from the spirits of Messrs. Webster, Calhoun, Clay, and others, communications obtained through one of the Miss Foxes in the city of New York, and in a circle constituted of such men as the Hon. J. R. Giddings. Mr. Calhoun is affirmed to have announced his own presence in an elliptical style peculiar to himself, namely, "I'm with you," and this was assumed as proof positive of his actual presence. It was forgotten that some persons present knew well what were his peculiarities in such forms of expression. As soon as he and the others began to make formal communications, however, all peculiarities of their earthly style and manner disappeared at once, and all adopted one and the same style, a style, too, utterly unlike and infinitely beneath what was so peculiar to each when in the body. Now, if such facts as these do not prove the exclusively mundane origin of these communications, we may well ask, what can be established by evidence? We cannot have higher evidence, when standing before a mirror, that it is our own image that we see reflected there, and that our presence is the cause of that reflection, than we have, in such facts as these, that these communications are nothing but the reflections of the thoughts of the mediums, and of the persons constituting these circles, and are caused by those thoughts, and not by those of spirits out of the circles. The time is not distant when the only sentiment of mystery connected with these manifestations will be that in the middle of the nineteenth century the belief could have obtained among any intelligent portion of the community, that such communications could have descended to us from the "undiscovered country."

VIII. FUNDAMENTAL FACTS DEVELOPED BY INDIVIDUALS THROUGH INQUIRIES MADE FOR SELF-SATISFACTION IN REGARD TO THE ORIGIN AND CAUSE OF THESE PHENOMENA, INDIVIDUALS WHO HAD FORMED NO DEFINITE THEORY UPON THE SUBJECT.

We now refer to an important class of facts which have been developed by inquiries put by individuals for the specific purpose of satisfying their own minds on the question whether spirits have, as a matter of fact, any connexion with these mysterious phenomena. The inquiries to which we now refer have generally been made by individuals who had formed no particular theory upon the subject, and made simply for the purpose named. They have assumed, and for the best of reasons, that if spirits are really and truly responding here, individuals will, of course, get no answers, if they call for those who cannot be present; and that if they can get the same answers from such spirits that can be obtained from any others, and in all respects the same evidence of spirit-presence and agency, then Spiritualism, whatever else may be true of these facts, must be false. These experiments have established undeniably the fact, that in all respects the same answers can be elicited, and the same evidence of an actual presence as the authors and cause of these communications, can be obtained from the following classes of spirits, as from any others that ever have been or can be evoked, namely, from the departed spirits of devils; from the departed spirits of individuals yet alive, or who never existed; from the departed spirits of the lowest orders of brute beasts, insects, and reptiles; and finally, from the departed spirits of shrubs and stones. All tests of identity, all indications of intelligence, of a knowledge of our secret thoughts, all forms of information, all kinds of manifestations, physical and mental, that can be obtained from any spirits whatever, can be obtained from each and every class above named. " I don't understand these mysterious occurrences," said the father of a certain medium, an honest and intelligent farmer; "but there is one thing that I do know about them, and that is, that we can obtain just as intelligent answers from the spirits of beasts, shrubs, and stones, as from any spirits that can be called upon. This I know absolutely; for I have made the experiment myself, till I am perfectly satisfied upon the subject." Mr. Ballou admits that facts of this kind do occur, and attributes their occurrence to a low order of spirits who are ready to appear in any characters that men desire. "This," he also says, "is the explanation given by truthful spirits." This explanation, however, is self-contradictory and absurd; for this low order of spirits exhibit all the intelligence that any others do. They have the same power to respond to our secret thoughts, to answer test questions, and to convey information of facts unknown to us. They will discourse as profoundly upon all subjects that can be named as any others whatever. Now what more decisive evidence can we have of any truth than is here presented, that these responses do not come from spirits? The facts of the case could not be as they are, if invisible intelligent beings were really and truly communicating with us in these manifestations. They could not, on the other hand, but be as they are, if the spirits constituting the circles were unconsciously producing the answers which they obtain to their own inquiries. In this case, and in this alone, any spirit named, whether existing or not existing, would give the same responses as any other.

The spiritualist, we know, has an answer ready for such facts. The individual putting such questions, he says, is in a dishonest state of mind, and therefore, by the law of spiritual communications, draws lying spirits to himself, and from these he obtains his answers. This answer, if admitted as valid, proves far more than the spiritualist intends. It renders demonstrably evident one fundamental fact pertaining to all these communications, the absolute impossibility of *identifying* at all any spirits which are communicating with us, if any are. If lying spirits can answer as correctly as any others all test questions given to identify the spirits who are communicating with us, it is absolutely impossible for us to determine whether the spirit communicating with us, on any given occasion, is not a lying spirit instead of the one we suppose. All ground of confidence, therefore, in the validity of any of these communications is taken away. It cannot be denied that all evidence of the *reality* or *validity* of all such communications is utterly annihilated by the facts before us, facts which cannot be denied.

But the assumption that the putting of such inquiries implies dishonesty in the inquirer, is wholly unauthorized. The questions are put for the single and honest purpose of determining the fact whether these responses do proceed from disembodied spirits or not. They are perfectly adapted to secure that result, and consequently may be, and no doubt often are, put with the most perfect integrity; a state of mind which, if the law of spirit-communication referred to is real, would repel and not draw to itself lying spirits. Truth-telling spirits, and they only, would be drawn into communication with the inquirer to solve his honest doubts.

The relation of the responses obtained under such circumstances to the state of the inquirer's mind should not be overlooked in this connexion. They are always in the fixed relation of consequence to that state as *antecedent.* As is the state, so are the responses. As the former changes and varies, so do the latter. This is the fixed law of their occurrence. If this fact does not reveal the state referred to as the cause, and the responses as the effects of the action of that cause, and therefore exclude the supposition of *ab extra* spirit-agency, what relations of antecedence and consequence can reveal that of cause and effect? None, it must seem, but those who are determined to be deceived can avoid the conclusion which we draw from such facts.

IX. THE SAME RESPONSES, AND THE SAME EVIDENCE OF SPIRIT-PRESENCE, CAN BE OBTAINED FROM THE SPIRITS OF INDIVIDUALS YET ALIVE, BUT SUPPOSED TO BE DEAD, AS FROM THE SPIRITS OF PERSONS ACTUALLY DEAD.

There is a class of facts which should not be overlooked in this connexion, a class against which no objection like that above alluded to can be raised. We refer to responses which individuals obtain when they, with the most honest desire for true information, call for the spirits of friends whom they sincerely *suppose to be dead, but who are yet alive.* In all such cases, all the evidence of actual presence and identity is obtained that is ever obtained in any instances whatever, and inquirers are just as certain to get responses when they call for the spirits of such persons, as in any other cases. We have two friends, for example, one of whom is alive, and the other dead, both of whom, however, we, with equal honesty, suppose to be in the spirit-world. We are just as sure to get an answer when we call for one of these spirits as for the other, and we can obtain, in all respects, the same evidence of actual presence and identity in one case that we can in the other. The facts cannot be denied. They would be as these are, if the responses originated within the circle. Could they be so, if they came from spirits out of those circles? But one answer can be given to such a question.

A child, for example, in an intelligent Christian family which we have known for nearly twenty years, years since became a table-moving, writing, and rapping medium. We have ourselves seen phenomena of the first class, and heard the raps connected with that child, and have fully satisfied ourselves that there is no intentional deception in the case. The evening after the child announced the fact that he was a medium, the family formed a circle by themselves, and when the rappings commenced, took the alphabet, and called for the name of the spirit present, if any was present, and was producing these mysterious sounds. The name of a young man who had been for a considerable period a member of the family, and had left for New Orleans in the spring of 1854, and from whom, though he had promised to write, they had never heard since, was given. In answer to subsequent enquiries, the following statements were all rapped out, namely, that on the 24th of May, 1854, he had died in New Orleans, of the yellow fever. Since that occurrence, that young man has reappeared among us, and thereby established the fact that he is not dead. In this case every question was put with the utmost sincerity, and there was nothing whatever to draw responses from lying spirits. Of this, however, the entire family are perfectly aware, that the answers obtained represented their own previous convictions of facts, and to those convictions they have sense enough to attribute the communication which they did obtain.

A somewhat remarkable case of this kind some years ago occurred in Cleveland. A young man went from that city to Chicago. From the latter city he wrote to his friends that he was to leave that place for St. Louis. For upwards of five months subsequent to the reception of this letter, no intelligence whatever was received of him, and it was supposed that he was dead. His mother, having accompanied a female friend, a devoted spiritualist, to the residence of a medium, and while listening to the communications which others were then receiving, felt something like a human hand grasp her own, as if for the purpose of an affectionate salutation. She asked the medium what that meant, and was told that it was an indication to her that a spirit was present who desired to speak to her. To her inquiry who the spirit was, the name of her son was given. She was then informed, as from him, that on his way down the Mississippi, the boat took fire, and he, in his fright, leaped overboard and was drowned. "You know, mother," said the spirit, "that while alive, I ridiculed Spiritualism. I am exceedingly glad to find it true, as I can now communicate with you." The mother was then requested to call again, at a time named, when he would have other important communications to make to her. The medium in this case was a speaking one, and the mother, though she had never met the medium before, nor had ever heard of her, recognised a perfect likeness to her son's voice and manner. She called as directed, and received other communications. She then called upon two other mediums, both total strangers to her, and through them also received substantially, as from her son, the same messages as before. To the question, How can I know that it is really and truly my son communicating with me? she was told in reply that he would accompany her home, and remain with her there till all doubts were removed from her mind. The disconsolate mother returned home with the most absolute conviction that her son was dead, and that she had communed with his spirit. On her arrival, however, she was met by that very son, who had returned during her absence. He had written home, but none of his letters had arrived, and this was the cause of the apprehension that he was dead.

Now this case, which we ourselves obtained directly from the family itself, this case, we say,—and others of the same character, to any number desired, might be adduced,—establishes most unquestionably the following facts: (1) There was here the most perfect honesty and sincerity in the mind of the inquirer, and the consequent absence of all causes which, according to the principles of Spiritualism, would draw lying spirits into rapport with her mind. (2) All conceivable evidence, physical and mental, of the presence of the particular spirit supposed to be present was given, that is or can be given in any other case. (3) Nothing is requisite to obtain all the evidence of the actual presence of the disembodied spirits of individuals who are yet alive, that can be obtained in reference to that of any person who is dead, but an honest conviction on the part of the inquirer that the living individual, whose spirit is called for, is actually dead. (4) To suppose that lying spirits can thus personate other minds, and none other, if any do, can respond, in such cases, is to annihilate all evidence that any other can have that he has ever communicated with any particular spirit, on any occasion whatever, on the one hand, and that all these communications, if from spirits at all, are not from "the father of lies" or his agents, on the other. (5) We need suppose no other cause for such responses but the state of the inquirer's mind, in the circumstances actually existing, to account for all the facts which here present themselves. The recollection of her son would, of course, be very vivid in the mother's mind, and this would give form to the words, voice, and manner of the medium. (6) It would be the height of absurdity, consequently, to refer such communications to any *ab-extra* spirit-cause. (7) If *such* are not, and no one will pretend that they are, to be referred to the agency of "the spirits," it would be a monstrous absurdity to refer any other of these communications to such agency. (8) No tactual impressions, no likeness in these communications to the voice, style, or manner of persons living or dead, can be any real proof of the truth of Spiritualism.

X. SIMILAR RESPONSES ARE OBTAINED IN THESE CIRCLES, BY DEVOTED SPIRITUALISTS, FROM THE SPIRITS OF PERSONS ACTUALLY ALIVE, BUT SUPPOSED TO BE DEAD.

We now adduce a class of facts perfectly similar to those above named, and which occur under circumstances that entirely free them from all the objections that can be raised, even by spiritualists, against the conclusions undeniably deducible from them. We refer to responses obtained in these circles by devoted spiritualists themselves, answers purporting to come from individuals *supposed*, and *honestly supposed*, to be dead, but who are yet alive, or never existed at all. Here, of course, there is the most perfect integrity in the inquirer's state of mind, and the consequent total absence of all causes to induce the presence and action of lying spirits. In precisely such circumstances, just the same kind of communications are obtained, and all test questions put to identify "the spirits" communicating are answered with the same correctness as in any other instances. A very striking case of this kind came under our own observation. A friend of ours was believed by herself, her physicians, and by all around her, to be in the very last stages of consumption, within one or two weeks, at the utmost, of death. At this time she was visited by a number of relatives, who were most devoted spiritualists, and who took very great pains, but without success, to interest her in the subject. She was feasting on more substantial realities than "the spirits" revealed to her. These individuals took their final leave of our friend, and returned to their distant homes with the most undoubted conviction that in a very few days she would be in eternity. A few weeks subsequently, the husband of our friend received from those individuals a letter containing a special and affectionate communication from the spirit of his departed wife,—a communication obtained from that identical spirit and none other, in the spirit-circles which these individuals attended. In that circle they inquired if the spirit of that supposed to have been dying, and consequently then dead, friend, was present. The answer was, yes. After all proofs of identity were given that are ever required, and all the circumstances of our friend's departure and her then happy state were given, a wish was expressed by her to send a communication of consolation, etc., to the bereaved husband that was left behind. This communication was then given and forwarded, as stated above. It so happened that that very disembodied spirit thus identified, and thus communicating with the living, was then with her husband in the body, and to the wonder of all around is yet alive, with a prospect of seeing years to come.

A very notable case of a similar character appeared in the public prints, as connected with Judge Edmonds and others. In a certain paper in the interests of Spiritualism, and published in California, a paper called *The Pioneer*, a professedly spirit-communication appeared, as from the spirit of a Mr. Lane. This communication was subsequently indorsed by "the spirits" in a spirit-circle as a genuine spirit production. It was then forwarded to Judge Edmonds, who forwarded to *The Pioneer* a communication which he had obtained, in the city of New York, from the spirit of this same Mr. Lane. On the appearance of this last communication, an editor of another California paper published the fact that he was well informed about Mr. Lane and his communications, that no such person ever had existed, and that the communication which first appeared in *The Pioneer* was of an exclusively mundane origin. Yet this very spirit appeared to Judge Edmonds, with all the evidence of an actual presence and identity, that he ever had of that of Bacon or any other spirit.

We recently met with a very intelligent Christian lady who utterly repudiates the claims of Spiritualism, a lady who was left a widow by the celebrated William Leggett of New York, and whose present husband is a devoted spiritualist. While a circle was being held in her own parlour, her husband being a member of it, and she sitting in another part of the room, and no one in the circle could obtain any communication at all, the question was asked, whether there was any spirit present that wished to communicate with Mrs. ——. Instantly a number of very loud raps were heard upon the top of the table. She was earnestly requested to enter the circle and receive communications. On her refusal to comply, individuals in the circle put questions themselves, and received ready answers to all their inquiries. The spirit responding purported to be that of a brother of Mrs. ——, a brother who had sailed some twenty years ago as the commandant of a vessel, from the port of New York, and had never since been heard from, the vessel and all on board having, no doubt, been lost. All particulars of the loss of the vessel, and the subsequent death of all on board, the brother having languished for thirty-six days on a raft, before he died, were given to her, as she affirmed, with a disgusting and even shocking minuteness. She had another brother, Stephen, from whom no tidings had been received for upwards of two years. The elder brother, on being questioned on the subject, affirmed that Stephen was with him in the spirit-land; that he had died on a steamboat, at a particular place and time named, on the Mississippi river; that he had six thousand five hundred dollars with him when he died; that this treasure was taken possession of by three individuals, one a female, who had since died, and with the greatest agony of mind had confessed the wrong to the spirit of the brother named above, etc. Soon after she received a letter from a sister in New York, saying, "I have just received a letter from brother Stephen, and he will be with us in two or three weeks." The statements pertaining to the elder brother could not, of course, be tested. Those pertaining to the other, however, statements equally specific and worthy of credit, she happily had the means of informing herself about. But one explanation can be given of the communications obtained in this instance. The husband of this lady knew about the brothers, honestly supposed them both alike to have been dead, and hence the responses obtained.

The fact is undeniable, that whenever there is an honest belief that an individual is dead, whether he is alive or never existed at all, even spiritualists can obtain all the evidence of the presence, identity, and agency of his spirit that can be obtained in any other case whatever. Any persons that in the presence of such facts will attribute these manifestations to "the spirits," and especially to particular ones, hold their minds open to any delusions that may be imposed upon them from any source whatever.

XI. MOST DECISIVE OBSERVATIONS AND EXPERIMENTS MADE BY INDIVIDUALS OF THE HIGHEST INTELLIGENCE AND INTEGRITY, FOR THE SPECIFIC PURPOSE OF DETERMINING THE NATURE AND LOCATION OF THE CAUSE OF THESE PHENOMENA.

We now invite very special attention to a class of facts of the most absolute and decisive bearing upon our present inquiries. We refer to certain observations and experiments which individuals have made, with this one specific purpose in view, namely, to determine the *location* of the cause of these manifestations, whether that cause pertains to the minds in the circles, or to disembodied spirits out of them. As the facts now to be adduced are perfectly fundamental in their bearing, we shall make a quite extensive selection from the great mass that lies around us, and which might be adduced, did our limits permit.

We will begin with a fact connected with clairvoyance, and then parallel it with another connected with these manifestations. Some years since, Rev.

J. H. S., then pastor of the Baptist church in Poughkeepsie, N. Y., met, on a certain occasion, several individuals at the house of a friend. Among the individuals present was a Mr. L., who first mesmerized A. J. Davis. Mr. L. expressed to Mr. S. much surprise that the latter should hold the doctrine of future retribution, when such palpable evidence to the contrary could be presented. "Here," he says, "is a young man now present whom I will introduce into a clairvoyant state, in which he will have a direct vision of the condition of the spirits of the dead. Let us see what report he will bring back of that state." This was done. As the young man was subjected to the actions of the odylic [mesmeric] force, his head, he being seated in a chair, was drawn between his knees, till his hair touched the floor. In this state he remained for about two hours, without apparent injury or wearisomeness. During this time many very wonderful facts were developed which we have not space to detail. At length Mr. L. introduced his subject among the spirits of the dead, that is, willed that he should have such visions, and asked him what he saw. With the greatest delight conceivable, he testified that all, *all* were happy, very, very happy. "What do you think of that, Mr. S.?" says the mesmerizer. "How can you resist such evidence?" "Put me in communication with the young man," says

Mr. S., "and let us see what will then appear." This was done. Mr. S., without speaking at all, fixed his attention upon one of the most depraved characters that ever appeared in this country, an individual who had been executed in that place, a short time previous, for murder, and who died as he had lived. Soon the clairvoyant began to scream, with the greatest anguish and entreaty conceivable. "Do let me off! Do let me off! I can't endure it," he exclaimed. Mr. S. asked him what he saw. The individual referred to, and to whom no allusion had before been made, was named. "Where is he?" asked Mr. S. "In hell," was the reply. "I can't endure the sight of him," exclaimed the young man. "Do let me off." "What do you think now, Mr. L.?" said Mr. S. No one can doubt the cause of these diverse and opposite visions in this case. They simply represented the ideas of those in mesmeric communication with the clairvoyant. That is all. Had he been put in communication with individuals holding every variety of sentiment that exists on earth in reference to a future state, his visions would, in succession, have represented them all, just as they did those of the individuals referred to, and that for the same identical reason.

We will now attend to a case of perfectly similar characteristics, connected with these manifestations. A gentleman of our acquaintance, now a member of the bar in Cleveland, held a discussion on this subject, some years since, in North Adams, Mass. That he might be prepared for the discussion, he called, in company with the leading physician of the place, upon a neighbour whose daughter was a medium, and requested the privilege of witnessing some of "the spirit" phenomena. The first evening was spent in witnessing physical manifestations. With these they were perfectly astonished and even confounded. The medium placing simply the ends of her fingers upon the top of a large table standing in the centre of the room, called upon the spirit of an individual who had previously died in the place to move the object referred to. It was moved accordingly. Our friend got under the table and attempted to hold it still. Yet the object, and himself with it, was drawn over the floor, his utmost efforts to the contrary notwithstanding. The physician placed a sheet of paper under the fingers of the medium, and drew it out while the table was being moved, and that without any sensible indications of pressure upon it. They consequently left, with the impression that they should be compelled to confess before the audience to the truth of Spiritualism.

On the next day they agreed with three individuals, leading members of the three denominations of the place, one a Congregationalist, one a Baptist, and the other an Universalist, to meet them the evening following at the house referred to, neither being informed at all of the object to be obtained, nor of the fact that either of the others was to be there. When the circle was formed, the Congregationalist was introduced. The same spirit was present that moved the table the evening before. In answer to inquiries put by the individual last referred to, the evangelical view of heaven, hell, and eternal retribution, was absolutely affirmed as immutably true. To the question, What mode of baptism is correct? *sprinkling* was rapped out. With a pledge of secrecy, he was then dismissed, and the Baptist called in. In answer to inquiries made by the latter, the same view of eternity as before was given. To the question, What mode of baptism is right? *immersion*, was rapped out. He being dismissed, the Universalist was introduced. The same spirit which had given the responses above stated, now denied the doctrine of retribution altogether, stoutly asserting the doctrine of universal salvation, and manifested a total indifference to the question of baptism, in any form. When the audience had assembled to listen to the discussion, these individuals were called upon to testify to the spirit-communications which they had received, and did so with a result which we need not specify. In a similar manner, every sentiment held by every people or sect on earth might have been absolutely affirmed and denied, by the spirit which responded in that circle, or by any other spirit which appeared there, or ever appeared in any other circle on earth, and that for the identical reason that precisely similar answers can be obtained from the mesmeric subject. Who, in the presence of such facts (and this is the immutable character of these manifestations the world over), can doubt their origin? It would be an impeachment of the common sense of our readers to argue the question.

The above case, while it bears with the most decisive weight upon the question of the location of the real controlling cause of these manifestations, clearly evinces the reality of an important fact—the honesty and sincerity of some mediums, of one, to say the least. Any person who was voluntarily, and by known but occult and deceptive means, producing these rapping sounds, would never, at the same sitting, rap out such contradictory communications. Many other facts equally palpable and undeniable, evince to our minds most indubitable evidence that many other mediums are not intentionally deceiving the public, but honestly suppose themselves organs of communication between the inhabitants of this and the spirit-land.

Let us now consider another case of a similar character to the one just adduced. A gentleman who was then at the head of one of the literary institutions of the state of Ohio, entered one of these circles, and inquired if the spirit of a dear friend, his mother, we believe, was present, and received an affirmative answer. Being perfectly assured that that spirit, if present, and no one in the circle but himself, did know his age, for the exclusive purpose of identification, he asked the spirit to reveal his age. To his surprise, precisely the right number was rapped out, namely, thirty or thirty-one years. To satisfy himself in respect to the *cause* of the answer, he fixed his attention distinctly upon another and different number, twenty-five, and asked the same spirit to give his age once more. The identical number upon which his attention was then fixed was given, and not the correct one given before. He asked if the doctrine of eternal retribution is true. He received an absolute affirmation that it is. He induced a voluntary doubt in his mind of the truth of that doctrine, and assumed that of the opposite one. To his questions now, his own mother stood revealed as an uncompromising Universalist. He asked, Which denomination of Christians is most nearly correct in doctrine and discipline? at the same time fixing his attention upon his own. That one sect was named. He fixed his attention upon another denomination, internally *assuming* that it was most nearly conformed to the Scriptures, and repeated the question just answered. This one sect was now designated. He thus went through the entire circle of denominations that occurred to his recollection, so putting his questions that the medium's mind was not disturbed, and found his own mother a Presbyterian, Methodist, Baptist, Episcopalian, Universalist, Christian, Unitarian, and anything and everything, just according to his own mere internal assumptions. He knew absolutely that such was not her character, and that upon no known or reasonably imagined laws of mind could he account for such responses as proceeding from any intelligent spirits, good or bad. On the other hand, he saw clearly that just such communications would be obtained if these manifestations are caused by the mental states of the individuals constituting the circles. He consequently left the circle, as any reasonable man would, with the undoubted conviction that the cause of these communications was within the circle, and not from disembodied spirits out of it. Just such answers may be obtained, and are obtained, in all these circles everywhere, in all cases where the inquirer acts with corresponding deliberation, and where the responses are not controlled by the influence of other minds present. Precisely similar and analogous experiments were made by Miss Catharine Beecher, with precisely similar results; experiments made in the most decisive forms, and so varied and repeated that a mistake is hardly conceivable, and by no means supposable. With the same identical results, a gentleman made very extensive experiments in the various circles in Great Britain. At one time, for example, he *imagined* that a great fortune had just fallen to him by legacy, in a certain city. He immediately received from "the spirits" an important communication, corresponding in all respects to his own imaginings, and having no other foundation in fact. What higher evidence can we have that any facts are exclusively mundane in their origin, than is here presented in respect to the facts under consideration?

Two gentlemen, partners in business in Cleveland, have given us the privilege of making use of the following facts, of which they were both witnesses. On one occasion they witnessed the following facts in mesmerism. We here repeat, on account of present bearings, a fact stated in another connexion, adding some circumstances not then stated. The mesmerizer agreed to induce the subject, a lady who was perfectly blindfolded, to sing, and to stop the singing the instant Mr. A. should raise his finger. When the singing commenced, the mesmerizer was standing some two or three feet from the subject, with his eyes fixed intently upon Mr. A., who was standing in a distant part of the room. When the singer had partly finished a very long note, Mr. A.

raised his finger. The voice instantly stopped, with the note half finished. As the mesmerizer willed it, the singing was resumed, and that note and the rest of the stanza were finished. After the lady was brought out of the magnetic state, Mr. A. saw her engaged in conversation with a friend, with the fingers of her hands interlocked together. Without uttering a word, or making a motion, he fixed his attention upon her hands, and willed that they should adhere together so firmly that she should be unable to separate them. When the conversation was finished, she, to her perfect surprise, found it impossible to draw her hands apart, till Mr. A., by an act of will, permitted it. These facts occurred in the presence of other most credible witnesses, who testify to their occurrence as here related.

On a subsequent occasion, these gentlemen visited, in company, a spirit-circle formed in Cleveland by Mrs. Fish and the Fox girls. Mr. A., when it came his turn to inquire, fixed his thoughts distinctly upon his father, who was then living, and with the same distinctness framed in his own mind the communications he should receive. Instantly the departed spirit of that father appeared, his name being rapped out in answer to the question, What spirit will communicate with me?—that spirit, we say, appeared and took from his son's mind the thoughts pre-existing there, just as the printed page is taken from the stereotype plate. He dismissed his father from his mind, and fixed his thoughts as distinctly as possible upon five or six other individuals. Immediately a corresponding number of raps were heard upon the top of the table. "Five or six spirits now respond to you," says Mrs. Fish. Such was the correspondence between the thoughts of the inquirer and the answers obtained, a correspondence which always obtains when there is the same deliberation and distinctness of thought on the part of the inquirer, and when the action of the invisible force is not disturbed by the mental states of others in the circle. Myriads of undeniable facts confirm this statement. Mr. L., the other partner, now communicated with "the spirits." Every question, whether put to the departed spirits of individuals living or dead,—and he communicated with each class,—was answered in exact correspondence with his own preformed conceptions. At length, having put a question, he instantly, by an act of will, confused his own mind, so that there was no thought in it to be represented. In a moment, the rappings stopped, just as the singing was interrupted in the instance above adduced. Thus he found that the action of this mysterious force was under his absolute control. He could induce, suspend, and direct its action at will, just as he could that of his own hand or arm. The same holds true, in all cases, when the same conditions are fulfilled. Everyone who has tried the experiment has found that correct answers can be obtained when the inquirer knows what the answer should be, and keeps his mind distinctly fixed upon it, and that everything is confused, or that no answers at all can be obtained, when he asks a question, and then either confuses his thoughts or turns them upon other subjects. If such facts do not reveal the relation of cause and effect between the mental states of individuals in these circles, and the communications there obtained, no such relation can, by any possibility, be established between any causes and facts in the universe around us.

The case which we next cite is, if possible, more fundamental and decisive in its bearings than any others that we have yet adduced. A gentleman of the city of Cleveland made very extensive and careful experiments and observations, for the purpose of satisfying his own mind in regard to the origin of these manifestations. He entered upon the inquiry with the earnest hope of finding valid evidence that these manifestations come from disembodied spirits. He was equally dissatisfied with the doctrine of eternal retribution, on the one hand, and with that of Universalism, on the other. The general teachings of the spirits appeared to affirm an intermediate view, which corresponded with what, to say the least, he wished to find reliable evidence for believing. He accordingly put, and received answers to, upwards of one hundred questions, in the circles of Mrs. Fish and the Foxes, in Cleveland. A large portion of these questions, probably more than one half, as he says, were asked mentally. The following are the most important facts developed :—

(1.) In every instance, without exception, the answer referred to the *subject-matter* inquired about. Here he found the immutable relation of antecedence and consequence, cause and effect. (2.) In every instance in which he knew what the answer should be, a perfectly correct one was obtained. (3.) When he was in doubt what the answer should be, those doubts were reflected, and nothing positive asserted. For example, a sister of his had died of a lingering disease, of the nature of which there was doubt among the physicians, and in his own mind, some five or six different diseases having been assigned, and none fixed upon with certainty. He inquired of the spirit of that sister, what was the disease of which she did die? All the diseases which he had heard suggested as the cause, and none others, were named, each designated with very feeble raps, and neither positively affirmed as the real cause. So in all other similar cases. (4.) When he was mistaken in regard to the facts about which he inquired, and when the spirits of whom he was inquiring did know, and could not have forgotten, the answers invariably corresponded with his mistaken apprehensions, and not with the real facts, as he subsequently became informed, and as they were known to the spirits professedly answering. For example, he inquired of the spirit of his own sister her age at the time of her death, he supposing, at the moment, that twenty-eight was the true answer, and that number was rapped out. On a subsequent reference to the family records, he found that she was really aged at the time upwards of thirty years. A friend of his had lost his life in California, by drowning, and that, as he had been informed, in a certain river, by accidentally slipping through a raft of logs. All the facts of the occurrence were given professedly by the spirit of that friend, as he had supposed them to be. From four individuals present when the event occurred, he subsequently learned that his friend actually came to his end in another part of the state, in another river, and by a totally different accident. The answer corresponded with the supposed, and not with the real, facts, as known to the spirit professedly communicating. He put a question to another spirit, pertaining to a transaction about which, as he well knew, that spirit was perfectly informed, and he, as he subsequently learned, himself had been misinformed. The answer corresponded with his misinformation, and not with the real facts, as known to the spirit professedly responding. (5.) To every question, without exception, pertaining to subjects of which he was ignorant, a wrong answer was obtained. As the result of his experience, he drew the following inferences :—

(1.) That disembodied spirits can have no connexion with these communications, and we envy not the candour or logical consistency of the individual who draws from such facts a different conclusion. (2.) That no information is ever communicated, in these circles, beyond what is previously known to the inquirer. We suppose that not one person in a thousand would draw any different conclusion from similar investigations in these circles, investigations conducted upon similar principles. The only exceptions that do occur are, as we suppose, some solitary revelations through clairvoyance (revelations which no one has reason to expect when he resorts to these circles), and certain answers corresponding to and evidently occasioned by acts of imagination and conjecture.

Let us now look at another very important case. A gentleman in Boston, a devoted spiritualist, while sitting in a spirit-circle, was struck with the revelation to his mind of the fact that the responses to the questions propounded by inquirers so frequently corresponded with the conceptions previously formed in his own imagination. This led to more careful reflection and observation, and finally to important experiments, in which he found that he could determine beforehand what answers should be given to any questions propounded by any persons present, and that he had, in a similar manner, been unconsciously directing the action of this mysterious force, and that while he had been supposing that spirits out of the circles had been doing it. A totally new theory pertaining to these so-called spirit-manifestations now stood revealed to his mind. He saw that mere reflections of the thoughts of individuals in the circles had been mistaken for the voices of spirits out of the circles.

A gentleman of very strong mesmeric power in the state of New York also found, after the most extensive experiments, that he could enter any circle whatever, and by simply willing it, could utterly silence "the spirits" so that no communications whatever could be obtained from them; that he could, in a similar manner, utterly confuse their responses, or determine beforehand the answers which should be given to any questions proposed by any persons present. The bearing of such facts cannot be mistaken. Any person that in their presence will attribute these manifestations to disembodied spirits, must be a spiritualist by dint of will, and because he is determined to be deceived.

VERY INTERESTING AND DECISIVE FACTS FURNISHED BY ONE OF OUR FORMER PUPILS.

We will now give important facts furnished us

by a former pupil of ours, a lady of superior education and intelligence. After her marriage, she had occasion to accompany her husband to Philadelphia. While at the hotel, a spirit-circle was held for several evenings in succession, and she was invited to attend them. Having, from her own reflections, been led to apprehend that the cause of the communications received was the thoughts and mental states of individuals in the circles, and not those of "the spirits," she determined to avail herself of the opportunity then presented, to satisfy her mind upon the subject. Soon after she took her place at the table amid the circle, the fact was indicated that a spirit was present who desired to communicate with the stranger, every person present being wholly unknown to our friend. "Before I question the spirit," she remarked, "there are two questions to which I desire to receive specific answers at the beginning, namely, Will the spirit give his or her name when I call for it? and, Will said spirit answer promptly the questions I shall subsequently put? These questions I desire that the medium shall put to the spirit, and herself obtain the answers in my behalf." The medium put the questions in order, and to each received an absolute affirmative answer. "Well," said our friend, "let the spirit now give his or her name." As soon as this was said, our lady friend, by a secret act of will, confused her own thoughts, and allowed no name whatever to be in her mind, nobody suspecting what she was doing. The alphabet was now read for the purpose of having, by successive raps, the letters of the name designated. But no raps were heard and no letter indicated, although the alphabet was read over repeatedly, and the medium and members of the circle entreated the spirit to respond as promised. At length, when all were in despair of inducing the spirit to respond as promised, our friend remarked that it might be that he had had occasion to retire for a time, and had now returned to the circle; and requested the medium to put the inquiry whether the spirit was then present and would now give his or her name when it should be called for. The question was put, as requested, and an affirmative answer was received. The name was accordingly called for, our friend, in the interior of her own mind, doing as she had done in the first instance, and that with the same result, no letter being rapped to. The medium was requested to ask a third time whether the spirit was indeed present and would answer to his or her name when it should be called for. Again an absolute affirmation of actual presence, and an equally absolute pledge to answer when requested, was received. The experiment of the two former occasions was repeated, with the same result. The lady requested that the spirit should be questioned once more in regard to presence and answering. This was done, and the pledge to respond was repeated a fourth time. As the lady now requested the spirit to give his or her name, she fixed her thoughts upon a particular name, and the first letter of that name, to the great satisfaction of the circle, was designated. She now dismissed that name from her thoughts, and fixed her attention upon another. The first letter of this was designated. This process was continued until the first letters of some half-a-dozen names were designated. The medium and members of the circle now exclaimed that nothing but a jumble of letters, and no name at all, was being given. So utterly confused and surprised were they at what had occurred, that they broke up the circle, and our friend retired to her room, all affirming that nothing of the kind had ever occurred in their experience before.

After this, the circle was formed again, and now such distinct and accurate responses were obtained that on the next evening our friend was requested to have another sitting, all being certain that now everything would be done to the fullest satisfaction. When the circle was formed on this occasion, "the spirits" intimated that they desired, not to answer questions, but to give sentiments and maxims. Our friend now determined, in the secret of her own mind, that she would run the course of the thoughts which were begun to be expressed, into some ridiculous endings. The first letter designated was "K." As soon as that was designated, she became impressed that the sentence which was to come out was, "Keep thy mouth," and felt certain that that was the thought present in all minds in the circle. She determined that the sentence given should be, "Keep thy money." All went right, of course, until the letter *o* was reached, and the question was whether this letter should by followed by the letter *n*, or *u*. Here, our friend said, she had a hard struggle, the thoughts of all but her own being evidently fixed upon the last letter designated. Holding her own thought strongly fixed upon the letter *n*, that was rapped to. The astonishment of the circle was irrepressible, and no persuasion could induce them to permit the sentence to be completed. One of the women present now asked of "the spirits" the question whether there was not an individual in the circle who was disturbing its harmony, and whom they desired to have excluded from the sittings, and received an affirmative answer. Our friend now determined, mentally, that that woman should be designated by "the spirits" as the disturbing spirit at whom they were offended, and accordingly fixed her thoughts upon that one individual. When each individual was named in succession, "the lot fell," not upon the stranger, but upon the woman referred to. All was "confusion worse confounded" in that circle, and all but our friend departed wondering with unutterable wonder at what had occurred. In her judgment, her own theory was fully verified, and the illusions of Spiritualism were fully understood. On this case we remark :—

1. All the facts presented indicate that the medium and her associates in that circle were acting with perfect integrity in respect to the facts before us, and believed with all sincerity that they were in actual communication with "the spirits."

2. Equally manifest is the fact that, as far as the mere action of this force is concerned in producing rapping sounds and other phenomena in these circles, there is no delusion or imposition.

3. That the action of the force developed in these circles is, when the proper conditions are fulfilled, controlled by mental states; an absolute accordance being obtained here between the most secret thought and visible and audible effects, and that in such a variety of decisive instances as to reveal a law of antecedence and consequence.

4. The mental states which here controlled the action of this force existed in the minds, or a mind, within the circle, and not in those of spirits from another sphere.

5. The fundamental error of Spiritualism is a mis-

apprehension in regard to the *location* of the mental states which control the action of this force in the production of these phenomena. As the reader shall carefully examine our facts in all their bearings, he will become absolutely assured that our doctrine of the mundane origin of these phenomena stands revealed as a strictly verified deduction of science. Let us now attend to other facts.

A professor of the Ohio Medical College, at the earnest solicitation of friends, visited on one occasion the spirit-circle of Mrs. Fish and the Foxes in the city of Cleveland. All his questions, the first excepted, his mind not being in a collected state at the moment, were answered with perfect correctness, though they pertained to subjects with which he alone, of the members of the circle, was acquainted; all his questions, we say, were correctly answered, till the spirit communicating, that of a sister, was requested to specify the given name of their father. The moment he put the question, his thought recurred to his brother, concerning whom he had just before been inquiring. The name of the brother instead of the father was immediately rapped out. The occurrence, he remarked, threw a flood of light upon his mind in regard to the origin and cause of these manifestations. The spirit professedly communicating understood the names of each of the individuals referred to as well as the professor himself, and would have corrected the mistake had it been that person that was communicating. No such correction, however, was made. He concluded, therefore, that his own thought caused the answer, and not that of a spirit out of the circle. Who can doubt the correctness of his conclusion? Had it been an intelligent mind out of the circle, especially the mind professedly answering, it could have made no difference whatever to what subject the thoughts of the inquirer should turn, after asking his question. If, on the other hand, the action of this power in the production of the answer was controlled by the mental states of the inquirer himself, then the accidental diversion of attention in this instance would occasion the identical answer that was received. On no other principle can its occurrence be accounted for.

This case also reveals the principle on which so many wrong answers are obtained in these circles to questions pertaining to subjects in respect to which both the inquirers and the spirits professedly answering are perfectly informed, and when such answers are not only unintentionally but unexpectedly obtained. It is by the accidental diversion of attention from the subject inquired about to some other subject. We shall have occasion to recur tc this class of facts again, as they will be seen to have a very important bearing upon the question before us. All that is now required is to suggest the principle in accordance with which they occur.

This case also suggests a class of facts of very conclusive and decisive bearing upon our present inquiries. It has been found, by careful observation and experiment, that the following relations, among others, exist between the mental states of the inquirer and the answers obtained, when such responses are not disturbed and modified by the undeniable psychological influence of other minds. (1.) If the inquirer fully commands his thoughts, and keeps his attention fixed upon the subject inquired about, the responses, whether right or wrong, will invariably relate to that one subject. (2.) If he knows what the answers should be, they will be almost, if not quite, invariably right, and if he does not know, and the spirit professedly communicating most manifestly does, the answer, excepting where a mere yes or no is required, and where, and on the principle of mere guessing, there is as much likelihood that the answer shall be right as wrong, the answer, we say, will be nearly as invariably wrong. (3.) When the inquirer is misinformed, and the true answer is known to the spirit professedly communicating, the answer will uniformly embody the misinformation of the inquirer, instead of the truth as known to the spirit; all the apparent exceptions admitting of a ready explanation, without supposing the interposition of spirits.

(4.) When the true answer is known both to the inquirer and to the professedly answering spirit, if the attention of the former is either intentionally or accidentally diverted and fixed definitely upon something else, this new thought, and not the answer referred to, will be embodied in the response obtained. (5.) If, either by accident or design, the mind of the inquirer becomes so confused that there is in it no thought at all to be represented, no answer whatever will be obtained. (6.) If the inquirer is not able, or does not think, to command his attention so as to prevent his thoughts becoming confused and wandering, the answers will perfectly accord with his mental states at the time, the answers being sometimes relevant and at others strikingly irrelevant, and sometimes right, and at others wrong; and that when the true answer, in every instance, is perfectly known both to the inquirer and the spirit professedly communicating with him. (7.) Let an individual write out a series of questions, the true answers to all of which are perfectly known to him and to the spirit of a deceased friend; let the former put those questions into the hands of an individual who knows nothing about the facts to which the questions pertain, and let this individual put these questions to that spirit, and the following will be the invariable result. If this individual puts the questions without forming in his own mind any imaginary answers, or fixing attention upon the subject at all, there will be either no responses at all, or they will all have the undeniable characteristics of mere imaginings, on the part of individuals who know nothing about the subjects referred to. If, on the other hand, he frames in his own mind a distinct and definite imaginary answer to each question, and keeps his thoughts distinctly fixed upon that answer when he puts the question, the response obtained will accord with his imaginings, and not with the facts as known to the individual who wrote the questions and the spirit professedly responding to them. Experiments of this kind have been tried in so many instances, and in such a diversity of forms, as to establish the truth of the above principle. If any still doubt, they can verify that principle by making the experiments themselves. (8.) Any inquirer who can command his own thoughts, and think with entire deliberation under such circumstances, especially if he has considerable mesmeric power, can, at will, make any spirit that shall professedly answer his call,—and such individuals can call up any spirit they choose,—give any answer he pleases to any question he may choose to put. He can make such spirit affirm and deny successively any sentiment that can be named, and contradict himself any number of times he pleases, provided always that the process is so conducted as not to disturb the medium, or break the odylic harmony of the circle. Most of the above statements have been most fully verified by the facts already stated. Others will be in those which we are about to present, and all could be still further by numberless undeniable additional facts which we might present. We affirm, without fear of contradiction, that these facts can be accounted for but upon the truth of the hypothesis which we maintain, namely, that these communications originate exclusively from the minds in these circles, and not from disembodied spirits out of the same. If such were their origin they could not but have these identical characteristics; and they could not have these characteristics if they did originate from intelligent minds, good or bad, out of these circles, minds governed by any mental laws known to us. We have made the above statements to prepare the way for the presentation of the following very interesting and important facts which we have obtained in the city of Boston, Mass. Our convictions of the truth of our hypothesis have been greatly strengthened by the perfect accordance which we have found to exist in the character and bearings of the fundamental facts developed by careful observers in this city, and those which we had previously collected and arranged by means of our own observations and inquiries. The individuals whose names and facts will now be presented will please to accept of our grateful acknowledgments for their kindness in furnishing us with facts so important, and especially for permitting us to use their names in connexion with these facts.

FACTS WHICH OCCURRED AT THE HOUSE OF REV. STARR KING.

The facts which we first adduce occurred at the house of Rev. Starr King, pastor of the Hollis Street Church, Boston. The circle was a select one, and the individual through whom the communications were obtained was the celebrated medium, Mrs. Hayden. The main questioner was an individual of great self-command, and of corresponding power of intellectual concentration. The circumstances then were as favourable, in all respects, as we can well conceive, for eliciting important and decisive facts. The first object of the questioner was to ascertain distinctly and conclusively whether the name of an individual of which he was thinking, and when no one present could have the least suspicion of what name he was thinking, could be spelled out, through the medium, by raps, and that when the medium could, by no possibility, have any knowledge of the movements of his hand when he should point at the requisite letters. He accordingly placed himself where the medium could not see him at all, nor any other person who could report his motions to her. The right name was thus given, and also the place where the individual bearing that name had died, namely, the Tremont House. He was, therefore, as he ought to have been, most fully satisfied that there was present a power through which his most secret thoughts could be externally expressed, and this, too, when he had given not the least indication to anyone what those thoughts were. He then wished to know whether his own mind controlled the action of that power in the production of such communications, or that of some spirit out of the circle, no other hypothesis being supposable in this case. To solve this one problem was the object of the questions subsequently put. He accordingly asked the spirit professedly communicating, how long a time it was since he died. "Twelve days," was the answer rapped out. "You are wrong there," replied the questioner, addressing the spirit; "it is only ten days since you died. I know absolutely that this is the fact, and you must be aware of it too. Please answer that question again." "Twelve days" were again given. Again and again he reasoned with the spirit on the subject, affirming absolutely to him that ten days was the only right answer. Again and again the same number as before was given. He then asked the spirit to designate the day of the week on which he died. Saturday was given. "You are wrong again," says the inquirer, "and you must be aware of the fact.

You died on Monday. Please correct the mistake." Saturday was given, as before. Again and again the spirit was told that Monday was the true answer, and was expostulated with for not giving it. Again and again, when requested to correct his mistake, Saturday was given. The man did die on Monday, and had been just ten days dead. How were these singular answers obtained? When the inquirer asked the spirit to tell the time which had elapsed since, or the day of the week on which he died, the inquirer would internally, and wholly unknown to anyone but himself, fix his thoughts, and hold them fixed, upon the number twelve, or Saturday, as the case might be. When he had reminded the spirit of his mistake, and asked him to correct it, he would then, while the response was being rapped out, fix his attention upon the wrong number or the wrong day, and the answer, in every instance, corresponded to that number or day, and not to the right one, as absolutely known both to the inquirer and the spirit professedly responding. Between the thought in his mind at the moment and the answer obtained, there was, even in this case, the fixed and immutable relation of antecedence and consequence, a relation so immutable and fixed as to demonstrate the existence between them of that of cause and effect.

The individual then called up other spirits, and went through precisely similar processes with them, and that with the same invariable results. A friend of his, for example, had died in the city of New York. After obtaining the evidence of presence and identity as before, the inquirer, secretly fixing his own attention upon Salem, then asked the spirit of that friend to name the place where he died. Salem was rapped out. He solemnly assured the spirit that he was wrong, affirming that New York was the right answer, and asked him to correct his error, the inquirer fixing his own attention, as soon as the request was made, upon Salem. This last name was given as before. So with many other spirits, with precisely similar results, no one present having the least suspicion of what the inquirer was doing, until he himself disclosed the fact, after he had finished questioning the spirits. In every experiment, he found it absolutely impossible to induce any spirit he could call up—and he could, we repeat, call up any one he chose—to give the true answer to any question he might propose, however absolutely that answer was known to himself and the spirit too, if his attention at the moment was only fixed upon some other answer, an answer known to himself, and the spirit too, to be false, and when the spirit was entreated not to give that answer, but the true one. He always obtained a correct response when he would allow his attention to be fixed upon it, and a wrong one when his attention, for the moment, was directed towards that and in all instances the answers perfectly accorded with the secret movements of his own mind. No person, we are free to say, will have the effrontery to assign any other controlling cause for these communications, than the mental states of this individual. From these most decisive facts, the following conclusions in regard to these communications are rendered undeniably evident: (1.) There is in nature a force whose action, when certain conditions are fulfilled, corresponds with our mental states, and is determined by the same,—a force through which our own thoughts may be reflected back upon us, as if they came from other minds, to us invisible, and apparently from the spirit-land,—a very important truth, unquestionably. (2.) There is also in this so-called spirit-movement a power by which, without any external motions or signs whatever on our part, our most secret thoughts may be revealed and expressed. (3.) This may be done in the total absence of all *ab extra* spirit-agency, none being supposable in the facts before us. (4.) No such revelations can be adduced as presenting any evidence whatever of an *ab extra* spirit-origin. (5.) We have no occasion to go beyond the force developed in these circles and the mental states of the individuals constituting them, to account for any revelations embodied in these communications, those pertaining to secret thoughts being, of all others, in themselves the most wonderful and unaccountable—

far more so than those which pertain to mere physical objects, however distant. (6.) We have the highest positive evidence of the exclusively subjective origin of these so-called spirit-manifestations. Any person that, in the presence of such facts, can draw any other conclusion, is, in our honest judgment, far removed, in his reasonings from facts to conclusions, off from the true line of scientific or common sense deduction.

The communications received by Mr. King himself, though not, in all respects, so decisive in their bearings, were yet very interesting and important, Being informed, by the appropriate raps, that a spirit was present who would communicate with him, he asked, first, for the initials of his (the spirit's) name, Mr. K. at the time fixing his attention upon a certain individual who had died some time before, an individual whom no one present but himself was likely to think of. The initials of the very name that rose in his mind were given. He then called for the name in full, and it was given accordingly. Many important test questions were then asked, and all, without exception, which came within the recollection of Mr. K. himself, were answered with the most perfect accuracy. The spirit was asked to give the title of the work which he prepared for the press just before his death, Mr. K. knowing what it was. The entire title was given accordingly. "Now give," says

Mr. K., "the first sentence of that work," the work being present, but Mr. K. having no recollection whatever what that sentence was. Several most abortive efforts were made to form a sentence; but nothing was expressed which at all corresponded to any part of the sentence referred to. Such facts leave no reasonable doubt upon the question of the origin of these manifestations.

IMPORTANT FACTS FURNISHED BY DR. BELL.

We now invite very special attention to some interesting and important facts which have been kindly furnished us by Luther V. Bell, M.D., who was at the head of the McLean Lunatic Asylum of Somerville, near Boston. For two years, as Dr. B. informed us, he had, as far as his official duties permitted, carefully observed and studied the spirit-phenomena, physical and intellectual, and that for two reasons—the interest which attaches to the phenomena themselves; but more especially from the fact that not a few of the inmates of that institution were there through the influence of this one cause. The following may be stated, as among the more important results of his investigations. We make our citations from "Two Dissertations on what is termed the Spiritual Phenomena, read at the meetings of the Association of Medical Superintendents of American Insane Hospitals, at Washington and Boston, in 1854 and 1855,"—dissertations, the manuscripts of which he very kindly put into our hands, with the permission to make such extracts from them as, in our judgment, the interests of science might seem to require. The following are the results of his observations, which were most carefully made through upwards of twenty sessions in the spirit-circles.

1. They most fully sustain the claims of Spiritualism, as far as the mere fact of *physical manifestations* are concerned, namely, the movement of heavy bodies, both with and without physical contact; their movement, too, in accordance with intelligence. We will give a single case in illustration, a case related in the following extract from Dissertation II.

"The following is the minute of one of the physical manifestations. Went to the house of Jonathan Brown, Jr., Esq., cashier of the Market Bank, with Mr. Homer Goodhue, just returned from the South. Mr. Goodhue for twenty years was the supervisor of our male department, and well known in character, at least, to many members of this association. He is a gentleman of orthodox faith, and not free from the prejudices of that denomination against this new thing as a religious element. He never before had been present, or seen any manifestations. In fact, he had never seen a 'medium,' or attended a 'circle.' Mrs. Brown and a young woman, Mr. Brown's niece, made up the list of the five persons present. This 'medium' is exceedingly small, not weighing more than eighty or ninety pounds, and yet her gifts appear to be very great in effecting infractions of gravitation, but not certain or strong in the other classes of powers. We sat in the double parlours joined with folding doors, or rather doors sliding on trucks along an iron rod projecting one-half to three-quarters inch above the level of the carpet. We began the operations by opening the family dining-table, and inserting two or three leaves, elongating it from about six to perhaps nine or more feet. I state this as it allowed an eye to be kept as to wires, etc. It had six legs, and was of such a weight that when the castors were all in a right line for motion I could with both my hands, and as strong a pull as my strength of fingers would allow, just put it in motion.

"After an evening's performance of all the usual responses, motions of the table with hands upon it, with the finger's ends just touched, etc., which were satisfactory, it was proposed, especially as the motions were unusually facile and free *with* contact, to make the trial *without* touch. I was master of ceremonies, and directed things to suit my own views. We stood on the sides of the table, three and two, and back from it from twelve to eighteen inches. Our hands were raised above it about the same distance. As the table was rather low and my height is unusual, I was able to see between the bodies of all present and the table. We spoke as if we were addressing persons in reality, and once in a while we received remarks from the 'spirits' as is assumed, the medium being 'impressed' and writing on paper before her.

"The table commenced its journey down the room, keeping midway, reached the iron crossing at the sliding doors, surmounted it, and passed on. One of us ran and pushed away a centre-table in the middle of the other parlour, intending to allow as long a journey as possible. It moved on, sometimes slowly, then with a rapid slide, a foot or two at once. At length it reached the end of the second parlour, as near as the mirror made it safe to go. I expressed my thanks to the 'spirits' for the completeness of the manifestation, and begged that they would gratify us by returning the table back to the point of beginning. It reversed its course. At a momentary halt, I suggested to the company that we should all gradually remove from it our bodies and hands, to see how far the 'influence' would extend. It was found that when we withdrew more than about eighteen or twenty inches, the motion ceased. And indeed on returning, the capacity of motion seemed to be lost for three or four minutes afterward, as if a certain accumulation of power were in progress. When the fore legs of the table reached the iron bar, it came to a dead stand. We waited, and the table heaved and trembled and creaked, but could not rise above the obstacle. Presently the medium was impressed, and wrote that if we would lift those two legs over the iron, they, that is 'the spirits,' thought they could bring the other four along. We did not hesitate to afford the suggested aid. Whereupon the spirits succeeded in moving the whole on, without interruption, until the table was as high up in the room from which it started as it was at commencing, but about four feet over from the central line at one side. I expressed my gratification at their success, but said, There is one thing more I wish you to do—move the table at right angles, so that these chairs will be right to sit in, as they were at first.' The table immediately moved at right angles as desired, into the precise position designated. This evening's performance now closed, no person of us having the remotest doubt as to the fact of this considerable motion having taken place with no human power. The entire space passed over was about fifty feet."

On this case we deem it important to make the following observations:—

(1.) Every circumstance which surrounds this case

combines with every other to remove it from the most distant suspicion of trick or fraud.

(2.) The fact of the movement of heavy bodies without visible contact is most fully established, and will not be questioned by any who have not fully made up their minds to blindly follow the maxim practically, at least, adopted by David Hume, that the occurrence of no strange event can be established by testimony.

(3.) Equally manifest is the fact that this movement was immediately caused by an attractive and repulsive physical force developed in the organisms of the individuals present and the object before them. We bring an object called the magnet within a certain distance of another object, a piece of iron, for example, and the latter object is drawn towards and after the former. We remove the object to a somewhat greater distance, and the phenomena of attraction disappear. It is thus that the existence of magnetism, as a force in nature, is demonstrated. How was it in the case before us? The table moved when, and only when, the hands of the individuals referred to were within a certain distance of it, and ceased to move when they were removed to a greater distance. We have, then, in these movements, the same evidence of the presence and action of an attractive and repulsive physical force, that we have, or can have, of the existence of magnetism, as such a force.

(4.) This force differs fundamentally from magnetism and electricity, and all other mere physical forces in nature, in this, that the *direction* of its action accords with acts of intelligence and will, and is often determined by the same. How perfectly were all those movements conformed to the mental states of the individuals constituting that circle, and how perfectly manifest is it that these movements were determined by the thoughts and wills of some minds within that circle, or without it. We can have but little, if any, more evidence that our physical organisms act in accordance with our own mental states, and are directed, in many important particulars, by the same, than we have that these movements were directed and controlled by the mental states and acts of some intelligences located somewhere, either in the circle or out of it.

(5.) We have only to suppose the presence of a power having the very attractive, repulsive, and mentally directed qualities which we see that this must have, together with the known mental states of the individuals constituting this circle, to account most fully and satisfactorily for every fact that occurred there, and this without the supposition of any *ab extra* controlling cause whatever. When Dr. Bell said, Let the spirits move the table so and so, the thoughts of every mind present were fixed intensely upon that one movement, and the unconscious, but really united and strong fiat of every will was, let that movement be made. Instead of its being a cause of wonder that the phenomena did appear under those circumstances, it would have been a miracle if they had not occurred. We have no more occasion to go out of the circle, and suppose the interposition of spirits, to account for these facts, than we have to go out of our bodies, and suppose the interposition of spirits, to account for the movements of our own physical organisms.

(6.) Not a solitary ray of light is thrown upon any of these facts, by referring them to the agency of disembodied spirits. If spirits did do it, it must have been by simply willing the motions which the individuals constituting the circles wished to have made. Why should we suppose that such power attaches to the mental states of the former, and not to those of the latter? If the mental states of spirits out of the circle have such power, much more must we suppose that those of minds in the organisms in which this force is developed would have the same efficiency. The supposition of the interposition of spirits, therefore, is the most uncalled-for hypothesis conceivable, to account for these facts, an hypothesis which throws not a solitary ray of light upon one of them.

(7.) Hence we remark, finally, that there is not in these facts, and if not in these, in none of the physical facts of Spiritualism, the least conceivable evidence of the controlling interposition and agency of spirits. The fact that the spirits were requested to move the table, and that it did move accordingly, as if in answer to such request, presents no such evidence at all; for the two following reasons, that, as we have seen in other cases, the same movements would have occurred had the object been commanded to move and no reference at all made to spirits, or if the same command had been given and the spirits challenged to prevent the movement. No such interposition is demanded to account for any of the facts, and they are, in all respects, what we know they could not but be, from the nature of the force developed, and from the relations of the minds present to the same.

2. The facts developed by Dr. Bell fully sustain the claims of Spiritualism as far as concerns any questions pertaining to the real existence of a power to obtain, through mediums, a revelation of our most secret thoughts, and to obtain also, as from spirits, correct answers to any questions pertaining to any subjects known to the inquirer and to the spirits professedly communicating with him, however remote such knowledge may be from the cognizance of the mediums, or of any other persons present. No candid person, we feel quite safe in making the affirmation, can read these dissertations without having every doubt removed from his mind on this subject. We

will give two examples. The first is contained in the following extract from the first dissertation :—

"I asked, 'Is any spirit friend of mine present?' Answer, '*Yes.*' 'Who is it?' Answer, '*Any one you may choose to question.*' I certainly felt that this was a sufficiently broad latitude, and my mind instantly elected, as the object of my converse, a deceased brother, the late Dr. John Bell, of New York city, because he was entirely unknown to anybody in the section where I resided, having been dead nearly five-and-twenty years, and never having been a resident of Massachusetts. In fact, he left New England about 1820. A gentleman at my elbow said to me, 'You need not speak the name of any friend you may call upon. Put your question mentally.' I did so, and then said, 'Is the spirit I have just thought of present?' Answer, '*Yes.*' 'Give me some proof by indicating the year of your decease.' I passed the pencil secretly over the numerals, and the figures 1-8-3-0 were successively indicated (1830). *This was the year.* I then remarked aloud, '*Coincidences are not proofs*,—confirm the fact of your presence by stating the place at which you were at your decease.' There was then rapped out on the alphabet the letters, t-h-i-b-a-u-d-e-a-u. When it had proceeded thus far, the medium and all the others acquainted with the processes, exclaimed,—'That is no word ; it is a mere jumble of letters : go back and recommence.' 'No,' said I, 'let him go on, and see what he will make of it.' The rapping continued,—v-i-l-l-e,—forming the word Thibaudeauville, a small town in Louisiana, near which my brother lived on a plantation, and at which he received and sent his letters. The fact of his death at or near that place could not have been known, probably, to any other person in Massachusetts except myself, and years had passed by since it had entered my mind. The medium was an uneducated young girl, living in the city of Boston, unknown to me; and the other parties present were three eminent clergymen, and the two gentlemen I have before referred to."

The next is taken from the second dissertation, and must stand for many other cases recorded, of equal pertinency :—

"Recurring again to my own experience, I entered upon a series of six weekly examinations with the same medium and associates, whose names would be recognised as among the distinguished in literature and theology of this vicinity. Having already received evidence, as I felt (as detailed last year), that I had obtained correct replies to mental questions, and that many things not possibly within the knowledge of any person present had been correctly given to me, I arranged my plans, 1st. To verify this in full, and ascertain whether there was anything known to me and a deceased person *alone* which could be reproduced. 2nd. Whether a correct reply could be got to anything known, *ex necessitate rei*, to the spirit invoked, but not known to the questioner, as subsequent inquiry should demonstrate. I had, as I thought, a very complete test, to understand which I must go into a brief domestic narration. I had a brother, Dr. John Bell (alluded to in my last year's experience), who died in Louisiana in 1830. He was settled in New York city as a medical practitioner. He was seized with hæmoptysis in 1824, and as the celebrated Laennec, whose pupil he was, had some years previously diagnosed pulmonary disease, his case was regarded as highly critical. Abandoning at once the brightest prospects of professional success, he decided to go to the South on horseback. Mounting his animal, he first made a farewell visit to his friends in New England. I was at the time of his visit here attending lectures at a country college, but learning that he would be in Boston about a certain date, I proceeded to that city. Arriving late at night I could make no attempts to find him, but early the next morning I set out to visit the various hotels, which were much crowded at that season, to meet with him. I succeeded in finding his name at what was known as the 'City Hotel.' On inquiring, I found that he had just settled his bill, and probably would be found about starting. I passed into the shed connecting the hotel and its stables, and there found him arranging his horse's stirrups, etc., preparatory to mounting to take his departure. I there had what I, and probably he, felt to be our last interview, and which in fact so proved, although his health was partially recovered, and he lived several years afterwards. This interview had always been very clearly recollected, and as I never had communicated it to any person, I had often remarked to my 'spiritual' friends that if any medium could reproduce that occasion in its essentials, I would admit that the spirit of my brother was present; indeed I must do so, because I could see no alternative. I may as well remark here, that I was too hasty in my logic, in proffering such admissions. At the first or second of the series of investigations, I was informed that the spirit of my brother would communicate. I took occasion to question him pretty thoroughly on such points as I thought none could know except myself or other immediate friends. I think the nature of the questions will leave no room for the suspicion that the medium, who was an entire stranger to us, and born since the events referred to, could have been 'crammed' into an ability to answer correctly. I will give the questions and answers, observing that every one except the last [given in another connexion], was perfectly correct and true.

"*Q.* When you went to Paris, as a medical student, who was your fellow passenger? *A. Wells.* N. B.

I had previously requested, as the communications were to be in the tedious alphabetical process, that he should reply in the briefest terms. A gentleman asked his Christian name. *A. John D.* *Q.* The name of the vessel? *A. Brig Caravan.* *Q.* On that voyage to France, where did you land? *A. In Holland.* N. B. At that date (1821) there was no direct French trade, and passengers were obliged to take circuitous passages. *Q.* You once obtained a medical prize: what was the subject? *A. Smallpox.* *Q.* Where was our last interview in life? *A. In Boston.* *Q.* Where in Boston? *A. City Hotel.* *Q.* What were you doing? *A. Preparing to mount my horse for a journey.* *Q.* A journey! where? *A. To the South.* *Q.* What part of the South? *A. Natchez.* *Q.* Who went with you? *A. James Dinsmore and Stephen Minor.*

"This Stephen Minor was a young gentleman of Natchez who had been sent north for an education, had become insane, and had been a resident for some years at the late Dr. Chaplin's private insane retreat at Cambridgeport. His friends took the opportunity of their going to Natchez to procure his return home. Mr. Dinsmore was a cousin of my brother, who remained with him at the South as long as he lived. I might observe that I am not conscious of this young man, Stephen Minor, having been in my memory for five-and-twenty years!"

We leave these cases to speak for themselves. Any persons that in their presence would deny the existence of the power under consideration, would not be convinced by any facts or arguments bearing upon this subject.

3. The facts adduced by Dr. Bell, while they most fully sustain his and our conclusion, that no valid evidence exists of a connexion between the extraordinary facts of this new science and another world, or with departed spirits, the same facts as fully sustain the truth of our present proposition, the exclusively and subjective and mundane origin of these manifestations. Two hypotheses are before us pertaining to the origin and controlling cause of these manifestations—the supposition that the action of this force is controlled, in their production, by the mental states of the minds in these circles ; and that it is controlled by those of spirits out of the same. Suppose that we find these communications bounded wholly by the range and limits of the former, and not by those of the latter, being generally correct where the former is, erring where they err, even when the spirits cannot but know the truth ; blundering where they blunder, varying as they vary, moving when and as they move, and stopping where and when they stop. In this case, all the laws and principles of science and common sense require us to affirm the truth of the first hypothesis. If, on the other hand, we find these com-

munications uniformly harmonizing with facts as they are when they are mutually known to the inquirer and the spirits professedly answering; that when he errs, they accord with the facts known to the spirits, and that when he is wholly ignorant, and the spirits are known to be well informed, the real facts, and not incorrect answers, are uniformly given, then we should be bound to adopt the latter hypothesis. We have already shown that the phenomena of Spiritualism are just what they would be, were the former hypothesis true, and just what they could not be, if the latter were true. This conclusion is most fully sustained by the facts adduced by Dr. Bell.

He affirms, in the first place, that during all his observations and experiments, neither himself nor any individuals associated with him were able to obtain, in a single instance, correct answers to any questions pertaining to subjects lying beyond the circle of their knowledge, and this when the questions pertained to facts of which the spirits manifestly answering, if any were, must have been fully informed, and could not have forgotten, or to subjects of which they might or might not, but positively affirmed themselves to have been well informed, and that in connexion with cases where the most surprising accuracy was preserved in statements, where the truth was known to the inquirer. Take the following as an example. The spirit of an only sister of the Doctor, who "had died and was buried in St. Augustine, East Florida, in 1830, and was a total stranger in this vicinity," responded on one occasion, and after having stated the place of her decease and burial, the following facts occurred.

"I then asked, 'With whom did you board when at St. Augustine?' *Mr. Wallen.* True. 'What physician attended you?' *Dr. Samuel Anderson.* The fact was, his name was Andrew. 'Who performed your funeral services?' *Mr. Nott.* 'What was his other name?' *Handel.* Now the fact was, that among the many visitors for health at that city was a New England clergyman of that name, who actually performed these services. These facts could be known to no other person but myself. I thought of them at the time, as the questions were put. I may remark, however, that I knew Dr. Anderson's Christian name *as well as I did my own.* These were but a few of the many questions of a domestic nature which I put, and which were all answered correctly, the responses being *all* known to me.

"I also made a series of inquiries, predicated on a previous arrangement with the family at home, by which every quarter of an hour they were to do some act, and I was simultaneously to ask what was doing. In every case, the spirit declared it saw distinctly what was doing, and gave a ready response. What was done, and what was said to be done, were acts of the same general nature, that is, putting the match in the bed, upsetting furniture, etc., but in no example was there any near coincidence."

In cases also where a mistake existed in his mind, and the real facts were known to the spirit professedly answering, the answers, as in cases which we have already adduced, corresponded with the mistake of the inquirer, and not with the knowledge of the spirit. At the same time, while a spirit would be wholly unable to answer while the facts remained unknown to the inquirer, a right answer would be given at once as soon as he became informed. The following extract—the first part of which contains the remainder of the long communication which Dr. B. held as with the spirit of his brother, and the other part presents other important facts developed in subsequent interviews—presents a full verification of each of the above statements.

"*Q.* Who was with you at the time of your death? *A.* Dinsmore, Sears, Whitney.

"Now I knew the true replies to every one of these questions, except the last, and they were all truly given. I had, of course, some anxiety, as all the others had been answered truly, to ascertain how the unknown one would prove. Fortunately Mr. D. was still alive in Kentucky, and I wrote him. He replied that he was *not* present at the death, as I had always *supposed* he was, and mentioned the persons who were. Neither of them was of those named!

"At another time, with another medium, this same brother appeared. As usual, he replied to all common questions I could frame, by any ingenuity, the replies of which were within my mind. After a while I said, 'My brother, I have brought here two letters which, on leaving home, I slipped out of a file of old date, and put in my pocket without looking at them. Now as you have answered certain things here (alluding to a selection of certain rolled up pieces of paper) which show that if you really are present you are capable of *seeing* clearly, I will unfold these letters behind me, and you will rap out alphabetically the names of the writers.' He replied that he could not do it.

"I made trial again of this important test some weeks after, by holding letters open behind me, which I had drawn from my file unlooked at. I first asked the spirit if he saw me 'clearly and distinctly,' as we saw each other, face to face. He replied that he did. I then said, 'Of course you can see and read this letter, or its signature, which I hold open behind me.' Some reply was made, a mere subterfuge, not *ad rem;* something about things being afterwards clear to me. I then cast my eye upon the signature, and saw who wrote the letter, and then remarked that I was now sure that we should get the name correctly, *because it was in my own mind.* The result proved the truth of my surmise."

On a particular occasion,—we now relate what was given to us verbally,—the spirit of a son of Dr. B., a son who had died some time before while a student in college, responded to a young man, a former associate and friend of the son. A very marked accuracy of memory, as far as related to things known to the inquirer, characterized the entire answers coming from this spirit, so much so, that the young man supposed that a mistake in regard to real presence and identity was hardly possible, and so presented the subject to Dr. B. The father then wrote out twelve questions pertaining to facts well known to himself and son, but wholly unknown to the young man, and requested the latter to take the questions with him to the circle, and when the spirit of the son should appear again, ask him to answer the same. This was done, and a prompt and unqualified response was given to each question. Not one of these answers was found to be correct, while the form of each was such as to render it certain that it was a mere guess suggested by the question itself, thus evincing the truth of the principle above stated, that in all such cases the answers will not only uniformly, if not invariably, be wrong, but will accord with the imaginings and guesses of the person putting them, and not with the facts as known to the author of them, and to the spirit professedly responding.

Such are the principles which control these manifestations, the world over. As to the individuals who, in their presence, will still hold on to the belief that their controlling cause is the mental states of spirits out of the circles, instead of the minds constituting them, we must "leave them alone in their glory."

THE STATEMENTS OF DR. BELL CONFIRMED BY KINDRED ONES FROM N. I. BOWDITCH, ESQ.

In the manuscript volume containing the above-named dissertations, is a letter from N. I. Bowditch, Esq., addressed to Dr. Bell, on the subject discussed in those dissertations. From this letter we take, with leave, the following extract, containing very conclusive corroborations of the general and particular statements of Dr. B. The character and standing of Mr. Bowditch, together with his well-known relations to Spiritualism, will add much interest and weight to his facts and statements.

"I have found my most successful sessions to be those where I was alone with the medium, or attended only by one friend. During the whole two hours I have had often entirely accurate answers to a series of mental questions, some of them such that the answer could not be known to any other human being than myself. For instance, I wrote certain lines as from a young girl, lately dead, to her father, describing her reunion with her deceased mother, the love they both bore him, etc. The answers gave the character of the paper, the number of its lines, and, at my request, accurately repeated the last lines of the last stanza, namely,—

> "'And while thy years of life shall last,
> Life's noblest ends still keep in view,
> By each dear memory of the past,
> To us, thyself, thy God, be true!'

"I am satisfied, as you are, that the answers are according to our *thought* or *belief*, even if erroneous. On two different occasions, once when I was in communication, a spirit gave its *own* name as William instead of Thomas, *because I thought it was William*. And, at another time, when a *friend* was in communication, a wife made the same mistake in her *husband's* name. My friend announced the mistake, as a gross failure. I suggested this disturbing influence, and shut up my eyes, while he tried the question again, and got the true name, Thomas.

"A strong and determined *will* can also get answers known to be *false*. Dr. H. T. Bigelow went with me to Mrs. Heyden (while we used pencils). The letters touched by him would be negatived (by single raps), some of them five or six different times ; but after knocking at a particular letter over and over again, *three* raps would at last come. Having once come, Dr. B. would say, Are you sure that this is the right letter ?—*three raps, or yes.* In this way he *compelled* the spirit to say that its name was 'Miserable Humbug'—that spirits lived on 'pork and beans,' etc., through a series of absurdities. Had I never been present at any other session, I should unhesitatingly have arrived at his conclusion, namely, that the medium knew (by his loud and emphatic pointing and striking at particular letters) where the raps were wanted, and *made them accordingly ;* and that it was all a delusion.

"Like you I have failed, in a single case, to *verify* as true a fact stated which at the time *was not in my own mind.* On the contrary, time and time again, answers have been made, without any words of doubt or hesitation, which have proved to be *false.* Sometimes, however, there has been a candid statement of *inability to answer.* I had asked mentally the number of my watch. It was given correctly—5,763. Mr. S. G. Ward was present, and said aloud, 'Can you give the number of my watch ?' Neither of us knew it. I repeated the question, and got, No. I said, 'Why ?' The alphabet spelt out, '*I cannot do it.*' I said, 'If W. shows it to me, can you then repeat it?' 'Yes.' Mr. W. opened his watch under the table and showed me the number, and I at once got the true answer. *Excuses* are sometimes made for palpable blunders. Thus the same young friend (dead only ten days before) gave Nathaniel Bowditch Mason instead of Alfred Mason, as the name of a young cousin who had died a few years before. *The true name was known to me.* I asked, 'How could you make such a mistake of name?' It was a mental question. The answer was, 'The fact is, I am so much absorbed in my new and beautiful home that *I have almost forgotten my own name.*'"

We make but two remarks upon the important facts and statements here presented:—

(1.) The particular conclusion which the friend of Mr. B. drew from the ludicrous facts which he witnessed, was occasioned by the assumption, on his part, that those responses were produced by spirits, or by imposition on the part of the medium. Had the third hypothesis been in his mind, he would undoubtedly, if well informed in regard to facts, have drawn the far more evident conclusion, that the action of this force was, in this case, governed by his own mental states, the supposition that such answers could come from spirits, good or bad, being out of the question.

(2.) The fact that such men as Dr. Bell and Squire

Bowditch, a devoted spiritualist, in all the widely-extended investigations which they have made, have never "been able, in a single case, to verify as true a fact stated, which was not in their mind at the time," goes very far to justify the very common opinion that no such revelations are ever obtained in these circles. For ourselves, we have yet, to our best recollections, to meet with the first individual, not a spiritualist, who has himself obtained any such communication, or witnessed its occurrence on the part of others. We still think, however, that such communications have, in instances exceedingly rare, been obtained, and that for the following reasons:—

(*a*) The evidence presented in such facts as are now before us, only renders the non-occurrence of such communications probable, and not certain.

(*b*) We think that adequate evidence of their real occurrence, in the form stated, is before the public.

(*c*) From the analogy of facts attending the action of this force, in other relations, there *ought* to occur just such facts as are authentically reported to occur in these circles, supposing no agency of spirits is ever exerted in them, and they ought to have the identical characteristics, and none others, that they do possess. For ourselves, we are rather embarrassed in the development of our theory with the infrequency of such occurrences, than with the real facts themselves, or with any of their characteristics.

Mr. B. says, "I have found my most successful sessions to be those when I was alone with the medium, or attended only by one friend." The reason is obvious. There were, in such cases, no other minds present, minds whose mental states would disturb the action of the odylic force, and whose thoughts would be consequently unconsciously intermingled with those of the inquirer. This fact strikingly corroborates the theory which we maintain. If spirits out of the body controlled the action of this force, it would make no difference how many living persons were in the circle.

IMPORTANT FACTS FURNISHED BY A NEW ENGLAND CONGREGATIONAL CLERGYMAN.

The next case which we cite was furnished us by a New England Congregational clergyman of unquestionable integrity and intelligence (names are withheld by special request), and presents so many interesting features bearing fundamentally upon our present inquiries, that we would invite very special attention to it. It presents a number of facts which he witnessed in a circle of which, by mere accident, he became a member, he having in the course of a walk for a totally different object called at the house of a friend whose daughter was one of his former pupils in an academy of which he had been for several years the principal, and was, as he learned, after he entered the house, a medium. A spirit-circle was accordingly formed, consisting of the teacher, the father, mother, and daughter, the gentlemen sitting on one side of the table, and the ladies on the other. The following are the prominent facts developed during this sitting, which continued upwards of four hours :—

(1.) The same evidence of presence and identity, the same ability to read correctly our secret thoughts, to reveal names, and ages, and any events of the past as they, one and all, stood in the mind of the inquirer, were manifested by the spirits of brutes, and even of inanimate objects, as are, in any instances, manifested by the spirits of men. It was found, also, that the great central wonder of Spiritualism, one spirit going after an absent one and returning with him at a specified time agreed upon, could be perfectly paralleled by the spirit of the brute. The spirit of a certain animal, for example, was asked if he could go and bring that of another that was named, and answered, yes. He was told to do it, and be back again in just one minute and a half by the watch. The instant the hand of the watch came over the right second, there was a rap to indicate the arrival of the spirit sent for. After affirming his actual presence, he was asked, as proof of his identity, to give his age. The precise number, nineteen, existing in the mind of the inquirer, was promptly given by raps. It was subsequently found that there was a mistake of several years in the answer given, thus most fully evincing the fact that the spirit of the brute fails precisely where and as that of man does. N. B.—Both animals were then alive.

(2.) This clergyman, by observations and experiments about which there could be no mistake, found that he could exercise an absolute control over the action of this power in the medium. When, for example, she would attempt to write, she being a writing as well as rapping medium, he could, by simply willing it, while no one had the least suspicion of what he was doing, stop her hand entirely, cause it to move up and down, so that the pencil should make nothing but dots on the paper, and then cause her to go on with the writing as before.

(3.) He also obtained the most palpable and conclusive evidence that the medium was in a mesmeric state, and that the other persons present sustained the precise relations to her that the mesmerizer does to the person mesmerized. For example, having occasion to reach his hand across the table to a letter of the alphabet, as his hand came near that of the medium, hers was instantly forcibly attracted towards his, so that the end of the pencil in her hand struck his with such violence as to leave a mark there, and to occasion some pain at the time. Recollecting that this was the first rude act that he had ever witnessed in her, he was led to look into her eyes, and immediately discovered, from her appearance, that she was in a magnetic state. To verify that thought, he said to her, "Your hand is fastened to the top of the table, and you can't take it off." The medium made every possible effort to withdraw her hand, but found it impossible to move it. "Now," says the minister, "your left hand must come up and be fastened by the side of the other." The medium declared, with the intensest excitement, that it should not be so. The hand, however, gradually came up, and when it came over the top of the table, descended upon it, as if suddenly drawn down by a resistless attractive force. By no effort could she move either hand, till, by an act of will, he released her. By subsequent experiments, he found that her entire powers, mental and physical, were under his absolute control. Without any external sign whatever, for example, he simply willed that she should turn round, and fix her eyes upon a picture that hung upon the wall of the room. Instantly she turned round and fixed her eyes upon the object referred to. He then willed that she should look steadfastly at an object in the hands of her mother, and her eyes were instantly fixed in that direction. When asked why she looked at those objects, her answer was, that, at that time, she wanted to do it. He then merely willed that she should leave her chair and seat herself upon the sofa, and she did so. At one time he made her weep at the thought that she had disobeyed her mother, nothing of the kind having occurred; and at another made her think that her own father was a rude and vulgar boy whom she had before seen. As a last experiment, he wished to know whether he could induce in her a mental perception of an object of which he had a remembrance, but which was unlike anything of whom she had any knowledge. He recollected having seen, in Virginia, years before, a cedar tree about twenty feet high, a tree the boughs of which were in a conical form, from near the ground to the top. The body of the tree was encircled by a trumpet vine, the blossoms of which, then in full bloom, completely covered it in all directions, just standing out in the midst of its foliage. Altogether it was the most beautiful object that he had ever seen in the vegetable kingdom before. He consequently stopped for some time to look at and admire it. The medium, as he well knew, had never in her life seen a cedar tree of that species, nor such a vine, and especially the two combined as in this instance. Nor had she ever heard of his having seen such an object. He wished to know whether he could induce in her, and that without uttering a syllable himself about the object in his own mind, a mental perception of that object. He accordingly put a book into her hand, requesting her to look into that mirror, and tell him what she saw. The book immediately became a mirror to her, and after looking into it a few moments, she exclaimed with the intensest delight: "I never saw so beautiful an object in my life. It is a tree; I never saw such a tree. It looks somewhat like a hemlock, and it is covered all over with beautiful flowers. They are shaped like a trumpet, and they are of an orange colour. I never saw so beautiful an object in my life." Thus, he said, she described that before to her totally unknown and unheard-of object as distinctly as he could have done himself, so perfectly was his own purely mental conception reproduced in her mind, and that without a motion on his part to afford the remotest indication of the particular object of which he was thinking.*

The reader will not be surprised to learn that through these important and fundamental facts the mysteries of Spiritualism stood distinctly revealed to the mind of this individual, and that from that time onward he has had the most unwavering con-

* Since writing the above, we have read the same to the individual from whom the facts were derived, and he indorses the whole as unqualifiedly correct.

viction that the medium after all is none other than a magnetic subject in whom the thoughts of those in the circles are, upon principles and laws purely natural, unconsciously reproduced, and for that reason received as responses from spirits out of the circles. There is not a solitary phenomenon of Spiritualism which does not fall in with this view, and when rightly apprehended does not affirm its truth. On the same principle that the medium's hand was so powerfully attracted towards that of her teacher, the table itself, or any other object between which and her organism the same force was developed in the same manner, would have followed her all round the room. Or, if it was developed between them, in different polarity, then it would have fled from her in apparent terror, running violently against certain objects, and from others. If the same force, as in some instances, was developed in still greater power, then there would have been a sensible jarring of surrounding objects, and rumbling sounds, as of distant thunder, or the far-off firing of ordnance. The medium was undeniably, at the same time that she was a writing and rapping medium, in a clairvoyant state. Suppose that, like the mesmeric subject of J. M. Brooke, Esq., she had possessed also, as might have been the case, the power of *independent clairvoyance* which that subject did possess. Then, while the thoughts of those who were present were reproduced in her, and embodied as spirit-voices in her communications, there would have been mingled with these the revelation of certain facts perceived, at the moment, by her on purely natural principles, facts unknown to any present, and all presented as from "the spirits." Thus we have the *new information* which is sometimes obtained in these circles,—revelations, none of which present the least indication of the presence and agency of "the spirits," but all of which are perfectly explicable on purely natural principles.

A passing remark is deemed requisite here upon a fact stated by Dr. Bell and others, as peculiarizing these revelations, the fact that the *thought*, and not the *language*, of the inquirer is commonly embodied in them. In general it is, as in the mental perception of the tree above presented, the thought only that is reproduced in the mind of the medium. Sometimes, but not generally, both the language and thought are reproduced. This accords with the statements of spiritualists as well as of others.

INTERESTING AND ILLUSTRATIVE FACTS FURNISHED THE AUTHOR BY A PASTOR OF ONE OF THE CHURCHES IN THE CITY OF CLEVELAND, OHIO.

An influential pastor of one of the churches in the city of Cleveland, Ohio, made to us personally the following statements, he being, as he stated, possessed of very strong mesmeric power. With the phenomena of Spiritualism he had made himself perfectly familiar. When in any circle he ever attended, he could, by secretly willing it, and doing nothing more, utterly suspend all manifestations of every kind, the operations always going on as before the moment he mentally suspended his secret prohibitory fiat. In a similar manner he could exercise any kind of control he chose over these manifestations. One evening as he called at the house of a friend, one of his members, he found a company of youths there engaged in discussing the merits of Spiritualism. On enquiry, he found that there was not present a single believer in the system. He then proposed that they should seat themselves with him around a table, and determine, as a matter of mere scientific inquiry, what results would follow. The dining-table was selected, and soon after the circle was formed the table began to move. It was soon found that the direction of its motions was under the complete control of one or two individuals, who were manifestly more affected by the power developed than the rest. If they willed it to turn round it would do so with great rapidity. At their bidding it would stop, turn round in the opposite direction, stand upon one or two legs, and tip out, by the alphabet, intelligent answers to any questions put to it, the answers corresponding to the thoughts of individuals present. It was asked to give the age of this clergyman. A certain number of motions up and down were made, and then they ceased. On inquiry, before the individual had answered the question whether a right answer had been given, it was found that the number designated was the precise number previously fixed upon by one or more of the controlling minds present, though it was wrong by some eight or ten years. Such were the manifestations obtained for the very purpose of proving Spiritualism false. Who can believe that spirits would produce movements thus to disprove their own favourite system? We might adduce many other cases of a precisely similar character. We should be guilty of infinite folly, then, did we attribute such acts to the agency of disembodied spirits.

XII. A PECULIAR CLASS OF FALSE ANSWERS CONTINUALLY OBTAINED IN THESE CIRCLES EVINCE THE EXCLUSIVELY MUNDANE ORIGIN OF THESE PHENOMENA.

We now call attention to a certain class of *false answers* which are continuously given forth in these circles. Of the false answers in general here obtained, we will speak in another place. We now refer to a particular class only, a class to which we have already alluded, namely, the continuous occurrence of false answers to questions pertaining to subjects well known both to inquirers and to the spirits professedly communicating, and in respect to which a failure of memory, or inadvertent mistake on the part of spirits is not supposable. The following statement of Dr. Bell is but the embodiment of the constant experience and observation of every one, as far as our knowledge extends, who has had any considerable personal experience in the spirit-circles:—

"The 'spirits' of your friends, while they announce to you many most extraordinary facts and truths, even in reply to unspoken questions, fail in many others, where you cannot yield them the charity of having forgotten, or being in ignorance. I do not now allude to the silly tests which many very sagacious persons have put, such as complex questions in mathematics, or in far-off dialects, as if spirits were presumed to be omniscient; or in relation to future events, as if they had the gift of foreknowledge. I mean that when you test your deceased relatives, while they are most free in expressing advice, etc., to you, with such simple questions as involve a recognition of the most marked events of your mutual knowledge, they constantly fail."

Now we affirm that such facts cannot be accounted for, in accordance with any laws of mind known to us, on the supposition that these communications proceed from intelligent beings, good or bad, who are holding intelligent communication with us, and who know whereof they affirm. Much less can they be accounted for on the supposition that they come from the particular class of departed spirits from whom they professedly proceed. No such facts characterize any forms of intercourse between any class of minds in the body. We know very well that the worst liars on earth do not thus falsify. Much less did our venerated parents, when with us in the flesh, as their assumed spirits now do, continuously falsify in regard to subjects well known to us and to them, and when they well knew that the falsehood must be at once detected. Never did such answers come to us from them when they were with us. How, then, can we suppose that such answers proceed from their spirits, when they come to visit and communicate with us, from their "angels' home"? It is impossible to account for such communications, even on the supposition that these communications generally are from fallen spirits. Devils even would not thus falsify.

On the other hand, if these communications are the unconscious echoes of our own thoughts, they could not but have these very characteristics. We ask a question, for example, and then before the answer is given turn our thoughts in some other direction. If the responses follow the current of our thinking at the moment, and are determined by the same, then a wrong answer will be obtained of course, and just the kind of answer that is obtained.

It is upon this one supposition only, that we can, by any possibility, account for the facts before us. A brother, as we have stated in another connexion, asks the spirit of a sister to give the name of their father, which is John, for example, and before the answer comes, his thoughts happen, by the laws of association, to be turned upon that of their brother, which is Thomas. If the answer is determined by the thought in the inquirer's mind at the moment, then Thomas, the name of the brother, and not John, that of the father, will be given, of course. This is the precise character of the false answers continuously given forth as by the spirits in these circles. We say that such facts cannot be accounted for but upon the supposition that these peculiar communications proceed, not from "the spirits," but that they are the unconscious product of the wandering thoughts of the enquirers themselves. We are perfectly sure that spiritualists will never attempt to account for these peculiar facts in accordance with their theory.

XIII. ENQUIRIES MADE FOR THE SPECIFIC PURPOSE OF DETERMINING, NOT ONLY THE LOCATION OF THE CONTROLLING CAUSE OF THESE PHENOMENA, BUT OF THE EXTENT OF THE CONTROL WHICH COULD BE EXERCISED OVER THESE PHENOMENA.

We now refer to a class of experiments which individuals have made for the purpose of determining, not only the location of this cause, but of ascertaining the *kind* and *extent* of control they could exercise over it. It is well known that no spirits, good or bad, will voluntarily render themselves the objects of the contempt and ridicule of those over whom they desire to retain a controlling influence, as the spirits undeniably do over the minds of men in this world. Yet we find among these communications numberless responses obtained for the express purpose of determining, in the first instance, how far they can be controlled, and, in the next, of rendering the whole subject ridiculous. If spirits do respond to inquiries drawing forth such responses, they must do it with a perfect knowledge of the designs of the inquirers, and of the tendency of the answers given to their questions. By no laws of mind can we account for responses given to questions which are put for such a purpose, and when the answers must be known to be adapted, most perfectly so, to secure the intended result and none other. Let us consider a few facts of this class, examples of which are everywhere occurring in these circles. The case of the gentleman in Boston to whom the spirit communicating revealed himself under the name of Miserable Humbug, and affirmed that spirits in the celestial spheres live on pork and beans, and all this in accordance with a previous determination in the inquirer's mind, is already before our readers, and is a case now in point. Let us consider another case of a similar character. When Mrs. Fish was in the state of Ohio, she visited the village of Hamilton for the purpose of multiplying disciples, not to hint a pecuniary motive. Her success, for a time, was wonderful, all who entered the circles being convinced. At length, some ten individuals agreed together to determine, by an experiment, what answers could be obtained from the spirits. They accordingly framed their questions and answers beforehand, and agreed upon a mode of questioning which would not awaken the suspicions of the medium. The departed spirit which responded to the first inquirer, gave his name as "the devil," affirmed himself to have been dead for two years, and to sustain to the inquirer the relation of uncle. The departed spirit which responded to the next inquirer was that of our informant, who was then in the circle. This spirit had been dead for six months, and died of hydrophobia. By this time some of the circle found it impossible to restrain their laughter, when Mrs. Fish remarked that the spirits were probably lying to the inquirers. On being informed of what had transpired, the circle was broken up, and the next morning she left the place. Who can believe that if intelligent minds stood behind this power, and directed its action, they would suffer themselves to be thus trifled with, and would lend their own voluntary agency to render themselves the objects of deserved contempt and ridicule? Yet "the spirits," in any circle on earth, will as readily respond to such questions as to any others, and will become, when the inquirer wills it, and has presence of mind and self-command sufficient to carry out his purposes, the agents of their own infamy or contempt. No limits can be set to the extent to which this power can be used for such purposes. Now we say that depravity itself never assumes such forms, and by no laws of mind can we account for such communications coming from disembodied spirits, either good or bad. If, on the other hand, our theory is true, nothing else could be expected. Just such phenomena, in that case, would appear, and in the very form which they now present themselves; and upon no other hypothesis can such facts, which, in legion forms, everywhere present themselves in these circles, be explained.

Since the child in the family to which we have referred became a medium, and since the communication from the spirit of a living person, supposed by them at the time to be dead, was obtained, the members of the family have been accustomed to amuse themselves by seeing what absurd communications they can obtain, as illustrations of the absolute control which they can exert over this mysterious power. The following may be stated as the results of their experiments and observations; and we have had an opportunity to converse with the family very often since these phenomena appeared, which was in or near the commencement of the year 1854. (1.) Any spirits will answer that they choose to call up. (2.) Any answers can be obtained from any spirits, that they will mentally conceive of and choose to have rapped or written out. (3.) They now obtain, as a general fact, absurd and ridiculous answers, answers indorsed by odd names, because they choose to have such and no others, the answers and names always according with their previous choice. (4.) Nothing is, or can be, more manifest to their minds than the fact that they themselves, and not spirits out of the body, control this force, in all the answers which they obtain. (5.) That control has remained just as absolute since they came to this conviction, as before; since they have utterly repudiated Spiritualism, as when they were sincerely inquiring whether it was true or not. A daughter of ours, when present on one occasion, while the force was being developed, willed secretly that her own name should be designated. This she did for the purpose of determining the real cause of these manifestations. Her name came out accordingly. Would "the spirits" thus disprove their own presence and agency, when, if Spiritualism is true they desire to convince all the world that they alone can originate such phenomena?

XIV. Important evidence obtained from the observations and testimony of individuals who have themselves been mediums.

We now invite very special attention to the testimony and experience of intelligent persons who have themselves been mediums. Facts derived from this source must be regarded as most decisive in their bearings, because such persons have had the best opportunities for examination; and when they have come to the full conclusion that phenomena presented through them are produced by exclusively mundane causes, their opinions and statements must be deserving of the greatest consideration. Among the cases falling under this class, we notice the following:—

We are well acquainted with a very intelligent gentleman, for example, through whom, when the proper conditions are fulfilled, all the phenomena of the spirit-rappings can at any time be obtained. He says that he has no conception that these phenomena are connected at all with any *ab extra* spirit-agency, and that for this reason, that when it is known what answer should be given to any question proposed, the true answer will uniformly be given, and when this is not known, the answer will be right or wrong, just as it happens. These are the uniform characteristics of these communications everywhere. If the inquirer or medium knows what the answer should be, it will be generally right. In all other cases, it has the characteristics of the most uncertain guessing. What facts can with certainty identify any communications as being wholly earthly, and not at all *ab extra* spiritual in their origin, if these do not?

We met some years ago a very intelligent lady who had been a medium, and who had presented such communications as to convince an aged atheist, among others, of the reality of spiritual existences. To us she remarked that when she first became subject to these influences she had no doubt whatever of their *ab extra* spiritual origin, so unconscious was she of any agency of her own in their production. But when she narrowly watched her own mental operations, and marked the perfect and regular correspondence between these phenomena and her own prior mental states, she was led to doubt the whole system of Spiritualism altogether. If all mediums were thus self-reflective, and thus honest, they would all, we venture to affirm, come to the same conclusion.

A scientific physician in the state of Michigan, who has, for a long period, been a writing medium, has, after similar observations and experiments, come to the same conclusion. There is a mystery about the subject, as he stated to our informant, President Fairfield, then of the Freewill Baptist College in that state, which he has never been able to explain. Yet the facts taken together precluded wholly the idea of their spirit-origin. They are too puerile, too self-contradictory and lawless in their character to admit of any such supposition.

The following case we cite from "Rogers' Philosophy of Mysterious Rappings." On many accounts it possesses much interest:—

"Now take the following case, the like of which we have seen in several other instances: Jane A. D., daughter of a physician, had become a 'writing and tipping medium,' and could obtain slight responses by the sounds. She believed herself to be a 'medium' for communications from a deceased cousin, who, with herself, had been passionately fond of poetry. Jane carried on these communications by herself for some time, for her own satisfaction, but mostly as a writing medium. She had not, after some few of the first communications, the slightest doubt of the reality of all this being the work of a pure spirit, until the following circumstance took place. A communication was made of a beautiful stanza of poetry, from what purported to be the spirit of her young friend, and was declared as original. Jane was so much delighted with the remarkable circumstance, and with the perfect sweetness of the lines, that she took them to her father and related the circumstances. He saw that the style of handwriting was that of his daughter's late friend, and was greatly amazed at the mystery. The fact of the identity of the handwriting was not, indeed, to be questioned; and since he knew his daughter to be truthful every way, he determined to examine into the wonderful phenomena. The following evening was, therefore, spent in experiments and conversation upon the subject. Everything was, however, to be kept profoundly secret in the family, as there was so much said in derision of the 'rappers.' 'That night,' says Jane, 'while I was dwelling on those beautiful lines, and my heart was swelling with joy that my own dear parents had become interested in the phenomena, it flashed across my mind that I had either heard or read the same lines before *somewhere.* But I did not wish to think so, and yet I desired to know the truth. It, at last, appeared, to me, fresh in my memory, the very place where and when I had read it. It was while alone and lonely, just after the setting of a beautiful September sun, and the lines were from that sweet poem of Longfellow, 'The Footsteps of Angels':—

> "'Uttered not, yet comprehended,
> Is the spirit's voiceless prayer,
> Soft rebuke, in blessings ended,
> Breathing from her lips of air.'"

No one can wonder that the confidence of this medium and that of her friends, in the doctrine of

Spiritualism, was utterly shaken by such an occurrence. This communication was, undeniably, exclusively mundane in its origin; and yet it bore upon its face all the evidence of an exclusively spirit-origin that any other does, or can do. It came *as* from a spirit. It was positively affirmed by that spirit, whose integrity could not be doubted, to have been original, and it was given in the *handwriting*, not of the medium, but of the individual whose spirit professedly originated it, and directed the hand that wrote it. The medium, too, had no consciousness, at the time, that any thought pre-existing in her own mind had anything to do with the subject. This single case, therefore, utterly annihilates the highest evidence ever adduced by spiritualists in proof of the spirit-origin of these manifestations; for it embodies the most fundamental facts which they ever do adduce for this end. At the same time, it presents the most conclusive proof of the truth of the opposite theory, that which we maintain as the only true one.

A few years since we met with an intelligent clergyman, one to whom we have already referred in another connexion, of the Episcopal Church, who had, for some years, had the phenomena of table-moving and other spirit-manifestations in his own family; himself, wife, and daughter, together being mediums. When these phenomena first appeared in his family, he sincerely believed in their real spirit-origin, and supposed that they could be reduced to scientific principles. After the most careful and extensive experiments and observations, however, he had come to precisely the opposite conclusion. In questioning any spirit, for example, some responses appear to indicate his actual presence. Others which arise in the same connexion, however, utterly preclude such a supposition; the supposition, too, that they do or can come from any intelligent minds out of the body, the communications, from whatever minds apparently proceeding, being often so utterly puerile, self-contradictory, and lawless in their character. "If there is in nature," he remarked, "a nerve fluid whose action accords with our mental states, and commonly with the ordinary random thoughts which run off from the surface of the mind, and these manifestations are the result of such action, they would, in that case, be just what I have found them to be." Now we affirm, without fear of contradiction, that a more striking and accurate description of the character of these manifestations can, by no possibility, be given, and this is most manifestly their real cause. The facts preclude any other supposition.

Of a precisely similar character and bearing is the following fact, which we find in the *North American Review:* "We are confirmed in our belief of the subjective character of these phenomena by a conversation with a highly respectable clergyman, who a few years ago, to his own surprise, found himself a writing medium, and was, for many months, in the frequent habit of writing under this singular influence, without premeditation, often without knowing what he was inditing, or whose name he was going to sign. He at first fell into the popular notion, but became gradually convinced, by the incongruity and absurdity of much he wrote, and by the dreamlike character of the whole, that he had been putting upon paper, not the behest of unseen spirits, but the results of some unexplained mode of his own consciousness."

We adduce but one additional fact connected with the class under consideration. A venerable lady, Mrs. C., of the Society of Friends, in Rhode Island, herself a medium, and who had, for a long time, been a most devoted spiritualist, requested the Hon. Mr. B., a member of Congress, whose wife, the sister of Mrs. C., had died some time before, to sit with her at a table, and receive communications from the spirit of their departed friend and endeared relation. Mr. B., though an unbeliever in Spiritualism, of course complied with the request, and for an hour or two held a very interesting conversation apparently with the spirit referred to. At length Mr. B. asked the following question:

"What did you do with those letters which passed between us before our marriage, letters which I committed to your care some eight or ten years ago, and you promised to preserve? I have searched for those letters in every place where I can even imagine them to be, and have not been able to find them. What did you do with them?" "I burned them," was the reply received. "Why did you do that?" "I thought that no good would come from preserving them," was the reply, "and therefore burned them. And now, as I assure you that I love you as truly and ardently as I did when with you in the body, you will not regret that I burned those letters." Subsequently those letters were found carefully preserved, as promised. The faith of Mrs. C. in Spiritualism itself was of course terribly shocked when this fact was made known. The conversation referred to presented all the evidence of real spirit-intercourse that can be presented in any case whatever, and no spirit could be identified, if that of her sister was not on that occasion. Yet the known character of her sister utterly precluded the supposition that such a reckless falsehood could proceed from her spirit. On the other hand, if the thoughts of the husband really determined the answer obtained, its character was accounted for, and this was the only explanation which the facts of the case admitted. How any individual, in the presence of such facts, can remain a spiritualist, is to us a greater mystery than is involved in any of the so-called spirit-manifestations of which we have ever heard.

XV. Disagreements and contradictions in these communications incompatible with the idea of their extra-mundane origin.

There are forms of disagreement and contradiction among these communications which are utterly incompatible with the idea of their *spirit*, and equally demonstrative of their exclusively *mundane*, origin. Differences of opinion do, on certain subjects, as we well know, obtain among men in the flesh, and, for aught that we know, may obtain among disembodied spirits. There are certain subjects, however, on which minds in the same locality never differ. There is no dispute in America, for example, in regard to any such question as this, whether Boston or New York is located on the Atlantic or Pacific coast. It is upon precisely similar questions pertaining to the spirit-world, that an irreconcilable difference of opinion does obtain among "the spirits." In regard to the *location* of the spirit-circles, for example, the *mode* of living and intercourse among spirits, their relations to other worlds, the *character* of spirits, whether all are good or not, whether evil spirits return to virtue, or eternally progress in sin and misery,—in regard to all such subjects, about which spirits can no more differ than living men can differ about the question whether grain harvests, in these northern latitudes, come in summer or winter, the most contradictory and irreconcilable accounts are given by "the spirits," and by spirits, too, of the highest orders that ever speak to us in these communications. In a spirit-circle in the city of Cleveland, for example, the spirit of Dr. Channing affirmed absolutely, Mrs. Fish being the medium, that there are no evil spirits at all in eternity, and that there is no unhappiness there; that when "the body dies, propensity to evil dies with it, and that *all* of man progresses in happiness." In the same circles another spirit, equally reliable, affirmed, with equal absoluteness, that while the good, in eternity, "eternally progress in goodness, the evil eternally progress in evil." A similar difference and contradiction obtain on all subjects whatever about which the spirits communicate. Let any one read the accounts given by the spirits of Paine and others, and in the publications of Judge Edmonds, about the spirit-circles, and he will perceive at once that here are contradictions which could not obtain among minds speaking from personal knowledge,—the subjects being of such a nature that there can be no motive to deceive, and no essential difference of opinion in regard to them among minds speaking from such knowledge. Just such a diversity, however, could not fail to obtain did these communications contain nothing but the reflections of human opinions on these subjects, and were determined by such opinions.

XVI. False communications which can be accounted for but upon the mundane hypothesis.

The last class of facts which we adduce, are the numberless false communications which are continuously received in these circles, communications pertaining to subjects of which we cannot suppose "the spirits" to be ignorant, and in respect to which it is the height of absurdity to suppose they would intentionally convey false information ; or to subjects about which they would not make positive affirmation if not well informed. Even men in the flesh do not falsify without a motive, and especially when they cannot but know that their falsehoods will soon be revealed. Now "the spirits" have not the common prudence of deceivers among men, in the particulars under consideration. They often, as is well known, give false information in respect to subjects of which it is absurd to suppose them ignorant, and where the error, as real spirits must be aware, will not fail, in a very short time, to come to light. We cannot but know that truthful spirits will not make such communications. They will not profess a knowledge of that of which they are ignorant. They will not assert as true what they know to be false, nor make positive assertions when they cannot but know that they should profess nothing but uncertain guessing. Nor will lying spirits do the same when they cannot but be aware that their attempted deceptions will soon be detected, and confidence in their communications will thereby be annihilated. Precisely such communications as these are continuously given forth in these circles. A friend of ours, for example, once requested a medium, who was then under the immediate control of "the spirits" as much so as any medium ever is, or professes to be, to ask "the spirits" how many gas-burners were then burning in the room where they were at the time. "I do not know," said our friend, "and keep your own head down, so that you will remain ignorant of the real number." On being asked by the medium, "the spirits" gave the number as four. After being requested to decide with perfect deliberation, they adhered to the number first given. The true number was found to have been *five.* The medium, who had been a professed Christian, had just before said that he had given up faith in the Scriptures to follow the higher light of Spiritualism. "There," said our friend to him, "you have rejected that blessed book which has been the light and consolation of the good in all ages, to follow spirits who, when put to the test, cannot count five."

One of the test experiments made by a gentleman in Cleveland, the gentleman to whom we referred in another connexion, was the following: While a circle was being held in an upper room, an individual present was requested to go below, and collect, in a particular place named, any number of individuals, from those known to be in the lower part of the house, that he should choose. When he had been gone a sufficient time, the spirits were requested to give the number of individuals, and their names, who were in the place agreed upon. Five names were rapped out. On inquiry it was ascertained that but two individuals were there. Such questions the spirits are everywhere and always ready to respond to, and for the most part, in doing so, are equally successful in betraying their ignorance and folly. Now, we affirm, from the known laws of universal mind, that no spirits, good or bad, would ever give forth such responses as these. They would, in such cases, not answer at all, or give only correct answers. Yet precisely such communications would, without fail, be obtained if our theory were correct.

In some cases, "the spirits" betray a degree of ignorance, or forgetfulness, which indicates progression in any direction, rather than towards higher and higher intelligence. Some years ago, for example, the whole realm of spirits seemed to have concentrated their efforts upon converting to the faith one of our leading editors. He was overwhelmed with spirit-communications, urging and entreating him to embrace the new doctrine. The spirits compelled the medium to write, and would then give her no rest till their communications through her were forwarded. At length a series of communications were sent him, each signed, "Your uncle." As he could call to mind no such relative who had died, he requested the medium to ask his uncle to give him his name in the communication next presented. The spirit, however, had forgotten his own name.

We will give but one additional illustration. Some years ago, while the people of America were in painful suspense in regard to the fate of an ocean steamer, the Atlantic, and when "hope deferred had made the heart sick" upon the subject, an individual who was desirous of crossing the ocean, and who shrank from doing it while in doubt of the fate of that vessel, entered a spirit-circle to obtain the desired information upon the subject. He was a most confirmed believer in "the spirits," and is, as we are informed, to this day. He inquired of "the spirits" if they could inform him of the state of that vessel. They positively affirmed that they could, and then stated absolutely that, after being destroyed by a terrible conflagration, it had gone to the bottom of the ocean with all on board, with two or three exceptions. These had escaped in a boat, and would probably survive to tell the tale of the terrible disaster. We have all the evidence that this communication came really and truly from "the spirits" that we have that any do. It was obtained in the same circumstances, through the same instrumentality. That it did not come from truth-telling ones is self-evident. That it came not from lying spirits is almost equally manifest from the principles stated above. This last supposition also totally annihilates all confidence in any spirit-communications whatever. The inquirer was in a perfectly honest state of mind. He wished to know the truth on the subject, whatever it was, and nothing else. If one honest inquiry may be answered by a lying spirit, all may be, and all these revelations may be nothing but "doctrines of devils." The supposition is altogether inadmissable, therefore, that real disembodied spirits of any character had anything at all to do with such a communication. This supposition, however, destroys all evidence that any of these phenomena whatever proceed from "the spirits," for this has all the evidence of such an origin that any of them have. Apply this principle to the positive affirmations which are continuously made by "the spirits" in these circles, and the supposition of their *ab extra* spiritual origin is rendered demonstrably false. They are affirmations which truthful spirits cannot, and lying spirits would not, make. On the other hand, they are precisely such affirmations as we should suppose would be made in these very circumstances, were they unconsciously produced by the individuals constituting the circles, and not by spirits out of them. They pertain to subjects about which the inquirers desire to be, and suppose that "the spirits" are, informed, and the answers accord with the mental states, the hopes, fears, opinions, or guesses of those who inquire of them. We must, we repeat, reject the supposition that this class of affirmations has an *ab extra* spirit-origin. Yet the same conclusion which thus forces itself upon us, destroys wholly all evidence that any of these so-called spirit-revelations have such an origin, for all are given forth in the same circumstances and are attended with the same identical evidence of an *ab extra* spiritual origin. How any intelligent persons can sit in these circles and witness the numberless positive affirmations which are there made, affirmations so many of which are known at the time by persons present, and if not then known, soon after ascertained, to be false, and yet suppose that real *ab extra* spirits have anything to do with these communications, is to us a mystery more inexplicable far than is involved in any question pertaining to the origin of these phenomena. A moment's reflection will convince anyone that truthful spirits would not, and could not, give such false answers. They would not, we repeat, profess knowledge when they were ignorant, nor make positive affirmations when they were only guessing, and not very prudently at that. Nor would lying spirits make the same affirmations, unless, a case not supposable, their object was to unmask their character as superlative liars, and thus destroy all confidence in their own communications. Yet these very communications or none others must be received as coming from "the spirits;" for all transpire in the same circumstances, and are attended with precisely the same evidence of an *ab extra* spiritual origin.

We here draw our argument, on this point, to a close. To our mind, the facts which we have adduced, facts the reality of which cannot be disproved, and will not, we judge, be denied, clearly and unmistakably locate the cause of these phenomena, however mysterious in themselves, within this mundane sphere, and as clearly and unmistakably exclude the supposition that that cause is any *ab extra* spiritual agency. We leave the subject with the reader, with the calm assurance that our facts will not be denied, nor our arguments invalidated, nor our conclusions rejected.

CHAPTER V.

TENDENCY OF SPIRITUALISM.

IN discussing the question next in order, *the tendency of Spiritualism*, we assume, first, that we have shown incontestably that all the so-called spirit-manifestations may be satisfactorily accounted for by a reference to exclusively mundane causes, and that to refer the same to any *ab extra* spirit-cause or causes, is consequently a violation of all the principles of science and common sense bearing upon the subject ; and, second, that, by arguments equally incontestable, we have proven that these manifestations are, in fact, produced by mundane and not *ab extra* spirit-causes. The question of *origin* being thus disposed of, we now advance to a consideration of that of *tendency*. This spirit movement is, no doubt, progressive, and progression is the great theme of its advocates. The question before us is, the *direction* of this movement. Progression may be in the direction of evil as well as good,—of darkness, ignorance, superstition, and even of idiocy, as well as upward and onward towards higher light, and more perfect forms of thinking and action. The question, *whence* a thought originates, is not so important as this: what is its character? The tendency of Christianity depends more fundamentally upon what is intrinsic in the truths which it reveals, than upon the mere fact of their origin; though mental harmony with the truth, and faith in its divine origin, are indispensable to its highest efficiency. Suppose that in "the spirit land," as well as in this world, there are myriads of idiotic minds, liars, and villains, and that they have found out a mode of communicating with mankind. Is the mere fact that *spirits* are communicating with us any reason why we should heed their communications, and frame our systems of belief, in regard to time, or eternity either, in accordance with their teachings? We are not to believe every spirit out of the body, any more than every spirit in the body. All spirits alike are to be tried by the same tests. The remarks which we have to make on the topic now before us, will be comprehended under three general divisions—the tendency of Spiritualism to the benefit or injury of mankind, *physically*, *intellectually*, and *morally*.

SECTION I.

Tendency of Spiritualism to the Good or Ill of Mankind Physically.

To show that Spiritualism benefits mankind physically, it must be proved that, in these circles, the health, not of the sick, but of those in a normal physical state, is benefited; and that, by visiting these circles, and subjecting ourselves to the influences there generated, the most perfect forms of physical development may be secured. That which is medicine to the sick, is poison to persons in health. If diseased persons are medicinally benefited by visiting these circles, that is a sufficient reason why individuals in health should avoid those places. We may safely assume that no intelligent individuals of this latter class ever visit these circles with the expectation of thereby lengthening life or of securing to themselves or posterity more perfect forms of physical development. Suppose, on the other hand, that the tendency of the action of the force there generated is to derange the physical system, and to derange it to such a degree as to disturb fatally the normal action of the mind itself. Then, as the masses of persons visiting these circles are in a normal state, mentally and physically, we should be bound to regard the tendency of Spiritualism, physically considered, as evil, and almost exclusively so, and that in a very aggravated degree.

"Catalepsy,"—one of the most terrible of all physical disorders,—"trance, clairvoyance, and various involuntary muscular, nervous, and mental activity," are among the effects attributed by Mr. Ballou to this force, as it acts "in mediums." The reports of our lunatic asylums everywhere disclose the appalling effects of the action of this terrible force in such persons. We once saw a speaking medium when "the spirits" were in him. We have no wish to have the spectacle renewed. We seriously doubt whether "the seven devils" in Mary Magdalen produced in her more revolting physical and mental manifestations than we then witnessed. Those terrible contortions and convulsions of the whole physical system, together with the wild and incoherent utterances,—we have often wished to banish the remembrance of them from our mind. What terrible thirst is often induced in such persons, under such circumstances! A single medium has been known to drink more than a dozen tumblers of water during a single evening. In other instances, the senses are utterly disordered. A tumbler of ginger water, for example, was handed to a medium in the presence of a friend of ours. She affirmed that it tasted like licorice. A tumbler of pure water was then handed to her. It was to her as bitter as wormwood, and so nauseating that she could not retain any portion of it in her mouth. Another medium, a strong man, when on his way to attend his spirit-circle, one of the coldest days of winter, found himself under the influence of this terrible force. He was utterly unable to stand upon his feet, and when subjected to the freezing cold, with his outer garments thrown off, the perspiration ran from him as from a labouring man under a vertical July sun. No wonder that early graves and our lunatic asylums are peopled to such an alarming extent from this class of individuals. We believe this force to be one of the life forces as ordinarily developed in the human system, and, for that reason, a death force when developed unduly, as it is, and from the circumstances of the case must be, in such persons.

Precisely similar effects in kind, though but in few instances in degree, must be produced in those who frequent these circles. A gentleman of our acquaintance, a very influential and devoted spiritualist, told us, some years since, that he received a special message from "the spirits," urging him to devote his time and influence to the promotion of this great cause, he having leisure and means and a liberal education. He accordingly introduced a medium into his own house, for the purpose of carrying out the plan proposed. The effect of frequent subjection to "the spirit" influence, however, was such upon his health, that the spirit of his own father told him that he must send the medium from his house and dismiss the subject from his mind, or his health would ere long be hopelessly prostrated. We state this fact merely in illustration of the physical effects produced by the action of this terrible power upon the human organism ; for such we honestly believe to be its unvarying tendency. Upon many the effect of sitting in these circles is such that it cannot be endured. A friend of ours, after sitting but a short time under such influences, had to be carried from the room, and more than two hours elapsed before she was able to return to her place of residence. A medium whom another friend accidentally met, some years ago, put one hand into one of hers, and placed the other upon the top of her head. Instantly our friend felt a very strong mesmeric force coming over her, she having frequently been subject to it before. We allude to this fact as another illustration of the identity of the mesmeric force and that from which these manifestations immediately result. On the subsequent evening, after she had been seated but a few minutes in a spirit-circle, by the side of the medium referred to, she found her eyes immovably closed, and herself unable to stir or speak. Her limbs became stiff and rigid, and her breathing very difficult, while the pulsation of the heart became perfectly unnatural; the feeling induced in her brain was as if a heavy mass of cold iron or lead had been laid upon it. At length, by the greatest effort, she was enabled to utter a scream sufficiently loud to indicate her condition to those present. She was accordingly taken from the circle, and after a time was restored to her natural state. Such is the effect of this power upon susceptible temperaments. Yet the tendency, in all other instances, is precisely the same, unless (cases of very rare occurrence) they happen to be affected with peculiar forms of disease upon which this force acts medicinally. For ourselves, we should deem it as criminal in us to subject ourselves to its frequent influence, as it would be to habituate our physical system to the continued action of small quantities of arsenic.

A power which acts with such terrible effects upon the physical, and especially upon the nervous, system, cannot fail to disorder, to a greater or less degree, if not fatally, the normal action of the mind. When the physical systems of individuals are so disordered, for example, that they cannot distinguish ginger water from licorice, or pure water from wormwood, which of their senses can we trust on any subject? What court of justice would receive the testimony of such persons in regard to any facts which they may affirm themselves to have witnessed when in such a state? To such individuals the most discordant sounds may possess an angelic melody, and the wildest vagaries of thought all the characteristics of the highest wisdom. These remarks apply, not only to mediums, but to individuals constituting these circles, and apply to the full extent to which they have become subject to the action of this force. When we read the communications there obtained, and find that sensible and even educated persons present regard them as embodying angelic thoughts, we affirm that but one account can be given of such facts, namely, that the minds of such individuals have become so disordered that they cannot distinguish the really beautiful, true, and good, from their respective opposites. The individual, for example, who could not distinguish ginger water from licorice, or pure water from wormwood, supposed herself speaking and acting under the immediate inspiration of the Apostle Peter. As thus inspired, her communications were received by her auditors. Yet when questioned, this apostle thus speaking and thus received, had forgotten the particular feast at which Christ was crucified, the names of the mountains on which Jerusalem was built, and all facts of a kindred character. The audience, however, which attended upon her ministrations, and which was gathered from one of the most intelligent and educated communities in northern Ohio, and was constituted of persons, numbers of whom, to say the least, were by no means void of intelligence, were not at all shaken in their faith in the reality of the Petrine inspiration of the medium, by such manifestations of ignorance. Her incoherent ravings, too, were received as the very height and perfection of inspired wisdom. To us such facts are far more mysterious than any others connected with Spiritualism, and can be accounted for but upon the supposition that mediums and the members of the circles around them are subject to a common mental disorder.

For these reasons we receive, with great caution, and with many and large subtractions, the accounts of very wonderful events, as having occurred in these circles. Such events almost invariably occur when spiritualists, with few or any exceptions, are present, and when the so-called spirit-power is operating with very great force. All these minds are under the influence of one common physically and mentally disordering force, a force which unifies the perceptions and thoughts of those upon whom it acts. A very ordinary event may *appear* to such minds as possessed of even miraculous characteristics. A single sound from some musical instrument is raised in the circle, or a combination of sounds, which, to an ear in a normal state, would grate harsh discord. To minds in the circle it may seem as super-angelic music. A single sound produced on such instrument, by some one in the circle, may subsequently reverberate in those minds as the highest melody proceeding from the object referrred to, when its chords are swept by invisible hands. The mesmerizer throws his handkerchief into the lap of his magnetic subject. To the latter it is a beautiful infant, a bouquet, a golden fringed mantle, a fur boa, or a terrible serpent, just according to the arbitrary imaginings of the former. So, to minds under the influence of the same disordering force, in these circles, some quite common event may successively assume a corresponding diversity of forms, all of which will appear to all these minds, not only absolute, but distinct and separate realities, which they unitedly and honestly suppose themselves to have witnessed. A member of Congress, for example, told us that while in Washington he once had occasion to step into the room of another member, who was a devoted spiritualist, and steady attendant on the spirit-circles, a man of high worth and much political eminence. In the window of that room lay a very beautiful paper-weight, of such a form that the rays of the sun shining through it were deflected so as to form a bright spot upon the wall. The occupant of the room, discovering the luminous spot, said, with much excitement, "I do wish I knew the cause of that light upon that wall. I do *wish* I knew what caused that light." Our friend, who had taken his seat by the window, passed his hand over the object referred to, and the light disappeared. "There," exclaimed the excited spiritualist, "it is gone. I do wish I knew the cause of that light." The hand was removed, and the exciting vision reappeared. "There, it has come again. I do wish I knew the cause of that light." Thus a very common event appears to one from whom the disordering force excited in the spirit-circles has not quite passed away. Let that man return to those places, and there again become subject to the strong action of that force, and what confidence can be reasonably reposed in the validity of any visions which he may have there? The most common events may put on the most miraculous forms conceivable, and, with all integrity, he may testify to their actual occurrence in such forms. No good, but much evil, physically considered, is to be expected to the majority of individuals who frequent these circles. Its physical results surely do not and cannot commend Spiritualism to our high regard.

SECTION II.

Tendency of Spiritualism to Benefit or Injure Mankind Intellectually.

The tendency of Spiritualism to benefit or injure mankind intellectually next requires our attention. In this respect, the highest conceivable claims are advanced in its behalf by its advocates. By it, "life and immortality," "things unseen and eternal," all that it concerns us to know, and all that is requisite to gratify a laudable curiosity pertaining to the future state, are rapped out with the most perfect distinctness before our minds. Under the tuition and guidance of "the spirits," fallen humanity is, at length, to be led out wholly from the dark and gloomy regions of ignorance, error, and superstition, to a limitless millennium of mental light and spiritual illumination. Our purpose is to bring the validity of these high claims to the test of a rigid examination. To have any claims to our regard, and especially to the high regard demanded for it, it must first of all present a *reliable source of information* pertaining to the objects which it professedly reveals. It must also do much for *the advancement of science*, and for *the purification and elevation of our literature.* It is in these three points of light that we shall consider the subject.

Spiritualism not a reliable source of information.

To us, it is a matter of no little surprise that those who seem to glory in nothing but discipleship of "the spirits" have never seriously raised the inquiry pertaining to the *reliability* of those revelations upon the assumed validity of which they are shaping their course, and determining their principles of action for an immortal destiny. Had they raised this one inquiry, and carefully applied those laws of evidence which conduct to a right conclusion in regard to it, we venture the assertion that there is not in the wide world a spirit-circle which would now be visited by any serious inquirers after truth upon the subjects referred to, with the expectation of receiving new and reliable information in regard to these subjects, any more than a circle of known maniacs would be visited for the same purpose.

"The spirits" are presented to our regard as *witnesses.* If they are intelligent, well informed, and truthful witnesses, and we can have evidence of the same, we may wisely and prudently resort to them for information upon subjects on which they may be willing to make communications. On any other condition than the perfect *reliableness* of their testimony, as a source of information, can we be justified, can we be justly freed from the charge of infinite presumption, in basing our belief in regard to the doctrine of immortality, or any other important subject, upon their revelations? Now no form of testimony can be shown to be valid but upon the following conditions: (1.) The witnesses must be *identified,* that is, we must know *who* are speaking, what are their names, and from whence they come. If it is a spirit out of the body, or in the body, that is giving testimony, we must, we repeat, know *who* he is. (2.) The character of the witnesses for truthfulness and veracity must also be fully established. The testimony of none but *truthful* spirits, known and read of all as such, should, for a moment, be admitted, on such subjects as those under consideration. (3.) Equally well established must be the fact that these witnesses are *well informed*, and not at all likely to be *deceived*, on these subjects. (4.) While there is the absence of self-contradiction, in the testimony of each witness, there must be a *substantial* agreement among the witnesses generally, on all fundamental facts. Is the testimony of "the spirits," granting that these communications do proceed from them, of this character? Can Spiritualism be shown to present a *reliable* source of information on the high themes and questions of our immortal destiny? We answer, no; and that for the following reasons:—

1. By no possibility can these witnesses be *identified*. No one can tell, when receiving a communication, from whom it comes, whether it comes from the spirit of man, from an angel, or a devil; much less can he, by any tests which he can apply, determine what *particular individual* is communicating. There is not a solitary test question that ever was put to identify spirits, to which as correct answers may not and are not obtained when put to spirits which are in the body, or never existed at all, as to any others. According to the fundamental teachings of Spiritualism, spirits can read our secret thoughts, and give answers to purely mental questions. Suppose we put a question pertaining to a subject unknown to any

person that is now, or ever has been, on earth, but ourselves and the particular spirit with whom we are professedly communicating. How do we know but that some devil has taken the true answer directly from our minds, or was present when the event referred to occurred, and thus learned about it, and is now answering in the name of the particular spirit invoked, and that for the purpose of perpetrating some fatal deception upon us on other subjects? The voice and manner and even the handwriting of individuals may be and are copied, when it is known absolutely that their spirits cannot be communicating at all. There is, then, no actual or conceivable tests by which the witnesses, in this case, can be identified.

2. Equally impossible is it to identify the *character* of these witnesses, supposing them to be spirits. That wicked spirits do inhabit some of the spirit-spheres, and do communicate with men, in these circles, accords with the fundamental teachings of Spiritualism itself. No principles or tests have yet been discovered by which we can determine the character or motives of any spirit that has ever appeared in any of these circles. All the tests which spiritualists have ever suggested on the subject, are sustained by no form or degree of evidence, on the one hand, and are most self-contradictory and absurd, on the other. It has been said, for example, that "the

pure in heart" will, by an immutable law of spirit-communication, draw spirits of a corresponding character into communication with themselves, while corrupt minds will attract corrupt and lying spirits. If this principle really obtains, as the law of spirit-intercourse, one fact is undeniable, namely, that bad men should, on no account, ever enter one of these circles; for they will thereby become possessed of "seven other spirits" more wicked than ever dwelt in them before, and "their last state be worse than the first." But, then, where is the evidence of the existence of such a law? Nowhere. It is a mere unauthorized assumption brought in to save a desperate cause. Granting that these are truly spirit-manifestations, we have not, and cannot have, the least evidence that any spirits but devils have ever appeared in a single spirit-circle on earth. There is no escaping this conclusion.

3. Not a solitary spirit has ever communicated in these circles, if any have, who does not present all the indications of being a most reckless liar that can be presented by any spirit, in the body or out of it. Take any spirit that can be named, for example, into an orthodox circle, and he will affirm absolutely all the articles of the evangelical faith, and assert, with equal absoluteness, that no spirits but "the father of lies" and his agents, have ever, in any circle, intimated the truth of any opposite sentiment. Change

the character of the circle, and on the same spot the same spirit will deny all that he has previously affirmed, and avow perfectly opposite sentiments. Change the circle a third time, and a hundred times in succession, and this same spirit will reveal himself a stern advocate of all creeds, and of no creed at all, just according to the sentiments of the company in which he happens to find himself at any given moment. We make these statements without reserve, qualification, or fear of contradiction from any well-informed persons in the community. If these are spirits who are speaking to us in these communications, we should be blind, and wilfully so, to undeniable facts, and to all the laws of evidence, if we did not brand the whole mass together as reckless liars, and utterly repudiate their testimony.

4. Not only is the testimony of each witness, in this case, thus self-contradictory, but upon no fundamental questions is there harmony among the witnesses themselves. It is impossible to bring "the spirits" to harmonize in their testimony on any such questions. On all subjects we have an endless chaos of contradictory affirmations. How, then, can Spiritualism benefit mankind by presenting us with a reliable source of information on any subject pertaining to this world or the next? If we follow "the spirits," we must hold all opinions and doctrines, and none at all, as true; we must revere the Bible,

as a revelation from God, and scorn it, as embodying a mass of "cunningly devised fables;" we must hold the doctrine of eternal retribution, and believe, with equal absoluteness, that all men will be saved; we must entertain the opinion that at death "*all* must appear before the judgment-seat of Christ," and that the spirit may wander for centuries, and, for aught that appears, to eternity, in the spirit-land, without seeing Him at all; we must hold that all evil propensities die with the body, and that the soul becomes perfectly pure as it enters eternity, and that it enters this state with the very character which it acquired while in the body, etc., etc. Who would regard such discordant revelations as these —and these are the only revelations of which Spiritualism can boast—a reliable source of information on any subject?

5. The same view of the subject is most fully confirmed by the concessions of leading spiritualists themselves. "The spirits," even according to Swedenborg, who claims the most ample experience upon the subject, "relate things exceedingly fictitious and full of lies. When spirits begin to speak with man," he adds, "man must beware lest he believe them in anything, for they say almost anything; things that are fabricated by them, and they lie; for if they were permitted to relate what heaven is, and how things are in heaven, they would

tell so many lies, and indeed with solemn affirmation, that man would be astonished." He further affirms that they will personate the characters of others, and make all manner of assertions, good and bad, in their names, so that it is perilous to deal with them at all. The following extract from the New York *Tribune* presents Judge Edmond's view of this subject:—

"But Judge Edmonds and his friends themselves acknowledge that spiritual intercourse is attended by numerous difficulties, and that it is hard to say how much credit is to be given to the communications of mediums. In the first place, the mind of the medium, as he says in the introduction to his second volume, lately published, influences the message; then the state of the atmosphere and of the locality have something to do with it; next, the harmony or discord of the mortals who are present. And, finally, many of the spirits themselves have a very decided propensity to mischief and evil. Of the latter, he remarks, 'Selfish, intolerant, malicious, and delighting in human suffering upon earth, they continue the same, for a while at least, in their spirit-home; and having, in common with others, the power of reaching mankind through this newly-developed instrumentality, they use it for the gratification of their predominant propensities, with even less regard than they had on earth for the suffering that they inflict on others. Sometimes it is, with a clearly-marked purpose of evil, avowed with a hardihood which smacks of the vilest condition of mortal society. Sometimes its fell purposes are most adroitly veiled under a cover of good intentions.'

"But how are we to know which is which? How are we to know whether the spirits speaking to Judge Edmonds as Bacon and Swedenborg—often speaking arrant nonsense, and never rising above commonplace—are not some of the veriest wretches whom he has, in his character of judge, committed to the gallows? What authority is there in anything they say, more than in the unsupported dicta of Jack and Gill, or any other inconsiderable mortal? If it be replied that their assertions are to be tested by our reason, or by the evidences to which we commonly resort in forming opinions, we rejoin that, in that event,—supposing them to be intrinsically worthy of attention at all,—they become simply intellectual or scientific data, and are not authoritative religious revelations. They are testimonies to a new experience of life, perhaps, given under dubious and conflicting circumstances,—are to be believed or not, as one may decide after investigation,—but in no sense veritable or commanding disclosures of spiritual truth. They are at best only assertions; and, until the spirits bring us, therefore, a great deal better credentials than they have yet brought us, or furnish us with better teaching than any they have yet furnished, the high claims put in for them cannot be sustained, and we are compelled to treat them as ghostly old quacks or jokers,—as of the classes spoken of by Swedenborg and Judge Edmonds, who delight either to mystify or poke fun at us poor mortals; for, as to their cosmogonies and descriptions of heaven, thus far, they seem to us the merest sentimentalities or stupidities, of which we can find scores that are superior any day on the shelves of any library."

We once put the question to one of the greatest, if not the greatest, of the spirit-leaders in the United States, whether he did regard these revelations as reliable sources of information on the subjects to which they pertain. He frankly replied that he did not. "There is not a medium on earth," he remarked, "whose communications I would commit myself to. If their revelations accord," he continued, "with sound philosophy, I believe them. If not, I disbelieve them." "That is," said a friend who stood by, "you believe these communications when they accord, and disbelieve them when they do not accord, with your own philosophy, and that is all. Every man must act upon the same principle, and we are all left just where we should be in the total absence of all such revelations." The apostle of "the spirits" was silenced, of course, and yet he was devoting his life to one end—the persuading of the public to hang their eternity upon the validity of these very revelations. We doubt whether an intelligent and honest spiritualist can be found who would not give the same answer to the same question as that above given; yet he is acting upon the same principle as the individual referred to.

Some individuals, and of these there are not a few, seem to be perfectly aware of the total unreliability of these communications, and yet maintain their faith in them, by mere dint of will. An individual, for example, sent a question to a certain spirit-circle, pretaining to a subject upon which he desired to obtain information. The question was attended with this singular statement: that if the answer obtained should finally turn out to be incorrect, it would not in the least shake his faith in the doctrine of spiritual communication. This fact, we hazard little in asserting, presents the precise attitude of the minds of almost the entire mass of those who consult and believe in "the spirits," throughout the world. They know that their faith hangs upon revelations whose validity is perfectly unreliable, and yet, by mere dint of will, they continue to believe.

There is one circumstance, which has, no doubt, great weight with many, that should not be overlooked in this connexion. While all the diversity and contradictions above described actually obtain in the teachings of "the spirits," yet a manifest and altogether preponderating majority of these responses actually harmonize in respect to certain important questions pertaining to the invisible world. Now here is a very singular assumption, namely, that amid a perfect chaos of conflicting voices, great questions pertaining to our immortal destiny are to be determined by a majority of responses, and that in total ignorance of the character of the respondents, especially when it is well known that if the majority of the inquirers held the principles of the evangelical faith, the majority of these very responses would be in favour of said principles, and not, as they now are, against them.

Another consideration has still greater weight with other individuals. They are under the firm conviction that they have had revelations from the spirits of departed friends, whose known characters and relations to the inquirers preclude the supposition that from such sources false revelations can come. Now the reliability of these revelations is utterly annihilated by the undeniable fact that even they are just as contradictory as those obtained from any other sources. In the wide and endlessly-diversified and contradictory catalogue of human opinions, there is not one, the mere doctrine of a future state excepted,—if even this be an exception,—which has not been affirmed and denied with the most perfect absoluteness by these the most reliable of all spirit-revelations. The spirit of the sainted mother of one individual affirms to him most positively the truth of all the fundamental articles of the evangelical faith, together with the solemn affirmation that all spirit-responses of an opposite nature are from the father of lies. Another individual obtains from his sainted mother responses equally absolute, and yet, in all respects, of precisely an opposite nature. These are the undeniable facts of the case; and they leave with us no grounds of doubt in regard to the real reliability of these revelations. Besides, the relations of "the spirits" to men in the flesh, as affirmed by these very revelations, and held by all who put faith in them, preclude totally the possibility of our knowing or having any adequate evidence, that we have, or can have, any specific communications with any particular individuals in the spirit-land. "The spirits," we are taught, are witnesses of our external acts, and can read, with perfect accuracy, our most secret thoughts. Hence the responses given in the spirit-circles to purely mental questions. Suppose that an individual in one of these circles inquires if the spirit of his sainted mother is present. That question can be answered by the father of lies as well as by her. Any response to such a question, therefore, is no certain evidence of her presence. A question is now put pertaining to a subject absolutely unknown, as he supposes, to any being but the inquirer, his mother, and God. How does he, how can he know but that the father of lies was present at the time, as a witness of that transaction, or that that fell deceiver is now reading his secret thoughts, and that from information obtained from one or both of these sources is giving forth the very responses which the inquirer vainly supposes can come from no being but the spirit of that mother, and all this for the purpose of ultimate deception on other subjects? The doctrine of spirit-revelations as given forth by "the spirits" themselves precludes totally the possibility of our knowing, or having any reliable evidence in regard to the identity of, the particular spirits from whom any given responses proceed, even granting the reality of such revelations.

Spiritualism has not benefited the world, as far as science is concerned.

But what has Spiritualism done for the advancement of science? It has, according to its own professions, brought to its aid the great leading minds of the highest celestial spheres, and those minds have carried us over the whole field of scientific research, in respect to the finite and infinite, time and eternity, matter and spirit. What is the result of this movement thus far? Have "the spirits" revealed to us any new and important facts in any of these great departments of human thought and inquiry, facts to the elucidation of which the great principles of science are to be applied? Spiritualism has revealed no such facts—not one. Have "the spirits" revealed any new and important *tests*, by the application of which truth may be distinguished from error? This is one of the grand consummations of science. Spiritualism, however, has won no laurels whatever in this important field. Have "the spirits" revealed any new principles, or truths of any kind, which may lead the mind forward in the march of discovery? This is what Bacon did while in the body. He discovered and elucidated great principles of science, under the influence of which humanity has been progressing ever since, and will continue to progress till the end of time. Bacon, after dwelling for centuries amid the illuminations of eternity, has, according to the teachings of Spiritualism, descended from the celestial spheres to instruct humanity once more. What new truth has the spirit of Bacon, or any other spirit, revealed, or even suggested, for the advancement and perfection of science? None at all. We have sounded the depths of these communications for such principles, and have found none. Others have done the same, with the same results.

In no respect is science under obligations to "the

spirits." Bacon, when on earth, and in the body, developed, as we have said, great principles, under the influence of which mind has progressed ever since. Dwelling, as he has been for two centuries, amid the light of eternity, what should we expect from such a mind were he now permitted to re-appear as the instructor of humanity? Would he not enlarge our vision, open new tracks for scientific research, and develop new principles, or more perfectly elucidate those we already know, and thus enable us to advance onward and upward in our search for truth? But the Bacon who now stands, before us as one of the celestial spirits, instead of enlarging our vision, needs to enter some of our primary schools, there to sit among children, and learn the very first principles of science. The same remarks are equally applicable to the entire circle of spirits who are speaking to us in these new revelations.

The spirits are continually harping upon human progression, and require us, as a means to this end, to yield ourselves to their exclusive and absolute guidance. They then reveal thoughts and ideas in dwelling upon which progression can result in but one direction exclusively—towards degrading superstition, mental imbecility, and idiocy. That divine revelation which Spiritualism would supplant, while it says almost nothing on this threadbare theme, reveals ideas and principles, upon which mind cannot but expand eternally, ever developing in that expansion higher and higher forms of beauty and perfection. When the great apostle of Spiritualism, A. J. Davis, was in Cleveland, Ohio, he remarked that the Mosaic dispensation had its origin in the back of the head, the Christian in the top of the head, and the new dispensation, that of "the spirits," in the front of the head; the first being the dispensation of *force*, the second of *love*, and the third of *wisdom*. When we read that statement, we were forcibly reminded of a fact which occurred in the place where Mr. Davis commenced his career as a "seer and clairvoyant." A young woman in that place became possessed of that form of clairvoyance in which, at all times, she could see and describe the internal structure of the human system with all the accuracy of science, and could name the parts affected with disease, and describe their appearance. After listening to a discourse from a certain speaker, she remarked that the mass of brains on one side of his head was much larger than that on the other, and that on one side there was a spot, about as large as a dollar, where there were no brains at all. We were forcibly impressed with the thought that if Spiritualism has its origin in the front of the head, there must be in all foreheads where it originates, and takes up its abode, spaces much larger than a dollar where there can be no brains at all, or anything else which can sustain the weight of scientific truth, or of great thoughts of any kind. Trophies in the field of science and human progression Spiritualism has yet to win.

Spiritualism itself utterly wanting in all the characteristics of a truly scientific movement.

But while Spiritualism has made no additions to science, it is itself, as an intellectual movement, utterly void of all the characteristics of true science. There never was a movement in which there was a greater carelessness, in the following fundamental particulars, than in this, namely, in the induction of facts,—in deducing conclusions from facts induced —and in the assumption of principles. To have introduced this new theory with any rational hope of obtaining for it a permanent influence over the public mind, its advocates should have been exceedingly careful to have introduced, as the basis of its high claims, no statements of facts but such as are sustained by the most reliable evidence. They should have been equally cautious in the deduction of conclusions, and none the less so in the assumption of principles. What has been their course in all these respects?

In the induction of facts, let us say, in the first instance, the history of the world does not present a case of greater carelessness and presumption. Their reliable statements, as far as they have any, are now so intermingled with mountain masses of statements which are utterly unreliable, or greatly exaggerated, on the one hand, and which are the grossest fabrications and impositions, on the other, that, by no possibility, can the public distinguish the one class from the other. We will allude to the following statements as illustrations. The first adduced was given in a public discussion held in Cleveland, on Spiritualism, years ago. During the progress of the discussion, Joel Tiffany, Esq., one of the debaters put forward by the spiritualists, called upon J. M. Stirling, Esq., to state some facts. Our extracts are from a pamphlet published by spiritualists themselves :—

"Mr. Stirling said, I could stand until to-morrow morning stating cases which have come within my own knowledge, of which none connected were aware. I was introduced to a lady in the cars near Boston, and soon ascertained that she was a spiritualist and a medium. She told me that she at one time received a communication, signed by Robert Rantoul, saying that he had an important matter to communicate. It will be understood that his estate was considerably embarrassed. The communication was as follows: 'I wish you to go to such a town where my commissioners are, and inform them that there are certain documents which they need, and the possession of which will save the estate a large amount of money.' She said that having gone to visit these friends, they had saved the estate $30,000. I was present in a circle in this city, in which a lady was told that her mother was sick, and wished her to come home immediately. I said to the circle, 'Now this will be a good test, for none of usk now this.' A few days afterwards the lady received a letter informing her of the sickness of her mother, and summoning her home."

By certificates obtained from the father of Mr. Rantoul, and from the two commissioners and the administrator to this estate, it has been proved before the public that not one farthing has been saved to that estate by Spiritualism. The report that $30,000 has been thus saved stands forth as a gross and shocking fabrication. Suppose, however, that the facts had all been found to have been in perfect correspondence with the statements made by Mr. Stirling. This would not justify him at all in having put them forward, as he did, as proof of the truth of Spiritualism. He is introduced to a female in the cars. Of her character he knew nothing but this, that she belonged to a class who had the highest motives to report themselves as the mediums of the most startling communications. Before any statements coming from such persons were given forth as the basis of such conclusions as were then sought to be established, the individuals above designated should have been written to, and the facts, when presented, given in the most reliable form. The above, however, is a fair example of the manner in which the great leading facts of Spiritualism are obtained and given to the public. Take another statement, given by Mr. Tiffany himself, during the progress of the same discussion.

"I was in a circle in which a communication was received by raps in a language which none of us understood. No one in the circle knew how to separate the letters into words as they were rapped out. They were all joined together. Some thought there was no sense to it, but I was of the impression that there was a connexion in it if anybody knew how to divide the letters properly into words. It was afterwards ascertained to be a communication in French, given by a mother to her son, who could not read French. The intelligence, in this case, was not in the circle, nor could anyone in the circle have any definite idea or thought that it was an intelligible communication."

Now what did this wonderful communication, as subsequently explained to the audience, turn out to be? The speaker, on a subsequent occasion, affirmed it to have been "a lengthy communication." But what was this lengthy essay given in French? A young lad was present in the circle who spoke French, and to the spirit of his departed mother he put a question in that language. The following "lengthy communication," in the same language, was then rapped out in reply, "My pretty little son." We do not say that the speaker meant to deceive us on that occasion. It is not unlikely that the minds of all in the circle were so disordered by the action of the odylic force, that they could not distinguish a long from a short communication. We adduce this case for this one purpose, to show that the real facts of Spiritualism, as far as they exist, are, by the carelessness of its advocates, to use no more offensive term, so intermingled with those which are sheer fabrications or utterly exaggerated, that the one class cannot be distinguished from the other. Myriads of illustrations are at hand to establish the same conclusion. Reports which have gone abroad of what has occurred in the spirit-circles are the most unreliable sources of information conceivable.

Equally careless have spiritualists shown themselves in respect to the *conclusions* which they have deduced from these facts. Individuals, for example, place themselves around a table, and call upon "the spirits" to move the object. The object is moved accordingly. Without inquiring at all whether the same phenomena may not be produced in the same circumstances, when "the spirits" are not invoked, the sweeping inference is drawn, that the truth of Spiritualism has been demonstrated. What a leap in logic does such a conclusion imply! Because a table, when certain conditions are fulfilled, follows the movements of our hands or bodies, what real basis can we find in such a fact for the conclusion that some disembodied spirit must have hold of the object, and be pushing or dragging it about the room? Other objects begin to perform some crazy antics, and we are called upon to infer that the room about us is filled with spirits. We may justly apprehend, if men continue long to reason thus, that posterity will say that in our day, logic, if nothing else, "had fled to brutish beasts, and men had lost their reason."

A similar want of scientific care has characterized this entire movement, in the *assumption of the principles*. The whole movement has, for example, been based upon one grand error, namely, the assumption that if the leading facts set forward by the spiritualists were admitted, the theory itself is established. Now this assumption ought to have received, at the outset, a most careful and rigid examination. But no such examination was ever given it. Never were men more confounded than were the spiritualists at Cleveland when they were told, at the commencement of the discussion above referred to, that their facts were admitted, and their conclusion deduced from them denied, and that on this single point we should join issue with them. For such an issue they were not at all prepared. The connexion between their facts and conclusions they had never examined. Had they carefully compared their facts with others equally well authenticated, which result from exclusively mundane causes, they would have perceived clearly that they had no facts which were not perfectly similar and analogous to those which result from such causes, and consequently none which present the least positive evidence of an *ab extra* spirit-agency. Under the influence of the assumption under consideration, Professor Ware, of Philadelphia, became a spiritualist. Professor Faraday had made certain experiments to prove that tables are moved by means of the pressure of the hands upon their surface. If he had established this fact, he would have annihilated all evidence in favour of Spiritualism, as far as this class of facts is concerned. Suppose he had failed to do this, it by no means follows from hence that Spiritualism is true. If tables are not moved by muscular pressure, it by no means follows that spirits do it. There is in such a fact no ground whatever for such an assumption. This, however, was the assumption of Professor Ware. He, consequently, having proved by the most decisive experiments that tables are not moved by mediums through this one means, became a spiritualist throughout.

The same remarks are equally applicable to all the basis principles on which this movement rests. Not one of them can sustain a rigid scientific examination for a single hour. Spiritualism has not only not made any contributions to science, but has, from its origin, in its process of self-development, violated all the principles of true science.

Spiritualism has done nothing to improve the literature of humanity.

But what have "the spirits" done for the benefit of humanity in the department of literature? Have they elevated the tone of thinking and utterance among us? Have they shadowed forth, through the creations of the imagination, the beautiful, the true, and the good, in more perfect and sublime forms than we had before? The elements of thought entering into the productions of "the spirits" ought surely to be altogether of a higher order; and these elements should be blended into higher forms of beauty and perfection than characterize mere mundane human productions. The spirits have tried their hands in almost every department of literature, such as music, poetry, fine writing, and even painting. As high as the celestial spheres are above the earth, so high should be their productions above those of men in the flesh. Is it so? Are "the spirits" better poets, better painters, better composers in music, and better writers, than our Miltons and Shakespeares, our Raphaels and Angelos, our Hadyns and Mozarts, and our Burkes and Irvings? Unless they are, no credit is to be awarded them in the department of literature. On the other hand, their productions tend most powerfully to degrade and debase humanity, by degrading and debasing our conceptions of immortality. We affirm, without fear of contradiction, that the plane of thinking and utterance presented by Spiritualism, is not only not above, but far below, that of humanity in this mundane sphere. For ourselves, we would hardly be willing to "loose, though full of pain, this intellectual being." Yet we would infinitely prefer annihilation to an eternity with "the spirits," if Spiritualism has given us a true revelation of the thinking and acting which obtains among them. We do not say that no examples of good poetry and fine writing may, in instances very few and far between, be found in the spirit-productions. But we do say that their general, and almost exclusive, character is such that humanity ought to be ashamed of them, if they were presented as the productions of men in the flesh, and in a normal mental state.

SECTION III.

Moral Tendency of Spiritualism.

The moral tendency of Spiritualism now claims our attention. As far as this department of our subject is concerned, we have no hesitation in affirming that the spirits have revealed no *new* moral principles of any kind. Nor have they disclosed any new applications of principles already known. They have disclosed no new sanctions to the idea of duty, nor have they encircled it with any new and more attractive motives to obedience. Before any utterances even professedly came to us from "the spirits," we had a system of morality absolutely perfect in itself, and equally universal in its applications; a system illustrated, exemplified, and commended to our regard by the instructions and example of One who knows perfectly "what is in man" and what fallen humanity needs, and in whose character every conceivable and possible form of virtue is visibly embodied in absolute perfection; a system, too, enforced upon us by motives and sanctions of infinite and eternal weight; a system, finally, to which absolutely nothing can be added, and from which nothing can be taken away, without visibly marring its beauty and perfection. Spiritualism comes in professedly as a higher light, to supplant "that dearest of books that excels every other," the only book that embodies this divine system of moral legislation. Yet every principle of duty which it does enforce, it copies, and very poorly too, from this rejected volume. At the same time there is intermingled in the moral teachings of "the spirits" principles of the most pernicious tendency. Let us consider a few facts and examples which tend to reveal and expose the moral tendency of Spiritualism :—

1. The known character of a large portion of the mediums, to say the least, does not present the system to our regard as tending to any moral good. If spirits are communicating to us, in these manifestations, they must know the character of their mediums, being not only able to witness their external acts, but to read their secret thoughts and purposes. If men in the flesh are known by the company which they keep, spirits must be known by the mediums through whom they voluntarily communicate. Spirits cannot preserve a character for moral purity when they will continue to communicate with us through persons whose character we and they know to be bad ; and nothing can be of a worse moral tendency than for circles to sit around such persons with the idea that through them communications are being received from spirits inhabiting the celestial spheres. The spirits surely have not been very careful to manifest their regard for moral

purity in the selection of their mediums. One such individual, for example, they will never communicate through, excepting when he is drunk, and then they are ready to use him for that high purpose. Others, in some cases, are known to be so morally impure as to exclude them totally from virtuous society, excepting when virtuous individuals gather around them in these circles, as the favoured mediums of "the spirits." One of the grand themes of spiritualists is the moral corruptions of the Church and ministry. They themselves, however, have not the effrontery to insinuate that the Spirit of God dwells with and communicates to men through persons thus corrupt. Yet these very men are loudly calling upon us to encircle mediums more depraved than they dare represent the Church to be, and to encircle these persons for the purpose of communing, through them, with the pure spirits from heaven itself. Nothing can be of a worse moral tendency than such associations.

2. The character of "the spirits" themselves, as they stand revealed before us, renders all our imaginary intercourse with them, as our intellectual and moral teachers and guides, of the most pernicious moral tendency. When we select for ourselves teachers and guides whom we know to be morally corrupt, or when we remain blind to the moral corruptions of such persons after their character stands revealed to us, we are subject to the most debasing

and pernicious moral influence conceivable. What is the moral tendency of Spiritualism in this one respect?

In general, we would remark, that *not one of "the spirits" bears the marks of even common honesty among men in the flesh.* There is not one of them who, when put to the test, will not make *false assertions* in respect to subjects in regard to which real spirits must know the truth, that will not *profess* absolute knowledge when their answers reveal them as profoundly ignorant, and will not make positive assertions when real spirits must know that they are only guessing with a perfect uncertainty in regard to the result, and all this in circumstances in which they must be aware of the fact that their falsifying will infallibly be detected. Now common liars, even among men, are not in any way guilty of such flagrant conduct. While, therefore, it would be very hasty in us to say that "all men are liars," it is using very mild language indeed to say that all "the spirits" cannot be anything else. What should we think of men who should be constantly making the false utterances which "the spirits" are in all spirit-circles throughout the wide world?

3. We affirm that meeting in these circles is adapted to generate influences and tendencies which naturally prompt to the worst sentiments and to corresponding actions, and finally to draw from

"the spirits" a similarly licentious morality; the immutable law of their teachings being to sanctify by their authority the sentiments, whatever they may be, of the circles which entertain them as teachers and guides. For men and women to get together in circles, and there, that spirits, they know not whom, and coming they know not from whence, may take the most complete control of their mental and physical powers, divesting themselves as far as possible of all independent thought or purpose, tends to but one result—to banish rational thought, and to impart to the sensual in man the most full and controlling development, and finally to prepare the mind to receive the most senseless puerilities as the perfection of wisdom, and the most licentious principles and sentiments as the highest and purest morality.

This we affirm to be the certain *tendency* of this mission of "the spirits," a tendency in which their moral character, supposing them to be real substantialities, is being distinctly unmasked. For ourselves, we would as soon inhale the malaria of our brothels and pest-houses as a means of moral and physical health, as subject ourselves to the teachings of "the spirits" as a means of intellectual and spiritual growth and development.

Summary statement of the tendencies of Spiritualism.

Spiritualism, then, we regard, with very few and slight exceptions, as, in its fundamental tendencies, "evil, and only evil continually," and that for the following reasons, among others:—

1. With the exceptions named, its medicinal effects in a few forms of disease, it tends to no form of good to humanity, physical, intellectual, or moral.

2. Subjection to the influences generated in these circles very strongly tends to a great, and in many instances fatal, derangement of the physical system of those in health, and to a corresponding derangement of their mental powers.

3. While it tends to unsettle our faith in a revelation absolutely sufficient and reliable in regard to all questions pertaining to human duty and destiny, Spiritualism induces a reliance for information on the greatest of human concernments,—questions pertaining to God, duty, immortality, and retribution, —upon sources the most unreliable and deceptive conceivable.

4. It tends to abstract and withhold our regard from all that is really great, beautiful, true, and good, and to generate an absorbing interest in the most childish subjects, and the most puerile and senseless forms of thought.

5. It tends, in the strongest manner, to degrade

and limit the action of the human mind, by giving to these senseless puerilities the greatest influence over it, in consequence of inducing the belief that they are the high forms of thinking descended to us from the high intelligences of the universe. Nothing but this one idea—the origin of these spirit-productions—has saved them hitherto from the universal contempt and ridicule of the world; and this is what imparts to them their great power to degrade and debase human thinking just as far as these productions become objects of public interest.

6. It presents, while it tends to nothing good, the greatest facilities for artful and unprincipled men and women to practise the grossest and most dangerous deceptions upon the public, and holds out to such persons the most persuasive motives to perpetrate such criminalities. To gain the greatest celebrity and influence, individuals of this class must become mediums of the most wonderful manifestations, physical and mental. Hence the so frequent resort to deception and imposition, on the part of mediums; and there is no place so favourable to the perpetration of such crimes as the spirit-circles.

7. While Spiritualism has already begun to develop the worst and most debasing moral principles that the seethings of human depravity have yet thrown upon the surface of society, the intrinsic

tendencies of the system render it certain that this is but the beginning of what is yet to be.

8. The influences naturally and necessarily generated in these circles, tend ultimately, with an unerring certainty, to secure an open and *unblushing* conformity to those principles.

Such is an honest statement of an honest estimate on our part, of the real tendencies of this system, as it now stands before the public. We leave the portrait to speak for itself.

CHAPTER VI.

MISCELLANEOUS TOPICS.

A FEW topics of a miscellaneous character, but which have an important bearing upon our present investigations, have been reserved for a distinct and separate consideration in the present chapter. The principles which we have elucidated will be found to be quite extensive and important in their applications. Through them many facts which have hitherto appeared utterly mysterious and inexplicable, admit of a ready and consistent explanation. We will specify a few of these facts, as examples.

SECTION I.

Special Facts connected with Spiritualism.

There is a certain class of what may be denominated special facts connected with these spirit-manifestations, facts upon which very special dependence is placed by spiritualists in establishing the claims of their theory, and which consequently demand a particular notice before closing our discussion of this subject. Speaking mediums, for example, will sometimes copy the manner and voice of persons they never saw, persons now dead. Writing mediums copy, in a similar manner, the handwriting of such individuals. Individuals, in these circles, and after having been subject to the influences there developed, have peculiar *tactual* impressions, as of individuals taking them by the hand, or grasping or affectionately touching their limbs, etc. In other instances still, spirits stand revealed apparently in visible form to mediums and others, and, as it seems to them, hold audible conversation with them. Finally, some mediums speak and write in languages with which they are totally unacquainted. Now we affirm in general that no argument can be legitimately deduced from such facts (their reality being admitted) in favour of Spiritualism, for the obvious reason that precisely similar facts occur from known mundane causes. Here, as we have already observed, lies the great error of spiritualists in all their facts and reasonings. They have entirely overlooked the fundamental and undeniable principle, that they must adduce facts which never result from the action of exclusively mundane causes, before they can infer, as even probable, the conclusion of an *ab extra* spirit-agency in the production of any phenomena in the world around us. Let us more particularly examine the different classes of facts above referred to.

Copying the voice, manner, and handwriting of individuals.

In regard to the class of cases in which mediums imitate, more or less accurately, the voice, manner, and handwriting of persons they have never seen, we remark that no argument can be adduced from such facts in favour of Spiritualism, for the following reasons:—

1. In the spirit-circles themselves these phenomena do occur, when no spirits at all, and especially the spirits supposed, can be present. The case cited above, which occurred in Cleveland, is a very striking and conclusive example of this class of facts. The manner, voice, and forms of expression of the young man are quite peculiar and unique; yet they were all so perfectly imitated by a total stranger, and that a female, that it seemed to his mother that her son stood directly in her presence, that son at the same time being not dead, but alive. No one also will have the credulity to suppose that the medium, a young lady in Boston, imitated the handwriting of her cousin through the influence of the spirit of that individual, or of any other disembodied

spirit. That which is done without the presence and agency of spirits, can never, without a violation of all the laws of correct reasoning, be adduced to prove their presence and agency.

2. These same phenomena occur under the influence of exclusively mundane causes, being the not uncommon facts which attend the action of the odylic force, as developed in cases of mesmerism and clairvoyance.

3. It would be an exception to the law which controls the action of this force, an exception for which no account could be given, did these facts not occur in connexion with these manifestations, supposing spirits to have no connexion with them.

Tactual impressions.

Precisely similar remarks apply to all the facts coming under the class of *tactual impressions.* The mother referred to, as soon as she came under the influence of the force developed in the spirit-circle, had the same sensations that she would have done had her hand been grasped by some friend in affectionate salutation; yet no spirit was there. A gentleman who had had great experience of the action of this same force, told us that on waking from sleep at one time, a sleep which occurred after he had been subject to the strong action of that force, all consciousness with him was confined exclusively to his right arm. He at first honestly supposed that his own body was that of another person lying by his side, and when he took hold of his own left hand, he supposed he had grasped that of another individual. These tactual impressions are, of almost all others, of the least weight in favour of Spiritualism. If just such impressions were not experienced in these circles, by those who subject themselves to the influences there generated, the facts of Spiritualism would be more unaccountable than they now are. If these impressions are conclusive for the presence and agency of the spirits of men as the cause of such phenomena, the sensations of persons in delirium tremens, and when affected with other forms of disease, are equally conclusive for the presence and agency of the spirits of serpents crawling over and encircling their bodies.

Seeing spirits.

But spiritualists proclaim, that mediums and others have at times, what seems evident to them at least, a direct and immediate *vision* of spirits, of their form, size, and complexion. That they have such visions we have no disposition to doubt or deny. The question for us to decide is, are these visions valid for the reality of their supposed objects?

That they are not, we argue from the following considerations :—

1. Many of these visions are of such a character as to preclude the supposition that they can be real perceptions of objects external to the organism of the percipient himself, and this class of visions must be held as valid if any are. Judge Edmonds, for example, affirms, that the spirits which he has seen are from three inches to twenty feet in height, the largest that he has seen being a majestic and well-proportioned female twenty feet high ; that he has seen spirits who have been eighteen thousand years in the celestial spheres, and yet retain the form of monkeys, while others have hoofs and horns, such as he has seen in pictures. This is what he stated on his western tour, in 1854, and his visions are just as palpable and valid as those of any other medium or spiritualist. Any persons who credit such visions as these, we shall not stop to argue with. They are entirely beyond the reach of reason and logic both.

2. Precisely similar visions occur when we know absolutely that spirits are not seen at all, because the spirits which do appear, if any do, are actually alive, and in the body, and at great distances from the percipient, when the visions occur. We shall hereafter, in another connexion, adduce a very striking case of this kind, a case in which a mother

when wide awake saw the spirit of her son, was addressed by him, and spoke to him in reply, and yet neither that spirit nor any other was present at all, as an object of vision, the son being at that very moment alive, and about sixty miles distant from the mother. The perception, in this case, was as distinct and palpable as in any that can be named. The mere fact that persons appear to themselves to see spirits, is therefore no certain evidence that spirits are present as objects of perception.

3. Precisely similar and equally distinct and palpable visions are well known to attend certain forms of disease, and also the action of certain medicinal substances introduced into the physical system, and that when no one has the folly to suppose that spirits are present as objects of perception. We have only to refer to the journals and productions of medical science to find the most abundant and absolute verification of the above statements. How absurd and unphilosophical it is, then, to refer to this same kind of visions as proof of the presence and agency of spirits in these so-called spirit-manifestations!

4. It is perfectly common for persons, under the action of the very force developed in the spirit-circles, to have visions, perfectly distinct and palpable, of objects which have no existence whatever.

The mesmeric and clairvoyant subject, for example, sees a meeting-house, a mountain, lake, ocean, or river; a man, angel, or devil; a serpent, a centaur, or spirit, and all with the greatest possible distinctness, just in accordance with the mere *imaginings* of the mesmerizer. On the supposition, therefore, that spirits have no connexion whatever with these so-called spirit-manifestations, it would be an exception to a general law, an exception for which no account could be given, if precisely the visions under consideration did not constitute a somewhat prominent portion of the leading phenomena of Spiritualism. Of the validity of its high claims, they present not the least shadow of evidence.

SECTION II.

Phenomena of dreaming, and premonitions of future events.

There are cases in which persons in sleep seem to have a direct and immediate vision of objects at a great distance from them. A case of this kind was, several years since, reported in the Cincinnati papers, as having ocurred in that city. A lady who had a very endeared brother in California, as she fell asleep, saw him in his log cabin rise suddenly and very carefully from his bed, and having girded on his weapons, look with an intense gaze at a certain opening in the wall at the head of his bed. Soon a hand holding a dagger was seen passing in through that hole, and passing on silently till the point of the weapon was directed to the spot where the brother had been lying down, a deadly thrust was given. The brother, in the mean time, with a single stroke of his bowie knife, completely separated the arm from the body without. A terrible cry was heard, and the brother, rushing out of the cabin, dragged in the body of the assassin, who was in the last agonies of death, in consequence of having shot himself with his other hand. Such, in substance, was the vision which was related by the sister the next morning, and subsequently became a matter of interesting conversation among her friends. A few weeks subsequent, she received a letter from her brother revealing to her the fact that on the very night in which she had the vision, the identical scene, in all particulars, as it then presented itself to her mind, actually occurred in his cabin. Whether this is an authentic case or not, and we see no reasons whatever to call in question its authenticity, facts of a precisely similar character do arise, and this case may consequently be taken to represent the class. Shall we regard this as a mere accidental coincidence, or an actual vision of what did occur? We take the latter supposition. How shall we account for the facts on that supposition? The brain of the sister, as we suppose, during sleep, came under the influence of the odylic force, and at the same moment happened to be in odylic rapport with the scene referred to, or more correctly, perhaps, with the brain of the brother. A vision of the scene, on that supposition, could not, from the nature of this force, but have occurred. This perception would have occurred had the individual been awake or asleep. The distance of the scene from the percipient made no difference whatever. In all ages, dreams of this kind have sometimes occurred, and in all cases, excepting when supernaturally induced, unquestionably from this cause.

We take the following case from "Rogers' Philosophy of Mysterious Rappings":—

"Rev. Joseph Wilkins, an English dissenting minister, relating the case of himself, says: 'Being one night asleep, I dreamed that I was travelling to London, and, as it would not be much out of my way, I would go by Gloucestershire, and call upon my friends.' Accordingly he seemed to have arrived at his father's house; but, finding the front door closed, he went round to the back, and there entered. The family, however, being already in bed, he seemed to ascend the stairs and enter his father's bedchamber. He found him asleep; but, to his mother, who seemed awake, he said, as he walked round to her side of the bed, 'Mother, I am going a long journey, and am come to bid you good-bye;' to which she answered

'Oh, dear son, thou art dead!' This, understand, was but a dream, to which the gentleman at the time attached no importance.

"He was, however, greatly surprised when, soon after, he received a letter from his father, addressed to himself, *if alive*, or, if not, to his surviving friends; begging earnestly for immediate intelligence, since they believed him dead. For that on such a night (that on which their son had his dream) he, the *father*, *being asleep*, and *Mrs. Wilkins, the mother*, being awake, she had distinctly heard somebody try the fore-door, which being fast, the person had gone round to the back, and there entered. She had perfectly recognised the footstep to be that of her son, who ascended the stairs, and, entering the bedchamber, had said to her, 'Mother, I am going a long journey, and am come to wish you good-bye.' Whereupon she had answered, 'Oh, dear son, thou art dead!' Much alarmed, she had awakened her husband, and related what had occurred, assuring him that it was not a dream, for that she had not been asleep at all.

"Mr. Wilkins remarks that this singular circumstance took place in the year 1754, when he was living at Ottery; and that he had frequently discussed the subject with his mother, with whom the impression was even stronger than on himself. *Neither death nor anything else remarkable ensued*; and he had no idea of a journey."

To us, the explanation of this fact, whose authenticity cannot properly be doubted, is quite easy and manifest. When two minds, or rather brains, happen to be in strong odylic rapport, the mental states of one are reproduced in the mind of the other. Distance of locality makes no difference whatever. In this case, the brains of the mother and son were in this relation, and hence the vision of the latter in a dream became an object of perception to the former when awake, just as the *imaginings* of the mesmerizer become preceptions in the mind of his subject.

In the same manner the brains of two individuals, when both are asleep, and at a great distance from each other, may come into odylic rapport with each other, so that the mental apprehensions of one may thereby be reproduced in the mind of the other, and thus each have the same vision or dream at the same moment. We received, several years since, from a gentleman whose testimony no one acquainted with him will doubt, a statement of an affecting fact of this kind which occurred in his own experience. When a youth, he had a pair of twin brothers whom he most tenderly loved. At length one of them died. His heart was then intensely entwined around the other, little Freddy, as he called him. At one time, when he was some fifteen or twenty miles from home, employed as a clerk in a store, he had in his sleep the following vision. He thought that at night he approached the front door of his father's residence, and on attempting to open it, found it fastened. He then went round to the back door and entered into a large kitchen, in a remote corner of which was a recess where his parents were accustomed to sleep. The room, as he thought, was at the time lighted up by a small fire which was still burning. As he entered the room, his mother extended her arms towards him, and exclaimed, "Oh, William!" As he came to her, and they were locked in each other's arms, she said to him, "Freddy is dead!" They then wept together, while the arms of each were encircling the other, for a long time, till, from excess of grief, he awoke, and found his pillow drenched in tears. About one o'clock in the afternoon of that day, his cousin drove up to the door. As they met, the young man exclaimed, "I know what you have come for. Freddy is dead." "Yes," was the reply, "Freddy is dead, and I have come for you." After he had been home a little while, his father said to him, "Your mother had a very singular dream last night. She thought that you came to the front door, and finding it fastened, you came round by the back door, and entered our room. As you entered, she extended her arms towards you, and exclaimed, 'Oh, William!' You came to her, and as each was encircled in the other's arms, she said to you, 'Freddy is dead,' and thus embracing each other, you wept together for a long time." The same identical vision had, as nearly as it could be ascertained, at the same time passed before the mind of the mother and the son, though they were separated at a distance of some fifteen or twenty miles from each other. People, if they choose, may call such events mere chance coincidences. We judge differently. We think that there must have been, at the moment, a medium of communication between those two minds, —the very one of which we are treating; a medium so relatively developed between them, that the thoughts of the one were reproduced in the other. To us, such facts, which, in some instances, do characterize human experience, admit of no other explanation.

Analogous facts of common occurrence in every-day life.

An invisible force which pervades all nature around us, and whose influence we are constantly experiencing, may not be recognised as present at all, excepting in its most powerful and startling occurrences. Of this, electricity may be alluded to as an example and illustration. Our physical system is no doubt continuously pervaded by electric currents, as is nature in its entireness all around us. Many events, also, are continually occurring around us, indicative, to the careful observer, of its presence and action. Its presence, however, is not distinctly recognised, till we witness some of its more startling phenomena, as in the thunderstorm. The same holds true of the odylic force. All nature is instinct with its presence and influence, and we are continuous spectators of its ordinary phenomena. From all the forces in nature, we think that it is distinguished by this one striking peculiarity: the *direction of its activity,* the proper conditions being fulfilled, *is as mental states, and is determined by the same;* and this, too, while, as an attractive and repulsive force, it acts with great power upon all other objects in nature. For ourselves, we believe, and we suggest this for the consideration of scientific men and of the public generally,—we believe, we say, that in the human organism it is the medium of voluntary muscular action, as well as of sensation. There must be in that organism some such force, a force which, while its own action accords with mental states, and is determined by the same, controls, also, in consequence of its peculiar properties, the muscular system, and thus becomes the immediate cause of all voluntary motion in the physical organization. This we believe to be none other than the odylic force of which we have been treating. When it is not sufficiently, or when it is excessively, developed in that system, we then have the various forms of cramp and convulsions, and also nervous developments. When developed in certain relative degrees in the organisms of two or more individuals, then the mental states of one are reproduced in the minds of the others. Where people are much together, in the ordinary intercourse of life, as in families, it becomes spontaneously developed between them to such an extent that they are often thinking each other's thoughts, or the thoughts of one are reproduced in the minds of the others. The father, for example, when sitting in the family circle, gives utterance to a certain thought. Nothing has been said before to lead to it, or to suggest it to anyone. Yet the mother and others remark, "I was just thinking of that very thing myself." Such facts occur so frequently, and in such connexions, as to preclude the supposition that such identity of thought, among so many persons, at such moments, is the result of mere accident. There must be some hitherto unrecognised medium of intercommunication by which the thoughts of one mind are reproduced in others. The hypothesis before us gives us such a medium, and thus explains such phenomena. An individual with whom we were once familiar has been separated from us for years, and for a long period has been totally out of our thoughts. He at length returns to our neighbourhood, we knowing nothing of the fact. As he comes within a certain distance of us, he suddenly and inexplicably becomes to us an object of distinct thought and remembrance. When he comes into our presence, we inform him that we were just before thinking about him, though he had not been in our minds before for years. Of more frequent occurrence are such facts, in common experience, relative to individuals who have been separated but short periods from each other. The common recognition of such facts among all classes of the community, has, as is well known, given rise to the old and somewhat vulgar maxim, that "the devil is always near when we are speaking of him." The maxim reversed would, no doubt, be more true, to wit, we are speaking of him when he is near, and for that reason. Facts which are so general, and so uniform in their character, in human experience, must, as we judge, have a common cause, and that cause must be something else than mere chance coincidence. We think that cause to be this: when individuals come into the vicinity of each other, the odylic relations between them not unfrequently happen to be such that the thoughts of one are reproduced, to a certain but limited extent, of course, in the mind of the other, and thus the thoughts of one are turned to the other. Thus we have these common facts of human experience. A moment's reflection will convince the reader that there is nothing incredible in such a supposition. The dog, for example, passes along where his master and many others had passed hours or days previous. The animal immediately distinguishes the track of his master from all the others, and thus traces him out. Such facts necessitate one of two conclusions. Either something passed from the organism of the master to the objects upon which he trod, and remained there till, and no doubt after, the time referred to, or owing to peculiarities of physical state and constitution, a cause in that organism developed in the objects touched, a peculiar force not developed to so great an extent before, and this force passing from the organism to those objects, or by contact of the organism developed in those objects, was the cause of the peculiar effect upon the animal, an effect by which the latter was enabled to follow the track of the former, and trace him out. Of the truth of one or the other of these suppositions there can be no doubt. Now if a mere momentary contact may produce effects from which such results arise, is it at all incredible that from the organisms of individuals, when in a certain vicinity to each other, and when certain conditions are fulfilled, influences should go forth from one to the other, by which common sensations shall be induced in the minds in those organisms, sensations through which the same thoughts shall be induced, at the same moment, in each mind alike? To us nothing is more reasonable than such a supposition, and nothing more accordant with the analogy of known facts in the world around us.

Premonitions of future events.

There are cases in which individuals have premonitions of coming events, premonitions which can hardly be regarded, with a show of reason, as accidental creations of the imagination which, by mere accident, happen to be true. We need not specify cases. It is enough to say that they have been matters of more or less frequent occurrence in all ages of the world. A gentleman, for example, had a vision of the shipwreck of a vessel on the coast of Hindostan, a shipwreck in which his own son was lost. Months subsequent to the vision, the events foreshadowed all occurred in exact accordance with the vision referred to. Yet the father was at the time in utter ignorance of the scenery where the event occurred, and of all the facts of the case. If our view of the nature and action of the odylic force be correct, the occurrence of such foreshadowings is no great mystery, but an event which is to be expected as a matter of occasional experience in the history of the race. When the brain happens to be in odylic rapport with the *causes* on which the occurrence of any particular event depends, the mind then has a vision of such events, however future, for the same reason that when in the same relations with distant objects it has a vision of the same. No person has as much reason to expect any such events in his own experience, as he has to expect to die from a stroke of lightning. Yet their occurrence in instances few and far between, in the experience of some individuals in a nation, should not be a matter of wonder or disbelief. Such, we are free to say, is our view, after a careful examination of facts.

SECTION III.

Phenomena of Ghost-seeing and Haunted Houses.

Had the son, in the case above stated, died in connexion with that dream, as it no doubt has happened in other instances of a similar nature, who would have doubted that the spirit of that individual had appeared to his mother? Yet undeniably no ghost did appear in this instance. The fact, then, that the spirit of one person is thought to appear to another individual, just at the time of the death of the former, or at any other period, is no certain indication at all that any spirit whatever is present as an object of vision. The vision may have been, and, till we have positive proof to the contrary, must be held to have been, a mere mental hallucination occasioned by the fact that the brain of the person dying happened, at the time, to come into odylic rapport with that of the subject of the vision. The fact, too, that persons have visions as of spirits, when no spirit can be supposed to be present, is also to be assumed as proof that *seeing* spirits is no evidence that spirits are present as objects of vision. One class of persons take certain medicines, others have certain forms of disease, and others spend a certain time in particular localities. In each case alike similar visions, as of spirits, occur. In the two former instances, no spirits are supposed to have been present, as objects of vision. Why should we suppose them present in the last? Nothing is more contrary to all the laws of scientific induction than such a supposition. There is known to exist a force in nature, which, when developed to a certain extent in the brain, induces visions as of spirits, ghosts, etc. All such visions, therefore, are to be attributed to the action of such cause, until facts occur necessitating a different supposition. We have, then, a clear and distinct explanation of the phenomena of ghost-seeing, which have troubled the world so much in past ages, and are beginning to trouble it again in the present. Wherever and from whatever cause the odylic force is developed unduly in the human brain, just such visions are from time to time to be expected; and when they do occur, we are, from the effect, to infer the presence of the cause. The fact that persons *speak* to the apparition, and seem to receive answers, does not alter the case at all; because just such facts do occur when no spirits are present, and the action of the force which occasions the vision equally accounts for such facts also.

What are haunted houses and places of a like character, but localities in which this same force is so developed that persons of peculiar temperament remaining in them for certain periods, become so affected with it that these forms of phenomena are induced, that is, visions as of spirits are occasioned? We have not yet read or heard of a haunted house all the facts connected with which may not be most fully and perfectly accounted for by a reference to this one cause. The spirits there seen, and the sounds and voices heard, are no more external to the minds and organisms of the percipients, than what the mother above referred to saw of and heard from her son was external to her mind and organism.

There is one other view of this whole subject also, that should not be overlooked in this connexion. It is not at all strange, but a matter to be expected, that phosphorescent and other luminous vapours should from time to time arise from graveyards and old, forsaken, and dilapidated and decaying buildings; and that in and near some such places, individuals of peculiar physical constitutional temperament should very quickly, in many instances, have the odylic force developed in their organisms. A number of most efficient causes of ghost-seeing here present themselves; causes sufficiently efficient to account for such perceptions in the total absence of all corresponding objects, that is, real visible spirits. Any such luminous substances rising in the night time in the form of columns, as they most naturally do, would, of necessity, to the terrified imagination of the beholder, appear as a human body wrapped in a winding-sheet, the form in which ghosts almost, if not quite, invariably appear. It is the opinion of some philosophers also, who have carefully investigated the subject, that the odylic force developed in such localities, sometimes, in ascending from the earth, spontaneously assumes a form somewhat like that of the human body, and in that form becomes visible to individuals present, especially if the same force is developed in their organisms. Then the same force in such organisms often occasions visions as of such objects, when nothing is perceived external to the organism itself. It is well known also that this force, as developed in particular localities, is attended with the very noises, jarring of surrounding objects, and movement of heavy bodies, which are witnessed in haunted houses. All these causes combined are abundantly sufficient to account for all the phenomena of ghost-seeing and haunted houses with which the world has, from time to time, been troubled, without the supposition of spirit-presence. All such phenomena differ fundamentally from the "angel visits" recorded in Scripture. The latter were intelligent manifestations made to answer important ends. The former are unintelligent manifestations bearing the very characteristics they would bear were they just what we have represented them to be. As such, then, we regard them, having assigned causes abundantly adequate to account for their existence as such phenomena.

SECTION IV.

Witchcraft, Fortune-Telling, Manner in which Mysterious Events are commonly treated.

There are two points of light in which the phenomena of witchcraft may be considered, namely, the leading facts set forth by those who, in past ages, have believed in such theory; and the conclusions which have been deduced from these facts. Hitherto there has, for the most part, been supposed to be a necessary connexion between the facts and the conclusion. Hence those denying the latter have generally ignored the former as mere illusions, and that without examination. Let us suppose that each of these questions be considered by itself, without any reference to the other, and that we commence with a candid and careful examination of the evidence that exists of the reality of many of the leading facts adduced by Cotton Mather and his associates, for example, in regard to the subject. We venture the opinion that few facts of the past will be found to be sustained by higher and more valid evidence than these. Our fathers will be found to have erred, not in regard to the facts,—many of them, to say the least,—but with respect to the conclusions which they deduced from those facts. It will also be found that there was, in all respects, the same connexion between their facts and conclusions that there is between those of Spiritualism now. We have precisely the same evidence of the agency of devils in the phenomena of Salem witchcraft that we have of that of the disembodied spirits of men in the so-called spirit-phenomena. If our fathers erred in their conclusions, two millions of people (the number asserted by spiritualists to hold their theory in America, at the present time) have shown themselves to be not more wise; for the same identical phenomena, physical and mental, were presented to reveal and prove the presence and agency of devils in one instance, that are or can be adduced to reveal and prove that of the disembodied spirits of men, in the other. Are physical objects now moved with and without physical contact, and that in accordance with intelligence? So they were then. Have we now various mediums through whom intelligent communications are obtained, as from the spirits of men? Through various mediums, equally intelligent and mysterious revelations were given forth, as from devils, then. The witch could do then all that the medium can do now. We are just as sacredly bound to admit the *mere facts* of witchcraft as we are to admit those of Spiritualism, and have just as high and sacred reasons for rejecting the conclusions of the believers in each alike.

One test which our fathers sometimes applied, in determining who were and who were not witches, will be found to be not so deserving of ridicule as has been supposed. We refer to the custom of putting individuals into sacks containing lead or stones, and then placing them upon water to see whether they would float or sink to the bottom, the former class being held as real witches and the latter not. We learn that the body of Frederica Hauffe would float upon water like a cork, and that it was very difficult to get it beneath the surface. For the same reasons, the bodies of witches, that is of those in whom the odylic force was to a certain extent developed, would thus float upon the surface of water. There, too, was an error, not in regard to facts, but in respect to conclusions to be deduced from such facts. Nor do we suppose that there is any ground whatever for the assertion so commonly made, that those who, in such trials, sank to the bottom, were left to perish there. They were unquestionably rescued by the spectators, and all arrangements were made for that purpose.

Nor, in our judgment, do our fathers deserve at all

the ridicule and censure heaped upon them by partial and prejudiced historians, for their so-called persecutions of witches. What were the real facts of the case? The witches, in the first place, *professed* to be in league with devils, and exercised their strange power as from them. Then they performed such mysterious and apparently supernatural feats that there appeared to the public no way of accounting for the facts but by admitting the claims set forward by this class of persons. They became the sources of great depravity and corruption, as well as objects of corresponding fear and terror in the community. Our fathers supposing, and most honestly too, that there was a necessary connexion between the facts which they knew and could not but know to be real, and the truth of the professions of the witches, under that knowledge and conviction proceeded against persons making such professions, and executed upon them what was then believed to have been required in the Word of God, in such cases. We believe that there is not the least reason for sympathy with those who were making such professions, or that their sufferings were beyond their guilt. Those who profess to be in league with devils, and perform, of choice, acts which can be accounted for, according to existing light and knowledge, upon no other supposition but that such professions must be true, have no reason to complain if they are treated according to their professions and acts. On the other hand, we are equally confident that our fathers, in what they did in the case, acted "in all good conscience before God" and man too; that they deserve of their posterity pity for their mistakes and commendation for their zeal, misdirected though it happened to have been. That the innocent, in some instances, suffered with the guilty, we have no doubt, and this should be and is a matter of deep and unfeigned regret.

If the theory which we have been endeavouring to establish be admitted, the phenomena of witchcraft wears no longer the veil of mystery. Connect with the so-called spirit-phenomena of our day the idea of an origin from devils, let our mediums simply believe themselves under a corresponding influence, and let that sentiment be entertained by those who visit these circles, and we should have all the phenomena of Salem witchcraft over again, and that without change or modification. Spiritualism and witchcraft are the exclusive results of a common cause. The phenomena of each are to be explained upon precisely the same principles. The facts in both cases alike are real, and the conclusions equally false; the conclusions, we mean, that the facts are the result of an *ab extra*, and not an exclusively mundane, cause. It would be interesting, did our space permit, to draw at length the parallel between the physical and intellectual manifestations attending these two movements—the one under the assumed control of devils, and the other under that of the departed spirits of human beings—and show how perfectly, with this one exception, they correspond with each other. This, however, is not necessary. All that is now required is to designate the cause of such phenomena, and to show how they may all be explained in the light of such cause.

Fortune-Telling.

The common supposition is that fortune-tellers are deliberate impostors, who, while they are in a normal state, and know themselves to be thus, profess to be possessed of a supernatural foresight of future events. For the most part, we have no doubt that this is the case. We are fully convinced, however, that this practice or art has its basis, in some instances, in an abnormal physical and mental condition of the professed seer, a condition induced by the odylic force, and in which the subject, the fortune-teller, sustains precisely the same relations to the individual present that the mesmeric or clairvoyant subject does to the mesmerizer. After the accustomed ceremonies have been gone through with, the fortune-teller goes into a manifestly magnetic condition, in which he or she speaks, as if a new power and influence had obtained full control over him. Soon the secret thoughts of the inquirer are disclosed, and facts in his history utterly unknown, as he fully believes, to any being on earth but himself. In the midst of these, there are incoherent predictions of things future, predictions which in but very few instances are realized in any form, but in some very distant and solitary cases very strikingly fulfilled. The power manifested in revealing things secret in regard to the past, inspires the inquirer with confidence in regard to the predictions of things future. Here we have another instance, or form, in which the thoughts of one person are transferred to the mind of another through the action of odylic force. A friend of ours, for example, a lady, once as she was at a distant place from that of her own residence, visiting from house to house, called at the residence of an individual of this class. She had never seen that person before, and was equally certain of being a total stranger to her. Finding that she was in the presence of such a person, our friend determined to satisfy her curiosity by seeing for herself what such an individual can do. After the usual ceremony of shuffling cards, etc., were gone through with, the fortune-teller evidently, our friend being acquainted with such manifestations, went into a magnetic condition. Soon she stated, among other things, that she saw the husband of the stranger in a *warehouse*, apparently examining it (he had gone on that errand at that very time) ; that one of her children was affected with a peculiar form of disease, and described with perfect accuracy his motions when under its action ; and then, among many other things, related facts in the past history of our friend, which she was perfectly certain no one on earth knew but herself. One prediction, very indefinitely stated, was uttered, which came to pass. "There," says the fortune-teller, after a while, "the influence has passed from me,—I can say no more." Who does not see here the results of known mesmeric or odylic relations between these individuals ; relations in which the thoughts and remembrances of one are transferred to the mind of the other ? A lady in Boston years ago told us of a similar interview which she once had with a fortune-teller in that city, an individual probably now alive. Our informant, whose word will not be doubted by those knowing her, was born and educated in the state of Maine, where her parents now reside. To the fortune-teller she was a total stranger, and from the circumstances of the case she felt the most undoubted assurance that her visit was totally unexpected, and that she was to the individual called upon an unknown and total stranger. When the proper conditions were fulfilled, the leading incidents of this stranger's life, from her childhood up, the peculiarities of her character as a child, special facts in her past history, utterly unknown as she fully believes to anyone on earth but herself, the peculiarities of the past and present residence of her parents, and of the scenery about the same, they having removed to another part of the state from that where her childhood and youth were spent,—all these things were detailed with the most astonishing minuteness and accuracy, and with a lifelike vividness, in the presence of which she seemed almost to live the past over again.

Of the leading facts pertaining to a celebrated character of this class, who lived in Paris during the early part of the present century, our readers are very probably aware. The name of the individual has escaped us. This, however, was true of her—all who visited her, from whatever parts of the kingdom or world they came, were astonished (and her fame drew vast multitudes from all parts to consult her) and not unfrequently confounded by the minute and specific revelations of their past history which they would receive through that pythoness. In her case, there would be equally strange revelations in regard to the future, and other facts unknown to her visitants; she, no doubt, while in a magnetic state, being a very powerful clairvoyant. Such facts accord with the history of many fortune-tellers, the world over. The manner in which their revelations, in regard to the past history of utter strangers resorting to them, are obtained and given forth, is quite obvious. In the magnetic or odylic state into which they are introduced by the various ceremonies performed, the remembrances of persons present in regard to their past history are, through the action of this power, and by virtue of its nature and relations to mind, reproduced in the mind of fortune-tellers, and given forth by them, on the same principles that A. J. Davis uttered the present thoughts of the lady in magnetic communication with him. Equally manifest is the manner in which revelations pertaining to the future commonly are obtained and given forth, through such individuals. The visitant has in his mind visions and plans in regard to the future. Social, and especially domestic, connexions may be formed, desired, or intended with specific individuals, or with imaginary personages imaged forth in the mind in conformity with the heart's *beau ideal.* In the presence of the fortune-teller, and in anticipation of such revelations, these plans and persons, real or imaginary, are of course suggested to the inquirer. Through his or her mind they are reproduced in that of the pythoness, and by her given forth as revelations communicated by higher powers to her mind. It is thus, no doubt, that the image of the person with whom conjugal relations are afterwards consummated is sometimes presented as a prophetic enunciation to the inquirer, and by him or her ever after regarded as proof of a real prophetic foresight in the fortune-teller.

Manner in which mysterious events are commonly treated.

Whenever mysterious events appear, and when inferences unfriendly to truth are drawn from them, the friends of truth are too apt, instead of acquainting themselves with the facts of the case, and thus becoming enabled to speak intelligently upon the subject, to deny the facts altogether, and that without examination, and at the same time to treat the whole subject with silent contempt, as wholly unworthy of their notice. To our mind, no course of procedure can be more unwise than this, especially among the teachers of our holy religion. They certainly should be able to speak intelligently upon all subjects which, in the public mind around them, bear upon the cause of truth and righteousness. Ignorance, in such cases, renders the religious teacher an object of contempt on the part of the opposers of the truth. It utterly annihilates also his power to benefit all who believe the facts ignored.

Nor does the evil stop here. The opposer of truth finds an excuse for ignoring altogether the great question of the divine origin of Christianity, and without examination denying its facts; and finds this excuse in the manner in which his facts and arguments are treated. We cannot ask men, with any rational hope of being heard, to listen with candour and wakeful interest to our facts and arguments, unless we listen with the same candour and interest to theirs.

By the same course also the friends of truth are sometimes found treating with contempt great facts, and the most legitimate deductions from the same, as in the case of geology and other kindred sciences, when they first unlocked their priceless treasures to the world. The friends of truth must ever regard themselves as bound to admit facts, however mysterious, when their reality is affirmed by valid evidence. On no other condition can they fully exemplify the love of universal truth required by the Gospel which they profess, or require men to admit the facts which lie at the basis of the claims of Christianity to a divine original.

SECTION V.

These so-called Spirit-manifestations and Scripture Miracles. Bearing of our previous Discussions upon the Doctrine of a General and Particular Providence. Conclusion.

Spiritualists everywhere claim that these so-called spirit-manifestations are attended with facts which have the same marks of being miracles that the great facts recorded in the Bible do. Indeed, it is now put forth, unblushingly, that this movement is attended with the same kind of supernatural events that Christianity was,—events, too, resulting from the very same cause; and that no one can repudiate the claims of Spiritualism, without being bound, in consistency, to repudiate those of Christianity. It is of no little importance, then, that we clearly distinguish these manifestations from real miracles, those recorded in the Bible especially.

What, then, is a real miracle, and what especially are the characteristics of the affirmed miracles recorded in the Bible? A real miracle, we reply, is *an event wholly unlike and unanalogous, in its essential characteristics, to any event resulting from mundane causes.* A miracle that can properly be used as a *divine* attestation of the truth of any proposition or doctrine, must be an event of such a character that its occurrence can be accounted for but by a reference to a direct and immediate interposition of *creative power;* and must sustain such relations to that proposition or doctrine that the reality of the event cannot be admitted without admitting such proposition or doctrine as a divinely-attested truth. Now we affirm the above to be the precise character of the so-called miraculous events recorded in the Scriptures. Such also is the relation of those events to the Scriptures, that the reality of the former cannot be admitted without admitting the divine origin of the latter.

What, on the other hand, is the character of these manifestations? There is not one among them, as we have seen, whose existence and entire characteristics may not be accounted for by a reference to purely mundane causes, and which is not perfectly similar and analogous in all its elements and features, to events which do result from such causes. All these manifestations, in the next instance, may be admitted, and with the most absolute logical consistency the claims of Spiritualism to an *ab extra* spirit-origin denied.

We will contrast a few miraculous phenomena revealed in the Bible with some claimed to be of a similar character connected with Spiritualism. We will begin with the leading miracles. It is well known that there are certain peculiar forms of disease which can, sometimes almost instantly, and at others in very short periods, be cured by the imagination, or certain medicines; there are others which cannot be affected by such causes: of the former class exclusively are the healing phenomena of Spiritualism. The latter class are among the most prominent miracles revealed in the Bible. The healing medium, by his passes, may, through the imagination of the subject, or through the medicinal influence of the odylic force thus excited in the patient, effect certain forms of cure. Over other diseases he has no power for good. Thus he may make as many passes as he pleases over a corpse, and he can never reanimate it with a living soul. He can make no approach whatever towards restoring to a maimed person his lost limb. Yet these last are among the most prominent of "the mighty works" performed by Christ and the sacred writers. The healing power of the medium has no efficiency excepting in the case of a few diseases. That exercised by Jesus Christ had an equal and absolute efficacy in respect to all diseases of every kind. In connexion with this fact, He did what the medium can make no approach whatever towards doing, that is, restoring lost limbs to the maimed, and raising the dead to life. The power, then, which originated the Scripture miracles, supposing them to have occurred, differs, not in degree, but in kind, from that claimed in behalf of Spiritualism.

The same remarks are equally applicable to the spirit of prophecy. Suppose that we have two classes of predictions, each one hundred in number, and relating to events which lie equally beyond the reach of mere human foresight. Of one class, but one in the whole hundred is fulfilled in any form; of the other, not one in the hundred fails in any particular. What higher evidence can we have that the intelligence which originated the latter class differs, not in degree, but in kind, from that which originated the former? the one being possessed of the most infallible, and the other of the most erring, foresight. Such, precisely, is the character of the predictions recorded in the Bible, and those put forward by spiritualists to sustain the claims of their system. The latter class bears all conceivable marks of a mere human, and the former of a divine, origin; the one indicating an origin from intelligence omniscient and absolutely infallible, and the other from one most limited and fallible. In all respects the miracles of Scripture stand in absolute contrast to the so-called mysteries set forth by the advocates of Spiritualism.

The advocates of Spiritualism claim that the miracles performed by mediums should rank, we repeat, with those recorded in the Bible. To bring the subject to a still further test, let this class of persons advance to one of our granite mountains, and after making their passes over the surface of the flinty rocks, see if that mountain, at their bidding, will open its sides and send forth floods of water sufficient to quench the thirst of three millions of people, together with their countless flocks and herds. Let these same individuals then approach the Ohio or Hudson river, and making their passes over the same, see if at their bidding the waters thereof will divide and stand in heaps on either side, while the people pass over dry shod, and subsequently roll on as before. And, finally, let them turn to the sun in the heavens, and see if on making their passes over his face, he will stand still for a season, or go "ten degrees" backward. When mediums can perform wonders even analogous to these, then, and only then, their mighty works may claim a rank among those recorded in the Bible. In the midst of these great events, there are some, of course, which might or might not be the immediate result of creative power. These standing by themselves could not be claimed as miracles, and could never, if they did stand thus alone, be appealed to as proof of the divine origin of Christianity. It is this last class exclusively—forms of healing, for example, which may result from miraculous interpositions on the one hand, or from mundane causes on the other—that Spiritualism copies or can copy.

Let us apply to these two classes of facts the principle of science to which we referred in a former part of this treatise, to wit, that when a given class of facts exist, and we know that a part of them is produced exclusively by one given cause, and that this cause is in itself adequate to the production of the whole, and therefore, to account for their occurrence, we are bound to refer them, in their entireness, to that one cause. Of the miraculous events recorded in the Bible, we know absolutely that none of these great central facts can have been the result of any cause but the direct and immediate interposition of creative power, and that this cause is perfectly adequate to account for all the rest. Admitting those facts to have occurred, we are required therefore, by the universal and immutable principles of science, to ascribe the whole together to this one exclusive cause. Of the facts of Spiritualism, on the other hand, we know with equal absoluteness that a part of them are the exclusive result of purely mundane causes, and that these causes are perfectly adequate to account for all the rest. By the same principles of science, therefore, we are bound to attribute all these facts to these causes. Thus it is that the facts of Spiritualism can be compared to Bible miracles only on the principle of contrast. This is the only relation that these two classes of facts do or can sustain to each other.

Bearings of our previous investigations upon the doctrine of a general and particular providence.

The idea very extensively, and almost, if not quite, universally obtains, at the present time, that all effects in the external universe around us, miracles excepted, occur in perfect accordance with the action of fixed and immutable material laws; that at the creation every particle of matter had its particular position assigned it relatively to every other; that all subsequent effects in the material universe are the necessary and necessitated results of the mutual action and reaction of all such particles, in accordance with the immutable laws of attraction and repulsion, of chemical affinities and of the vital forces; and that, consequently, each material event is a link in a chain of necessary causes and effects, and can by no possibility, excepting through a miraculous interposition of creative power, be otherwise than it is. Suppose that, with that view distinctly in mind, we are about to kneel in prayer, and that the object of the prayer is to secure the occurrence of some particular event in nature—rain in time of drought, or the restoration of a sick friend to health, for example. What effect is this view of the facts of the universe likely to have in exciting or suppressing a spirit of prayer for the objects named? Is it a view adapted to excite in us the belief that prayer "avails much" for the attainment of such objects, and consequently to excite in us sentiments of hope and the exercise of earnest, fervent, and humble but confiding and persevering importunity? According to the view before us, the sick man has a certain amount and form of disease, from which he can recover but through a certain process, a process which cannot be shortened or protracted by our mental states. The drought, too, is the necessary result of the combined action of the entire particles of matter constituting the material universe, and must continue till removed by such action, action which can but move on in the line of necessary causation. Prayer, however fervent, can have no avail whatever, to secure the result referred to, unless it avails to secure a miraculous interposition of creative power, an event which no one anticipates. In the presence of such a view of the operations of the material universe, the mind can no more have faith in the availing efficacy of prayer to secure such results, than it can believe that the same thing can, at the same time, exist and not exist. This view also, almost of necessity, will extend itself in our minds, from the material over the movements of the moral and spiritual universe. While we regard the one as controlled, in all its movements, by fixed and immutable laws of cause and effect, laws the results of which prayer can have no avail to change, we shall hardly fail to regard the moral and spiritual universe as governed by similar laws, laws whose results are equally beyond the availing efficacy of prayer. Prayer, in the presence of such a view of the material, moral, and spiritual universe, may remain as a mere form; and in no other state can it well remain. It will not avail, to change these results, to inform us that God, foreseeing, at the beginning, the prayers of His people, arranged the current of events so that they should accord, in important particulars, with prayer. From the nature of the case, such an arrangement could reach such contingent events but in a very general and limited manner. It is, in itself, also, a view of Providence in no way adapted to call forth "effectual and fervent prayer" for *specific results*—the form which prayer generally ought to assume. The actual results of this view of Providence are precisely accordant with the above presentation. Prayer made for any such results as we are speaking of, is, and no one will deny the fact, little more than a form, and as a form even, it exists to a very limited extent. The spirituality of the Church is, in our solemn judgment, being "spoiled through philosophy."

If we turn from this cold and cheerless view of Providence, to the Scriptures, we find, not only a want of correspondence, but a total and irreconcilable opposition between it and their most positive teachings, on this subject. According to such teachings, God is ever with us, as "a very present help in trouble," perplexity, and want; able and ready to respond, by specific providences, to our individual and specific necessities and filial requests, and that equally in regard to the demands of our physical and spiritual natures. All alike stand revealed as equally appropriate objects of prayer, objects in respect to which special and specific answers are alike and equally to be anticipated. There can be no doubt on this subject.

If we retire from the Bible and the philosophy of Providence under consideration, into the depths of our own moral and spiritual being, we shall find every principle and demand of that nature in fixed and immutable correlation to the former and in opposition to the latter view of Providence. We wander through nature in a state of cheerless orphanage, till God is present to us, in all the movements of Providence, in the very parental and special relations revealed in the Scriptures. Now we take the ground that the real providence of God, in the movements of the material creation, accord with the teachings of the higher philosophy revealed through the Scriptures and the moral and spiritual nature of humanity, and not with the teachings of the material philosophy before us, a philosophy which, as we shall see, has taken into the account but a *part* of the material forces of nature, and therefore fundamentally errs in its teachings pertaining to the procedures and laws of divine providence in the material universe.

As preparatory to the elucidation of the subject before us, let us, for a moment, contemplate the physical organism of man. In and connected with this organism two distinct and, in some respects, opposite classes of purely physical forces are continuously operating. There are the vital and chemical forces sustaining the organism itself, and producing all the phenomena of circulation and nutrition, and the attractive and repulsive forces, including all the particles thereof, and holding the organism itself, like any other ponderous body, in connexion with external nature; then in the same organism there is, as we have seen, another force, which, in accordance with mental states, acts upon the muscular system, and becomes thereby the medium of voluntary motion, and may, consequently, not inappropriately be denominated the will-force.

Now this will-force (the odylic force, as we have seen) not only pervades the human organism, but all nature too; and through it, as we have also seen, when the proper conditions are fulfilled, the most astonishing effects may be voluntarily and intentionally produced upon surrounding objects. We will, for example, that the hands of individuals in magnetic communication with us shall be immovably fastened to the table or other objects, or that their fingers shall remain interlocked so that they cannot draw them asunder, and these results, all the possible efforts of those individuals to the contrary notwithstanding,—these results, we say, follow in accordance with our wills. Either these events were the result of direct miraculous interpositions, or there is in all nature around us the very force of which we are speaking, a force through which such voluntary results may be produced; the facts themselves, the reality of which cannot be denied, admitting of no other explanation. It is a first and universal principle of science, that the government of God over the material universe (that being the only department of creation of which we are now speaking) shall accord with the nature of *all* the forces actually existing therein. If there are—and none doubt the fact of their existence—forces in nature which act in fixed and immutable accordance with the laws of attraction, repulsion, chemical affinity, etc., then we should expect to find a class of events, like the movements of the heavenly bodies, for example, events which move on in changeless antecedence and consequence, and which prayer can never avail to alter. If, on the other hand, there is in nature another and different force, a will-force of immense power and influence over all other material objects, a force whose action is controlled by mental states and directed by the same, then the immutable laws of science would require us to suppose that another class of effects are continuously occurring around us, effects which are the results of successive and immediate acts of divine volition through this very force,—effects immediately produced as existing and special exigencies require, and which are no more to be regarded as miracles than the other class referred to. As thus acting in and controlling nature, God would ever be present to us, as accessible by prayer, and as the immediate and special "rewarder of them that diligently seek Him." Healing mercies, rain in times of drought, sunshine in long-continued storms, and "present helps in *all* times of trouble," might be expected in answer to special prayer, and this without the mind being chilled and repelled from a throne of grace by the idea of an immutable concatenation of causes and effects throughout nature, a concatenation which nothing but miracles can avail to break or to alter, miracles which no one believes prayer would avail to secure in our behalf. To this one view of Providence, a view in accordance with which special prayer for specific blessings may receive specific answers through events which would not otherwise have occurred at all, and this without miracles, and in perfect accordance with God's ordinary method of controlling events in the world around us,—to this one view of Providence, we say, a view which also accords with the entire teachings of inspiration on the subject, and the immutable demands of our moral and spiritual nature, philosophy itself, we believe, is now advancing, and the faith of the Church will ere long not be "spoiled through philosophy," but confirmed by its teachings. The proposition that God governs the universe, "not by special, but by general laws," we utterly disbelieve, when presented as the exclusive view of Providence. We equally repudiate the universal proposition that He governs the universe, not by general, but by special laws. We think that in the order of Providence, both principles are harmoniously blended. Events falling exclusively under the first class of laws are not objects of prayer, and are never so presented in the Scriptures. Those, on the other hand, falling under the second class, are such objects—events the current of which God, without miracles, may, in the exercise of His sovereign wisdom and love, continuously vary in adaptation to the continuously varying necessities and filial requests of His creatures, just as the acts of the earthly parent vary to meet the ever-changing wants and affectionate petitions of his children. This view of Providence, which certainly accords with the teachings of inspiration and the demands of our moral and spiritual natures, will yet, we think, stand revealed as the only one which philosophy itself permits.

Conclusion.

Such is Spiritualism. We have examined its high claims, and found them empty and vain. We have handled the spirits, and found them absolute insubstantialities. We have scrutinized the facts set forth as the basis of the system, and found them wholly mundane in their character, and presenting no evidence whatever of a super-mundane origin. Our aim in all our investigations has been a far higher one than the mere overthrow of a dangerous and insinuating system of delusion and error, namely, in the first instance, to lay the foundation for a full and satisfactory explanation of certain mysterious facts in nature and the experience of humanity, facts which have been in all ages very fruitful sources of superstition, religious delusion, and unbelief; and, in the next place, to prepare, as far as may be done in such a connection, for a better understanding of the ways of Providence, on the one hand, and of the real claims, on the other, of that divine revelation which constitutes the last and only hope of fallen humanity. Our reasonings and deductions thus far will speak for themselves, and we leave them to the candid judgment of the reader.

Watson & Hazell, Printers, London and Aylesbury.

www.ingramcontent.com/pod-product-compliance
Lightning Source LLC
LaVergne TN
LVHW021147110826
845150LV00005B/1142
9781425548032